THE
Beautiful
TREE

JAMES TOOLEY

THE *Beautiful* TREE

A personal journey into how the world's poorest people are educating themselves.

CATO INSTITUTE
WASHINGTON, D.C.

The Cato Institute gratefully acknowledges the generous contribution of Steve
G. Stevanovich to the production of this book.

"Stopping by Woods on a Snowy Evening" from THE POETRY OF ROBERT
FROST edited by Edward Connery Lathem. Copyright 1923, 1969 by Henry
Holt and Company. Copyright 1951 by Robert Frost.
Reprinted by arrangement with Henry Holt and Company, LLC.

Library of Congress Cataloging-in-Publication Data

Tooley, James.
    The beautiful tree : a personal journey into how the world's poorest people
are educating themselves / James Tooley.
        p. cm.
    Includes bibliographical references and index.
    ISBN 978-1-933995-92-2 (alk. paper)
    1. Poor—Education—Developing countries.   2. People with social disabilities—
Education—Developing countries.   3. Tooley, James—Travel—Developing
countries.   I. Title.

LC4065.T66 2008
371.909172'4--dc22   2009004899

Cover design by Jon Meyers.

Printed in the United States of America.

CATO INSTITUTE
1000 Massachusetts Ave., N.W.
Washington, D.C. 20001
www.cato.org

To Pauline

Acknowledgments

First, I want to thank all the educational entrepreneurs I have met over the years who are actively serving poor communities. Some of those I am working with now, who deserve my deepest appreciation and admiration, are M. Anwar, Reshma Lohia, Yasmin Haroon Lohi, K. Surya Reddy, K. Narsimha Reddy, M. Wajid, Ghouse M. Khan, S. A. Basith, M. Faheemuddin, Alice Pangwai, George Mikwa, Fanuel Okwaro, Theophilus Quaye, Ken Donkoh, B. S. E. Ayesminikan, and Liu Qiang. For assisting in funding and associated advice and support over the years, I want to thank (in roughly chronological order) Neil McIntosh; Michael Latham; Tim Emmett; the late Sir John Templeton; Jack Templeton; Charles Harper; Arthur Schwartz; Chester Finn; Peter Woicke; Stuart, Hilary and Andrew Williams; Theodore Agnew; and Richard Chandler. Colleagues and friends who have supported and encouraged me in my endeavors include Khan Latif Khan, Jack Maas, Gurcharan Das, Nandan Nilekani, the late Kwadwo Baah-Wiredu, I. V. Subba Rao, Hernando de Soto, Christopher Crane, Parth Shah, James Shikwati, Thompson Ayodele, Lanre Olaniyan, Barun Mitra, S. V. Gomathi, P. Paul Saran, Sailaja Edla, Chris and Suzie Jolly, Naveen Mandava, Bob Leighton, Deepak Jayaraman, Leonard Liggio, Jo Kwong, Terence Kealey, Linda Whetstone, and John and Chris Blundell. For helping me to build the first embryonic chain of low-cost private schools in India, I thank Paul Gabie and the Orient Global team. Simon Kearney gave me useful comments on the manuscript, as did five anonymous referees, to whom I'm deeply grateful. Andrew Coulson has been the kind of editor and supporter an author dreams of, through good times and bad. Finally, I give thanks to my friends, colleagues, and students at Newcastle who've been an indispensable part of my life and work: Elaine Fisher, Karen Hadley, Nuntarat Charoenkul, Ekta Sodha, Liu Qiang (again), James Stanfield, Sugata Mitra, Richard Graham, and Pauline Dixon—to whom this book is dedicated.

Contents

1. A Discovery in India . . .

What Everyone Knows

My first real job was as a mathematics teacher in Africa. Right out of college, a couple of years after Zimbabwe's independence from Britain in 1980, I went to help "Comrade" Robert Mugabe build his new socialist society. And what better way to assist than through public education?

During my interview with the minister of education at the Zimbabwe High Commission in London, I asked to be assigned to a rural school so that I could really help the poor. He smiled, clearly understanding my motivation, I thought. To my chagrin, I found myself posted to Queen Elizabeth High School, an all-girls school right in the center of Harare, the capital. Queen Elizabeth had originally been a whites-only elite institution, although when I joined it had a mixture of races ("African," "Asian," and "European," as they were classified).

"This government wouldn't waste you in the rural areas!" the (white) headmistress laughed when I arrived, meaning to compliment me on my mathematics degree. She explained that many daughters of politicians from the ruling party, Zanu-PF, were enrolled in her school, and of course they would look after themselves first! I dismissed her cynicism, putting it down to racism, and the incongruence of my assignment to administrative error. I also found my niche in the school; it seemed all the children trusted me, so I was able to help them get along with one another. But I spent as much of my spare time as possible in the rural "communal lands," experiencing the realities of life there firsthand. In the process, I developed links between an impoverished rural public school and my own, bringing my privileged urban pupils there to help them appreciate all that Mugabe was doing for the *povo*—the ordinary people.

Two years later, I managed to engineer an assignment to a public school in the Eastern Highlands. I lived and worked in a small

1

school set on a plateau beneath the breathtakingly beautiful Manyau Mountains, from where the calls of baboons echoed as dusk fell and women returned from the river carrying buckets of water on their heads; leopards apparently still hunted at night on the rugged mountain slopes. I defended Mugabe's regime to its critics, for at least it was engaged in bringing education to the masses, benefiting them in ways denied before independence. Before long, once richer urban people properly paid all their taxes and the international community coughed up a decent amount of aid, it would be able to make education free for all. That would be truly cause for celebration.

After all, everyone knows that the world's poor desperately need help if every child is to be educated. Help must come from their governments, which must spend billions of dollars more on building and equipping public schools, and training and supporting public school teachers, so that all children can receive a free primary school education. But governments in developing countries cannot succeed on their own. Everyone knows that they, too, need help. Only when rich Western governments spend much more on aid can every child be saved from ignorance and illiteracy. That's the message we hear every day, from the international aid agencies and our governments, and from pop stars and other celebrities.

As a young man, I believed this accepted wisdom. But over the past few years, I've been on a journey that has made me doubt everything about it. It's a journey that started in the slums of Hyderabad, India, and has taken me to battle-scarred townships in Somaliland; to shantytowns built on stilts above the Lagos lagoons in Nigeria; to India again, to slums and villages across the country; to fishing villages the length of the Ghanaian shoreline; to the tin-and-cardboard huts of Africa's largest slums in Kenya; to remote rural villages in the poorest provinces of northwestern China; and back to Zimbabwe, to its soon-to-be-bulldozed shantytowns. It's a journey that has opened my eyes.

Read the development literature, hear the speeches of our politicians, listen to our pop stars and actors, and above all the poor come across as helpless. Helplessly, patiently, they must wait until governments and international agencies acting on their behalf provide them with a decent education. So we need to give more! It's urgent! Action, not words! It's all I believed during my early years in Zimbabwe. But my journey has made me suspect that it was,

2

however well intentioned, missing something crucial. Missing from the accepted wisdom is any sense of what the poor can do—are already doing—for themselves. It's a journey that changed my life.

Something quite remarkable is happening in developing countries today that turns the accepted wisdom on its head. I first discovered this for myself in January 2000.

In the Slums of Hyderabad, a Discovery . . .

After a stint teaching philosophy of education at the University of the Western Cape in South Africa, I returned to England to complete my doctorate and later became a professor of education. Thanks to my experiences in sub-Saharan Africa and my modest but respectable academic reputation, I was offered a commission by the World Bank's International Finance Corporation to study private schools in a dozen developing countries.

The lure of faraway places was too enticing to resist, but I was troubled by the project itself. Although I was to study private schools in developing countries, those schools were serving the middle classes and the elite. Despite my lifelong desire to help the poor, I'd somehow wound up researching bastions of privilege.

The first leg of the trip began in New York in January 2000. As if to reinforce my misgivings that the project would do little for the poor, I was flown first class to London in the inordinate luxury of the Concorde. Forty minutes into the flight, as we cruised at twice the speed of sound and two miles above conventional air traffic, caviar and champagne were served. The boxer Mike Tyson (sitting at the front with a towel over his head for much of the journey) and singer George Michael were on the same flight. I felt lost.

From London it was on to Delhi, Chennai, and Mumbai. By day, I evaluated five-star private schools and colleges that were very definitely for the privileged. By night, I was put up in unbelievably salubrious and attentive five-star hotels. But in the evenings, sitting and chatting with street children outside these very same hotels, I wondered what effect any of my work could have on the poor, whose desperate needs I saw all around me. I didn't just want my work to be a defense of privilege. The middle-class Indians, I felt, were wealthy already. To me it all seemed a bit of a con: just because they were in a "poor" country, they were able to latch onto this international assistance even though they as individuals had no pressing need for it at all. I didn't like it, but as I returned to my room and lay on the 500-thread-count Egyptian-cotton sheets, my discomfort with the program was forced to compete with a mounting sense of self-criticism.

Then one day, everything changed. Arriving in Hyderabad to evaluate brand-new private colleges at the forefront of India's hi-tech revolution, I learned that January 26th was Republic Day, a national holiday. Left with some free time, I decided to take an autorickshaw—the three-wheeled taxis ubiquitous in India—from my posh hotel in Banjara Hills to the Charminar, the triumphal arch built at the center of Muhammad Quli Shah's city in 1591. My *Rough Guide to India* described it as Hyderabad's "must see" attraction, and also warned that it was situated in the teeming heart of the Old City slums. That appealed to me. I wanted to see the slums for myself.

As we traveled through the middle-class suburbs, I was struck by the ubiquity of private schools. Their signboards were on every street corner, some on fine specially constructed school buildings, but others grandly posted above shops and offices. Of course, it was nothing more than I'd been led to expect from my meetings in India already—senior government officials had impressed me with their candor when they told me it was common knowledge that even the middle classes were all sending their children to private schools. They all did themselves. But it was still surprising to see how many there were.

We crossed the bridge over the stinking ditch that is the once-proud River Musi. Here were autorickshaws in abundance, cattle-drawn carts meandering slowly with huge loads of hay, rickshaws agonizingly peddled by painfully thin men. Cars were few, but motorbikes and scooters ("two-wheelers") were everywhere—some carried whole families (the largest child standing in front; the father at the handlebars; his wife, sitting sidesaddle in her black burka or colorful sari, holding a baby, with another small child wedged in between). There were huge trucks brightly painted in lively colors. There were worn-out buses, cyclists, and everywhere pedestrians, whose cavalier attitude toward the traffic unnerved me as they stepped in front of us seemingly without a care in the world. From every vehicle came the noise of horns blaring—the drivers seemed to ignore their mirrors, if they had them at all. Instead, it seemed to be the responsibility of the vehicle behind to indicate its presence to the vehicle in front. This observation was borne out by the legend on the back of the trucks, buses, and autorickshaws, "Please Horn!" The noise of these horns was overwhelming: big, booming, deafening horns of the buses and trucks, harsh squealing horns from the auto-rickshaws. It's the noise that will always represent India for me.

All along the streets were little stores and workshops in makeshift buildings—from body shops to autorickshaw repair shops, women washing clothes next to *paan* (snack) shops, men building new struc-tures next to the stalls of market vendors, tailors next to a drugstore, butchers and bakers, all in the same small hovel-like shops, dark and grimy, a nation of shopkeepers. Beyond them all rose the 400-year-old Charminar.

My driver let me out, and told me he'd wait for an hour, but then called me back in a bewildered tone as I headed not to the Charminar but into the back streets behind. No, no, I assured him, this is where I was going, into the slums of the Old City. For the stunning thing about the drive was that private schools had not thinned out as we went from one of the poshest parts of town to the poorest. Every-where among the little stores and workshops were little private schools! I could see handwritten signs pointing to them even here on the edge of the slums. I was amazed, but also confused: why had no one I'd worked with in India told me about them?

I left my driver and turned down one of the narrow side streets, getting quizzical glances from passersby as I stopped underneath a sign for Al Hasnath School for Girls. Some young men were serving at the bean-and-vegetable store adjacent to a little alleyway leading to the school. I asked them if anyone was at the school today, and of course the answer was no for it was the national holiday. They pointed me to an alleyway immediately opposite, where a hand-painted sign precariously supported on the first floor of a three-story building advertised "Students Circle High School & Institute: Registered by the Gov't of AP." "Someone might be there today," they help-fully suggested.

I climbed the narrow, dark staircase at the back of the building and met a watchman, who told me in broken English to come back tomorrow. As I exited, the young men at the bean-and-vegetable counter hailed me and said there was definitely someone at the Royal Grammar School just nearby, and that it was a very good private school and I should visit. They gave me directions, and I bade farewell. But I became muddled by the multiplicity of possible right turns down alleyways followed by sharp lefts, and so asked the way of a couple of fat old men sitting alongside a butcher shop.

Their shop was the dirtiest thing I had ever seen, with entrails and various bits and pieces of meat spread out on a mucky table over which literally thousands of flies swarmed. The stench was terrible. No one else seemed the least bit bothered by it. They immediately understood where I wanted to go and summoned a young boy who was headed in the opposite direction to take me there. He agreed without demur, and we walked quickly, not talking at all as he spoke no English. In the next street, young boys played cricket with stones as wickets and a plastic ball. One of them called me over, to shake my hand. Then we turned down another alleyway (with more boys playing cricket between makeshift houses outside of which men bathed and women did their laundry) and arrived at the Royal Grammar School, which proudly advertised, "English Medium, Recognised by the Gov't of AP." The owner, or "correspondent" as I soon came to realize he was called in Hyderabad, was in his tiny office. He enthusiastically welcomed me. Through that chance meeting, I was introduced to the warm, kind, and quietly charismatic Mr. Fazalur Rahman Khurrum and to a huge network of private schools in the slums and low-income areas of the Old City. The more time I spent with him, the more I realized that my expertise in private education might after all have something to say about my concern for the poor.

Khurrum was the president of an association specifically set up to cater to private schools serving the poor, the Federation of Private Schools' Management, which boasted a membership of over 500 schools, all serving low-income families. Once word got around that a foreign visitor was interested in seeing private schools, Khurrum was inundated with requests for me to visit. I spent as much time as I could over the next 10 days or so with Khurrum traveling the length and breadth of the Old City, in between doing my work for the International Finance Corporation in the new city. We visited nearly 50 private schools in some of the poorest parts of town, driving endlessly down narrow streets to schools whose owners were apparently anxious to meet me. (Our rented car was a large white Ambassador—the Indian vehicle modeled on the old British Morris Minor, proudly used by government officials when an Indian flag on the hood signified the importance of its user—horn blaring constantly, as much to signify our own importance as to get children and animals out of the way.) There seemed to be a private school on almost every street corner, just as in the richer parts of the city. I visited so many, being greeted at narrow entrances by so many students, who marched me into tiny playgrounds, beating their drums, to a seat in front of the school, where I was welcomed in ceremonies officiated by senior students, while school managers garlanded me with flowers, heavy, prickly, and sticky around my neck in the hot sun, which I bore stoically as I did the rounds of the classrooms.

So many private schools, some had beautiful names, like Little Nightingale's High School, named after Sarogini Naidu, a famous "freedom fighter" in the 1940s, known by Nehru as the "Little Nightingale" for her tender English songs. Or Firdaus Flowers Convent School, that is, "flowers of heaven." The "convent" part of the name puzzled me at first, as did the many names such as St. Maria's or St. John's. It seemed odd, since these schools were clearly run by Muslims—indeed, for a while I fostered the illusion that these saints and nuns must be in the Islamic tradition too. But no, the names were chosen because of the connotations to parents—the old Catholic and Anglican schools were still viewed as great schools in the city, so their religious names were borrowed to signify quality to the parents. But did they really deliver a quality education? I needed to find out.

One of the first schools Khurrum took me to was Peace High School, run by 27-year-old Mohammed Wajid. Like many I was to visit, the school was in a converted family home, fronting on Edi Bazaar, the main but narrow, bustling thoroughfare that stretched out behind the Charminar. A bold sign proclaimed the school's name. Through a narrow metal gate, I entered a small courtyard, where Wajid had provided some simple slides and swings for the children to play on. By the far wall were hutches of pet rabbits for the children to look after. Wajid's office was to one side, the family's rooms on the other. We climbed a narrow, dark, dirty staircase to enter the classrooms. They too were dark, with no doors, and noise from the streets easily penetrated the barred but unglazed windows. The children all seemed incredibly pleased to see their foreign visitor and stood to greet me warmly. The walls were painted white but were discolored by pollution, heat, and the general wear-and-tear of children. From the open top floor of his building, Wajid pointed out the locations of five other private schools, all anxious to serve the same students in his neighborhood.

Wajid was quietly unassuming, but clearly caring and devoted to his children. He told me that his mother founded Peace High School in 1973 to provide "a peaceful oasis in the slums" for the children. Wajid, her youngest son, began teaching in the school in 1988, when he was himself a 10th-grade student in another private school nearby. Having then received his bachelor's in commerce at a local university college and begun training as an accountant, his mother asked him to take over the school in 1998, when she felt she must retire from active service. She asked him to consider the "less blessed" people in the slums, and that his highest ambition should be to help them, as befitting his Muslim faith. This seemed to have come as a blow to his ambitions: his elder brothers had all pursued careers, and several were now living overseas in Dubai, London, and Paris, working in the jewelry business. But Wajid felt obliged to follow his mother's wishes and so began running the school. He was still a bachelor, he told me, because he wanted to build up his school. Only when his financial prospects were certain could he marry.

The school was called a high school, but like others bearing this name, it included kindergarten to 10th grade. Wajid had 285 children and 13 teachers when I first met him, and he also taught mathematics to the older children. His fees ranged from 60 rupees to 100 rupees per month ($1.33 to $2.22 at the exchange rates then), depending on the children's grade, the lowest for kindergarten and rising as the children progressed through school. These fees were affordable to parents, he told me, who were largely day laborers and rickshaw pullers, market traders and mechanics—earning perhaps a dollar a day. Parents, I was told, valued education highly and would scrimp and save to ensure that their children got the best education they could afford.

On my second visit, I arrived at Wajid's school in time for morning assembly at 8:50 a.m. The event was completely run by the children, especially the senior girls. Wajid told me that the experience was important to ensure that they learned responsibility, as well as organizational and communication skills, from a very early age. The

8

assembly began with about 15 minutes of calisthenics to the rhythm of drums played by the senior boys. Then there were announcements and readings from newspapers—chosen by the senior students to reflect items of interest to their classmates. There were a prayer and some songs—some religious, some patriotic—sung by selected students or by the entire school. Then three children from each class were chosen at random to relate something they had learned during the week. They used the microphone up front to address the assembly. Most, however young, seemed accomplished at this form of public speaking. The assembly closed with a song and a prayer, then all the children filed out past selected senior boys and girls, who checked their uniform and appearance.

Wajid's mother had apparently established the school to serve the community out of a devotion to the poor. And when I first started visiting the private schools, I assumed that they all must be run on a charitable basis—for how else could schools that charged such low fees survive? This seemed fair enough and fit in well with my understanding then of how the poor could gain access to private education. But the reality turned out to be far more interesting. As I traveled from school to school, I jotted down details in my field notebook of the number of children, the fees charged, and the number of teachers and their salaries. Back in my hotel room, I did some quick calculations and it dawned on me that running these schools must actually be profitable—sometimes very profitable—whereas other times they just break even. I mentioned this to Khurrum. He said that profit wasn't a great issue for them, but certainly they viewed themselves as businesspeople, as well as people who served the poor. This could of course explain why there were so many private schools—because it's easier to attract business investment than philanthropy.

Typical of the schools that had clearly been started with a business motive in mind was St. Maaz High School, situated near the state prison. (As I passed the prison one day, the prison guard ushered me in and gave me a guided tour; I was accompanied by the large entourage of school owners who went with me everywhere during my visit. I'm sure the guards didn't count us as we entered, so I don't know how they were sure that we were the only ones to leave.) St. Maaz was run by Mr. Sajid, or "Sajid-Sir," as everyone called him. Sajid-Sir was in his late 40s, and he clearly had a passion for teaching and for inspiring others. Teaching, he told me, kept him fresh, and it was his hobby as well as his livelihood; to him, he said, teaching was like acting. His aim was to instill a love for the subject he taught, mathematics. Mathematical allusions peppered many of his conversations. Interacting with his children and parents in Urdu, at a function organized for my visit, he had the assembly roaring with laughter, holding onto his every word. He told the gathered crowd: "There are three corners of the triangle, parents, teachers, and students, and this triangle must not be a scalene triangle; no, it must be an equilateral triangle. Am I right?" We all agreed. "Of course," he said.

Sajid-Sir had begun teaching in his early 20s, inspired, he told me, by the way that he managed to teach his younger brother the basics of mechanics by demonstrating the principles on an old bicycle (his brother is now a mechanical engineer). At first, he began, in his own words, as a "door-to-door teacher-salesman," traveling by bicycle to teach all six compulsory subjects to children in their homes, for a nominal sum. After three years at this enterprise, he founded a small school in 1982, with 15 students sitting on the floor of a tiny room in his rented house. From there he progressed over the next 19 years to an enrollment of nearly 1,000 students when I first met him, on three rented sites—one for the nursery and primary grades and one each for the boys' and girls' senior sections. The boys were housed in very cramped, dirty buildings on the periphery of a marriage function hall. (When it was not otherwise in use, the school could use the function hall for assemblies and other purposes.) The girls' site was a more attractive, although still-cramped, three-story building, about half a mile away. But Sajid-Sir had just bought a new site nearby with his accumulated surpluses, he proudly told me, to develop into a unified school. And that is exactly what happened over the next few years; he upgraded his facilities.

Few of Sajid's teachers had the state teacher-training certificate. The same was true of most private schools in the poor areas I visited. Indeed, it was a mystery at first why anyone would want to teach in the private schools, as their salaries were apparently lower than the public schools—perhaps only 20 or 25 percent of what the latter offered. So why would teachers choose to teach there when they could command much higher salaries elsewhere? The answer was simple: they couldn't get jobs in the public schools. Sometimes, such jobs were meted out as a means of political patronage, I was told. Since ordinary people couldn't get them, they taught in the private schools. But the lack of government teaching credentials was probably the chief reason. Many teachers in the private schools did have degrees; some even had higher qualifications, such as a master's in mathematics or sciences. But these credentials would not make them eligible to teach in public schools. For that they would need a government teacher-training certificate. The private school owners were disparaging about this: "Government teacher training," Khurrum told me, "is like learning to swim without ever going near a swimming pool; . . . our untrained teachers learn to teach in the well."

Learning in the well for Sajid meant training his own teachers. He told me that he instructed his new teachers personally, in what, above the heavy noise of the traffic in his office, I thought he described as the "Beard" method. Later I realized it was the "BEd"— Bachelor of Education—method. A lesson must have five parts, he said: an introduction, where the topic to be explored is fit into the context of students' existing knowledge; announcement of topic; presentation; recapitulation; and evaluation (usually through homework). Before he allowed a new teacher to teach in his school, he or she had to observe Sajid teaching. Then Sajid watched their first few lessons, made detailed notes, and challenged them on particular points.

I watched many lessons by teachers he had trained. One young woman with an MSc in inorganic chemistry, wearing a pale burka without a veil, taught about the derivation of salt and water from hydrochloric acid. I had never liked chemistry in school: if she had taught me, I think I would have loved the subject. She was very clear, lively, animated, and engaged her class throughout. There was nothing labored about her approach; the whole lesson moved forward smoothly. She taught without notes and seemed completely on top of her subject. At the end, she summarized the lesson, expertly managing the class so that all seemed to have understood, and set a three-part homework assignment. As she finished, Sajid stood and touched her bowed covered head. He had tears in his eyes as he said, "Thank you, wonderful."

Not all the teachers were as young. The schools also had older, sometimes much older, teachers. One was Mr. George Anthony, who taught English at Khurrum's Dawn High School. He was a

11

marvelous, sprightly, civilized Indian gentleman of 91 years, with dyed jet-black hair and thinly dyed lines for eyebrows, moustache, and sideburns. He had retired from his government job years before, but was dedicated to learning, "to the passing on of the greatest that has been thought and said to young minds," he told me, which is why he filled his retirement with teaching. He had this passion, and a passion for rationalism and improvement, along with a respect for tradition. ("Us old timers prefer the old names," he said of the change of the city names from Bombay to Mumbai, and Madras to Chennai).

I first met George Anthony as I toured Dawn High School, where he was teaching the senior boys Bertrand Russell's *Knowledge and Wisdom*. Then all the older children were called to a function to welcome me, and George gave a moving talk, which clearly inspired the children, about the value of discipline and self-improvement. He told them of the importance of punctuality, and of how, through pursuing their own self-fulfillment tempered with duty to others, they could make India great.

Back in Khurrum's office, we sat down for tea just as the electricity in the Old City went off. In the dim light of evening, Khurrum showed George a *Reader's Digest* manual, with a title something like *Everything You Need to Know about Almost Everything*. "They've brought this book out," said Khurrum. "Oooh," cooed George excitedly, flicking through the pages, "They bring out such excellent books." My suspicions were raised by the condition of the cover; I looked inside and saw the 1986 publication date. It was a very sweet moment.

Another older teacher was Mr. Mushtaq, who ran Scholars Model School. Scholars was on a very narrow lane, right across from the Government Boys Primary and Boys High School. On the same lane, I could see three other private schools. So what's the public school like? I asked innocently. Mr. Mushtaq laughed. "It's a government school," he said flatly, as if no other description or explanation was required. He was another refined, educated gentleman, of 66 years, who spoke with a quiet passion about his love for English literature. He had taught in college for 36 years, he told me, and "to keep my mind active, and to continue giving back to my people, I teach in the upper classes now." He told me of the authors he loves to teach, from Shakespeare and Milton to Charles Dickens, and his favorite poet Robert Frost. "Did you know that Robert Frost was poet laureate in the time of President J. F. Kennedy?" he asked me. I didn't know that. He continued: " 'I am not a teacher, but an awakener,' that's how Robert Frost described himself. If I can awaken a love of literature in my children, then what more would I want to achieve?" Then he quoted his favorite poem in full, in hushed, reverent tones: "Stopping by Woods on a Snowy Evening":

> Whose woods these are I think I know.
> His house is in the village though;
> He will not see me stopping here
> To watch his woods fill up with snow.
> My little horse must think it queer
> To stop without a farmhouse near
> Between the woods and frozen lake
> The darkest evening of the year.
> He gives his harness bells a shake
> To ask if there is some mistake.
> The only other sound's the sweep
> Of easy wind and downy flake.
> The woods are lovely, dark and deep.
> But I have promises to keep,
> And miles to go before I sleep,
> And miles to go before I sleep.

When he finished, the other school proprietors who had accompanied me on my visit nodded their appreciation in the cramped, stuffy, noisy office, deep in the vibrant heart of the slums of the Old City. Mr. Mushtaq explained the underlying metaphor, that "sleep is death in the poem, and there is an implied character here of a hearse—'. . . gives his harness bells a shake.' " "I'd love to see snow one day," he said quietly.

These teachers seemed pretty good to me. But how would largely untrained, low-paid teachers compare with their trained, well-paid counterparts in the public schools? How would the children achieve under them? As I toured the schools, I realized it was something that I had to find out. And how many children did they serve, I wondered? What proportion of poor families used private education in the Old City? Clearly, the official figures would be no help here, as so many children were in "unrecognized" schools, operating below the state's radar. Khurrum thought the figure might be as high as 80 percent in some areas. Again, I had to find out.

Clearly, Sajid and the school managers like him were businesspeople. But they didn't seem remotely like "businessmen ripping off the poor," as someone from the World Bank was to opine when I told her of my "discovery" on my return to Delhi. It seemed grossly unfair to characterize the school owners I was meeting in this way. On the contrary, they seemed dedicated to the children in their charge, going out of their way to help improve the education being offered. At my first meeting with Sajid, he invited me and several other private school managers into his office to look at some "play away" equipment and games he had recently bought, at some expense. The other school owners positively cooed about how these could help their children learn. And the first weekend of my visit, I was invited as a guest of honor to open a two-day science fair at M. A. Ideal High School, in the slums behind the high street of Kishanbagh.

M. A. Ideal, named after Mohammed Anwar, the founder, had been started when Anwar was a young man of 23, in 1987, when he taught about 40 children sitting on mats for 10 rupees (about 60 cents at the contemporary exchange rate) per month in two rented rooms. When I visited, his school had around 400 students (over half were girls) in his own buildings. For the science fair, the whole school was turned into something resembling a bazaar, with all the students, individually or in pairs, contributing an exhibit they designed, with guidance from teachers where necessary, illustrating some aspect of science. The exhibits included the dissection of a (at first, to my consternation, live) frog; a working model of the largest hydroelectric dam in Andhra Pradesh; a demonstration of how candles in different-sized jars burn at different rates; one showing how water is sucked into jars when candles burn, and why; another showing the boiling temperature of water; and yet another showing what happens when magnesium burns (complete with formulas for the chemical changes). Young children had exhibits showing different classifications of vegetables and fruits, brief descriptions of the differences between city and village life, or models of lungs and nervous systems, all cut out of polystyrene. For the whole weekend, people from the neighborhood and fellow members of the Federation of Private Schools' Management came to see the exhibits and question the students.

And the following weekend, there was a two-day cyber-olympics, involving a dozen or so schools from the federation. On day one, it was sports. In the rough school playground, girls played a sedate game called *Kho-Kho,* and there was a girls' jump rope competition in the street outside. The boys played a rough game, *kabbadi,* whose main aim was to pull one's opponents to the ground, while holding one's breath and emitting the phrase *"kabbadi, kabbadi, kabbadi . . ."* to prove that you really were holding your breath. If you stopped, you were out. Young Muslim girls, heads covered, were watching the boys and shouting excitedly to their favorites. Then there were straightforward footraces, with boys sprinting up the dirt street barefoot, the guest police inspector blowing his whistle for them to start. The second day of the cyber-olympics featured singing, drawing, essay writing, and GK (general knowledge) competitions. Sajid was one of the judges of the singing competition, endearing himself to the gathered students with his spirited performance of various songs in Urdu, including a moving rendition of "We Shall Overcome."

Seeing the school owners giving up their entire weekends seemed a mark of their commitment to the children under their care. And I discovered something else remarkable as well. At New St. Maria High School, I met the wonderful correspondent Maria, whose twin sister also ran a private school nearby. She told me that her school was built on a "lamentation," pointing to the picture above her desk, of a young girl who was two years old. "My daughter expired," she says, "and I had to have an operation so that I could not have any other children. So I decided to open a school, to give to children everywhere." "You now have 700 children," I said. "Yes, 700 children. And I have scholarships for 130 of these, named after my daughter. And every year on her birthday, I give out these scholarships."

Maria's generosity to the poorest of the poor turned out to be not that unusual. For those children who had been orphaned or who were from large families, the school entrepreneurs typically offered free or subsidized tuition. What kinds of children were assisted? As I toured the private schools of the Old City, I heard some of their stories.

Nine-year-old Saba Tabasum and her two sisters had free tuition at Master Mind Private School. Her father, who was educated up to primary-school level, was currently bedridden, due to an accident at work. Her mother, who was illiterate, worked as a maid in the neighboring houses to earn a living for the family. The three children and parents survived on the mother's income, which was approximately 200 rupees ($4.44) per week. With this money, she tried to educate her three daughters, pay the household expenses, and pay her husband's medical bills. Saba was good in her studies. She was one of the best students in her school and wished to become a teacher.

Peace High School gave five-year-old Shakera Khan and her three sisters 40 percent concessions. Their father, who was illiterate, worked in a shoe shop earning daily wages of up to 100 rupees ($2.22). However, if he didn't sell any shoes, he would return home empty-handed. Their mother was also illiterate but tried to help out by working as a day laborer for 25 rupees to 30 rupees (56 cents to 66 cents) per day.

Ten-year-old Farath Sultana also attended Peace High School. Her father works as a cleaner in a mosque and earned a monthly salary of 700 rupees ($15.55), which he admitted was not enough to feed his four family members. The family lived rent free with relatives who helped them get through each month by providing food. Both the mother and the father were illiterate, but they wanted their children to be educated. Peace High School provided both Farath and her six-year-old brother free tuition because of their critical financial position.

It appeared that these private schools, while operating as businesses, also provided philanthropy to their communities. The owners were explicit about this. They were businesspeople, true, but they also wanted to be viewed as "social workers," giving something back to their communities. They wanted to be respected as well as successful. A major motivation—many of the owners had a similar story—was their status in society. Khurrum told me: "I have an ambition of running a school, of giving good knowledge, and of building good character, good citizens, good people. We have status, as leaders of schools, people respect us, and we respect ourselves."

But the central mystery was why parents were sending their children to these schools at all. For however low the fees, the public schools were free. In public schools, children got free uniforms, free rice at lunchtime, and free books. And however much I enjoyed visiting the private schools and witnessing the dedication of their managers, the condition of the buildings worried me. They were crowded, many dirty, often smelly, usually dark, and always on some level makeshift. One was even in a converted inner-city chicken farm. So why would parents choose to pay to send their children to schools like these? The school owners told me that the public schools were just not up to scratch. Teachers didn't show up, and if they did, they seldom taught. I was told of public schools in the Old City that were becoming denuded of students, even though the teachers still commanded high salaries. One public school nearby apparently had 37 teachers but only 36 pupils. Other schools had more children, but the same story of the lack of teaching prevailed.

But of course the school owners might be biased. I wanted to hear what parents thought. At New Hope School, in a narrow two-story building with three classrooms upstairs and a main room downstairs, I spoke with nine mothers, all dressed in black burkas. Three fathers also came and sat away from the mothers on the other side of the room. I asked them about the public schools. They were totally disparaging. Teachers partied at schools, they said, or taught only one class out of six, and treated the children like orphans. There was no question that they wanted their children out of the public schools.

At Peace High School, a large group of parents came at the end of the school day to talk to me, congregating under a colorful tarp that Wajid had provided to shelter them from the sun. Mothers mainly, Muslims dressed all in black, some veiled, some half-veiled, some not veiled at all, interspersed with a few Hindu or Christian women dressed in colorful saris. The mothers were very forthcoming. There was no way they would send their children to public schools, one said. But aren't the teachers well trained? I asked. Yes, they might be very good at studying, but they are not very good at teaching. "They even beat the children very badly, treat them as slaves," said another.

Again, such parents might be biased—after all, they'd made a financial commitment to send their children to private school, so they might feel the need to defend that decision. I had to go to a public school to see for myself. Khurrum readily agreed to take me, and he seemed on surprisingly good terms with the deputy district education officer who accompanied us. The building looked fine from outside—much, much better than the crowded conditions I had found in the private schools. It was a well-apportioned, three-story structure, with a large playground and prominent signboard and a spacious and comfortable principal's office. Upstairs, the first class we visited had 130 students cramped together, all sitting on the floor, there being no desks or chairs anywhere in the school. The other teachers are absent today, I was told unapologetically by

17

the head, "so we're teaching them altogether." "They'll be absent every day," the deputy district education officer said—the first of many comments from government officials that impressed me—if that's the right word—with their matter-of-fact candor when addressing the failures of the system for which they were responsible. There were two other classes with similar numbers of children, whereas all the other classrooms were empty. Perhaps such crowded classrooms were the reason why parents preferred the private schools? But were they really better, I wondered, or were parents mistaken?

Finally, I learned of the school owners' frustrations with government regulations. At first, I was baffled to hear how often the government inspectors called on their schools—perhaps three to five times a year—showing a surprising dedication to quality and standards, I thought. Then Khurrum took me to one side and told me that they didn't come to inspect, only to "be made happy." I was naive enough then to be shocked, until others told me the same story as I was brought into their confidence, and realized that bribing officials was an unfortunate but necessary way of life in their community. Very quickly, I too become quite blasé about the presence of bribes— "unofficial payments" as they were labeled in Sajid-Sir's meticulous accounts. There were simply too many regulations to meet—"how can I have a playground of 1,000 square meters?" said Wajid of Peace High School, pointing to the crowded street where his school was situated. Detailing his problems with government inspectors, and his desire for official recognition, he said something I'll never forget: "Sometimes, government is the obstacle to the people." So they had to resort to bribery to remain registered or to keep the inspectors from closing them down. This was in stark contrast to the way the managers of the wealthy elite colleges that I was simultaneously investigating for the International Finance Corporation responded when I asked them about difficulties with regulations and inspectors: "Regulations?" they would nonchalantly say, "Oh, if anyone gets in my way, I pick up the phone to the CM," that is, the chief minister.

I realized that something quite remarkable was going on in the back streets of Hyderabad. It seemed that my expertise in private education might have some relevance after all in my urge to help the poor. Clearly, what was happening must have implications for the way we viewed education in developing countries? If so many parents were choosing to send their children to private schools because they perceived that the public schools were so bad, this was surely a profound discovery that would interest the development experts? I was in for a rude awakening.

2. . . . That Was No Discovery After All

The 500-Pound Gorilla

Oddly, my "discovery" was no discovery at all, or at least not to some people. Leaving Hyderabad, I returned to Delhi to meet again with World Bank staff before moving on to continue my "field trip" in other countries. I was eager and excited to tell them what I'd discovered in the back streets of the Old City of Hyderabad and to gain their insights on the way forward.

They weren't at all impressed. I met with a group of staff members in their pleasant offices, replete with potted ferns and pretty posters of cute children. Most, it was true, had never heard of private schools serving the poor, and they were frankly puzzled about how schools charging only $10 a year could exist, except through charity. And they told me that I had found some nongovernmental organizations working in the slums, opening a few schools, that was all. They told me this, assuming I was simply misguided, even though I had told them it was something else altogether. However, one of the group, Sajitha Bashir, had herself seen a few private schools in Tamil Nadu, although she insisted there were none in Karnataka, where she was now doing a study, so they weren't a universal phenomenon. In front of the group, she launched into a tirade against such schools: they were ripping off the poor, she said, run by unscrupulous businesspeople who didn't care a fig for anything other than profits. This didn't gel at all with what I'd seen in Hyderabad—how could such people devote their weekends to science competitions and cyber-olympics if money was their sole motivation? I was not at all convinced and hesitantly related some details of what I'd found. No one considered my information very significant. Those who hadn't heard of these schools simply shrugged, and the meeting soon dissolved.

Afterward, Sajitha took me downstairs for coffee, clearly trying to be helpful in letting me see the errors of my ways. So the private schools might be there, some *might* even be better than the public schools, but that's only because they are *selective*. "They take the cream of the cream," she said (and I had to force myself to remember that we were talking about parents earning a dollar or two a day), leaving the public schools much worse off. Anyway, continuing the theme that only a few were any good, she continued, "Most of the schools are shocking, there is a shocking turnover of teachers, they're not trained, they're not committed, and the proprietors know that they can simply get others because there is a long list of people waiting to come in." She paused to take a sip of her coffee: "All educators, 100 percent, believe that what the private schools for the poor are doing is untenable in modern educational theory. The rote learning, the cramming, they're just crammers ripping off the poor."

But her main problem, clearly based on well-intentioned personal convictions, was the question of equality. Because some children, the poorest of the poor, are left behind in the "sink" public schools, the private schools were exacerbating inequality, not improving the situation at all, she said. For that reason, we must devote all our efforts toward improving the public schools, not get carried away by what was happening in a few private schools. For Sajitha it was clear: if many—or even a few—parents had higher aspirations for their children and wanted to send them to private schools, then "they should not be allowed to do so, because this is unfair." It's unfair because it makes it even worse for those left behind. This puzzled me. Why should we treat the poor in this homogenous way? Would we—Sajitha and I—be happy if we were poor, living in those slums, and unable to do the best for our children, whatever our meager funds allowed? But I said nothing. As we parted, amicably enough, she told me that there was quite a bit of development literature about private schools for the poor in any case, and so I shouldn't go on too much about my "discovery," as I had done today, as people would only laugh. She gave me a couple of references to look up.

And she was right. I wondered at my own poor detective work in not having located these references before. Perhaps my own lack of recognition for what was taking place was excusable: For in the writings she pointed me to, and subsequent ones that I found, discussion of private schools for the poor was somehow veiled, or referred to tangentially, and ignored in subsequent writings. It was certainly not headlined in any conclusions or policy implications—to which many of us lazily turn when we digest development writings. It was almost as if the writers concerned were embarrassed or bewildered by private schools for the poor. They could write about these schools in passing, but instead of their leaping out at them as something of great significance—as they had to me when I first "discovered" them in Hyderabad—they didn't seem to impinge in any significant way on the writers' policy proposals or future discussions. Even for those who didn't deny the existence of private schools for the poor, everyone, it seemed, altogether denied their significance.

The more I explored those references, the more baffled I became. It was one thing to argue that "education for all" could be secured only through public education supported by international aid if you were unaware of private schools for the poor. But as soon as you knew that many poor parents were exiting the state system to send their children to private schools, then surely this must register on your radar as being worthy of comment in the "education for all" debate? Apparently not.

Following Sajitha Bashir's lead, I turned to the work of Amartya Sen, winner of the 1998 Nobel Prize in Economics. He'd coauthored a substantial volume, *India: Development and Participation*, which gave tantalizing glimpses of something remarkable concerning education and the poor. But this was totally ignored in his conclusions. I read the conclusion to the chapter on education and found nothing to upset what everyone knows: "Universal elementary education is a realizable goal," he had written, if only it is made "a more lively political issue."[1] More government spending is needed, I read, and government must be more actively involved in "opening more schools, improving the infrastructure, appointing more teachers, simplifying the curriculum, organizing enrolment drives, providing free textbooks," and so on. And he also trotted out the standard line on private education, that the "privileged classes" are "the main clients of unaided private schools." All standard fare—private education is about the elites and has nothing to do with universal primary education, which is the stuff of governments and politics. Nothing to upset the development applecart there.

But then wedged between these two quotes, I found not only an extraordinary description of the basic failings of public education but also the observation that many of the masses, including the poor, are now using private schools! I read that, even by 1994, the latest statistics he was using, in *rural*—that is, predominantly poor—India, enrollment in primary private schools was already above 30 percent, and there was "a further acceleration" of the numbers by the late 1990s, "especially in areas where public schools are in bad shape." In urban areas, the trend was even more startling, with the proportion in private schools estimated at 80 percent or more. As I read this, it seemed hard to reconcile these statements with the notion that private schools were patronized mainly by the elite—for it was surely stretching the definition of the privileged to include more than 80 percent of urban and more than 30 percent of rural people! What was going on?

Rather than further explore their choices, Sen criticized poor parents for making them: in villages in Uttar Pradesh, he wrote, poor parents' response to nonfunctioning public schools was "to send their sons" to study in "private schools." He'd used this comment to castigate parents' misguided preferences for educating their boys, rather than their girls. But as I read it, it seemed that he'd missed the most important point; *in passing only*, he'd thrown out a comment about the poor using private schools, only to ignore it in his later discussion! How odd was that?

The significance of this evidence was lost entirely in his subsequent comments and conclusions. Only a few pages later, he supported concerns about growing educational inequality with the warning of a "distinguished educationist" that public education "is crumbling everywhere because proliferation of private schooling has siphoned off the concern of the educated and vocal middle class." Again, surely it wasn't the "educated and vocal middle classes" that were the "problem," but from the evidence he'd already given, the less educated and politically inarticulate masses? It's as if a 500-pound gorilla was in his living room, but he didn't want to offend anyone by mentioning it. Why didn't he see the significance of his own evidence? Or was I the one who was reading too much into these passing references?

A major source of Sen's evidence was the *Public Report on Basic Education* (the PROBE Report), a detailed survey of educational provision in four northern Indian states. Sajitha Bashir from the World Bank had also given me a copy of it. I read it with growing amazement. It too was clear that "even among poor families and disadvantaged communities, one finds parents who make great sacrifices to send some or all of their children to private schools, so disillusioned are they with government schools."[2] Here was another source pointing to the phenomenon of private schools for the poor—why weren't they better known then? The PROBE team's findings on the quality of public schools were even more startling. When their researchers had called unannounced on a large random sample of government schools, *in only half* was there any "teaching activity" at all! In fully *one-third*, the principal was absent. The report gave touching examples of parents who were struggling against the odds to keep children in school, but whose children were clearly learning next to nothing. Children's work was "at best casually checked." The team reported "several cases of irresponsible teachers keeping a school closed or non-functional for several months at a time"; one school "where the teacher was drunk"; another where the principal got the children to do his domestic chores, "including looking after the baby"; several cases of "teachers sleeping at school"; and one principal who went to school only "once a week . . . and so on down the line." The team observed that in the government schools, "generally, teaching activity has been reduced to a minimum, in terms of both time and effort." Importantly, "this pattern is not confined to a minority of irresponsible teachers—it has become a way of life in the profession." But they did not observe such problems in the private schools serving the poor. When their researchers called unannounced on their random sample of private unaided (that is, receiving no government funding) schools in the villages, "feverish classroom activity" was always taking place.

So what was the secret of success in these private schools for the poor? The report was very clear: "In a private school, the teachers are *accountable* to the manager (who can fire them), and, through him or her, to the parents (who can withdraw their children). In a government school, the chain of accountability is much weaker, as teachers have a permanent job with salaries and promotions unrelated to performance. This contrast is perceived with crystal clarity by the vast majority of parents."[3] Accountability was also the factor highlighted by Amartya Sen. Low teaching standards "reflect an endemic lack of accountability in the schooling system."[4]

Other books that I was pointed to offered the same peculiar sense that something significant was being unaccountably downplayed. I read the summaries at the beginning and end of *The Oxfam Education*

Report, a standard textbook for development educationalists, and again I found only the accepted wisdom that governments and international agencies must meet the educational needs of the poor. The introduction states that there is an educational crisis because governments and international agencies have broken their promises "to provide free and compulsory basic education."[5] Then in the conclusion, I read that there is hope, but only if countries, rich and poor alike, renew their commitment to "free and compulsory education." As long as national governments spend more, and richer countries contribute billions more in aid per year, then we can achieve universal primary education by 2015. There is nothing exceptional about that, I thought as I read.

But then again, hidden away in a chapter titled "National Barriers to Basic Education," was the extraordinary (but downplayed) observation: "The notion that private schools are servicing the needs of a small minority of wealthy parents is misplaced. . . . It is interesting to note that a lower-cost private sector has emerged to meet the demands of poor households." Indeed, there is "a growing market for private education among poor households." The author of the report, Kevin Watkins, pointed to research indicating large proportions of poor children enrolled in private schools and commented, "Such findings indicate that private education is a far more pervasive fact of life than is often recognised." I put the book down and thought, that's unexpected, isn't it? Something as surprising as large numbers of the poor using private schools is surely worthy of comment in the conclusions, isn't it? Not a bit. The fact that the poor are helping themselves in this way was deemed unworthy of further mention in the introduction or conclusions. It was all a nonissue as far as the *Oxfam Education Report* was concerned.

The consensus on this surprising phenomenon, coupled with the consensus that it lacked any real significance, struck me as incredible after my first visit to Hyderabad. That poor parents in some of the most destitute places on this planet are flocking to private schools because public schools are inadequate and unaccountable seemed to me to be hugely significant territory for development experts to concede. The more I read of this evidence, the more it appeared that development experts were missing an obvious conclusion: If we wish to reach the "education for all" target of universal quality primary education by 2015, as agreed to by governments and nongovernmental organizations in 2000, surely we should be looking to the private sector to play a significant role, given the clear importance of its role already? Couldn't we be trumpeting parents' choices, rather than simply ignoring what they were doing?

Curiously—at least to me—this was *not* a conclusion reached by any of the development experts. The *Oxfam Education Report* was typical. Let me repeat: it was quite explicit that private schools for the poor were emerging in huge numbers and that these schools were more accountable to parents than government schools for the poor. Notwithstanding any of this, its position was that "there is no alternative" but blanket *public* provision to reach education for all. The PROBE Report also showed that private schools existed and were doing a much better job than government schools, but it nevertheless concluded that we must not be misled into thinking that there is a "soft option" of entrusting elementary education to private schools. It conceded that, although it had painted a "relatively rosy" picture of the private sector, where there was a "high level of classroom activity . . . better utilisation of facilities, greater attention to young children, responsiveness of teachers to parental complaints," this definitely did *not* mean that private education was an answer to the problem of providing education for all.

No Soft Option

Why not? For the past eight years, I have devoted myself to exploring this conundrum that something the poor were doing for themselves seemed to be systematically ignored by development experts and those with power and influence in these areas. Inspired by my first encounters with private schools for the poor in Hyderabad and my sense that the people working within them did not resemble the caricatures painted by development experts, I realized that I had to do some research for myself. I acquired a modest grant from the British education company CfBT for a small-scale project in the slums of Hyderabad, investigating 15 schools to find out more about their educational and business models. It was indicative, but couldn't really answer any of the challenging questions, and I couldn't convince people like Sajitha Bashir at the World Bank that I was really on to something. Fortunately, Jack Maas of the International Finance Corporation gave me additional consultancies in a range of developing countries; now when I visited a country, I took time off from my evaluation of posh private schools and colleges whenever I could and went into poorer areas to see if I could find the same thing I'd witnessed in Hyderabad.

In Ghana, taking time away from evaluating a proposed computer training franchise, I met the elderly but sprightly Mr. A. K. De Youngster, who looked on with pride as the children in De Youngster's International School began their day with a hearty rendition of "How Great Thou Art," in the school he started from scratch in 1980. Then there were 36 children in a downstairs room in his house, and he, an experienced headmaster, opened his doors after pleas from township folk, unhappy even then that public schools "were not doing their level best" for their children. When I met him, 22 years later, he had four branches to his school, with 3,400 children, charging fees of around $50 per term, affordable for many of the poor. And for those who couldn't afford it, he offered free scholarships. Seated in his office beneath a rickety fan that blew the sweat across his forehead, he chuckled as he told me that at age seven he had written to President Eisenhower from his village in West Ghana asking for help with his studies. "The Americans wouldn't help me," he smiled, "so I learned to help myself."

And I flew to Somaliland, the bit of northwestern Somalia that has declared independence from that troubled state but is recognized by no international agency. In stark contrast to my first trip to India, I traveled from Dubai in a 1950s' vintage battered Russian snub-nosed, four-propeller plane, which had to stop to refuel in Aden. Outside the battle-scarred town of Boroma, a city of 100,000 souls on the road to the Ethiopian Highlands, I met with Professor Suleyman, the vice chancellor of Amoud University, the first private university in Somaliland. Boroma had no water supply (donkey carts delivered water in leaking jerry cans), no paved roads, no streetlights, and apparently no way to dispose of the numerous burned-out tanks left over from its recent civil war. But it did have two private schools for every public school.

From the top of a rocky hill, Professor Suleyman pointed out the location of each private school in the town below. He told me: "The governor asked me, 'Why are you putting your energies into building schools? Leave it to the Ministry of Education.' But if we waited for government it would take 20 years. We need schools now." "Anyway," he continued, "in government schools, teacher absenteeism is rife, in our private schools we have commitment."

We visit one at the foot of the hill, Ubaya-binu-Kalab School, with 1,060 students, charging monthly fees of 12,000 Somaliland shillings, about $5. The owner told me that 165 of the students attended for free, the poor again subsidizing the poorest.

These were all useful insights into something that seemed remarkable to me happening around the world, but I needed more evidence. I needed to do a larger, global study to explore the nature and extent of private schools for the poor. Who would possibly be interested in funding this work? I submitted proposals to the international aid agencies and was turned down. Then I got lucky. I was to present the results of my small-scale Hyderabad research at a conference in Goa, India. Present was Charles ("Chuck") Harper, senior vice president of the John Templeton Foundation, a philanthropic organization that gave most of its grants for research on the overlap between science and religion. But, it turned out, it was also interested in exploring "free-market solutions to poverty." The bad news, I realized with a sinking feeling, was that Chuck would be leaving before my talk. So one morning, I cornered him, told him as much as I could about my findings in the slums of Hyderabad and about the tantalizing glimpses I'd had elsewhere. I told him that I thought I might be onto something interesting and said, why don't we go out into the poorer areas of Goa, and you'll see it for yourself. It was a big risk: I'd never been out to the poorer areas of Goa. Perhaps what I'd found in Hyderabad wouldn't exist elsewhere in India? Perhaps Sajitha Bashir of the World Bank was right about private schools for the poor being only localized in India? We hired a car, skipped the morning's lectures, and drove. We came upon a group of slender women in dowdy saris carrying heavy loads on their heads as they worked on road improvements. "Where do you send your children to school?" we asked. They didn't understand a word we said. We drove on, off the main road and into a little village: I needn't have worried. In front of us was a private school of the sort I'd described. Then we found another, and another. Driving back to the plush hotel where the conference was based, Chuck told me that I should submit a proposal to the foundation, and it would receive a sympathetic hearing.

Over a year later in April 2003, I was ready to start the research—promising to examine in more depth the phenomenon of private schools for the poor in India, in a range of African countries, and in China, too. The John Templeton Foundation was taking a risk: I might find nothing at all—perhaps the few schools I'd seen on my sporadic visits were just that: not the tip of the iceberg but the totality of what I might find. I suspect some of their academic referees told them that. But they funded me anyway. Beside me from the beginning was Dr. Pauline Dixon, the vivacious and entertaining economist from Newcastle University, who had come to academia later than most after spending several years as a jazz pianist. She was my indispensable support throughout, involved in researcher training, data collection and analysis, and writing up the final results.

The first study up and running was in the Old City of Hyderabad. We created a research team based in a small nongovernmental organization, the Educare Trust, in Hyderabad and trained them in how to collect the data. We then selected 3 (out of 35) zones, Bandlaguda, Bhadurpura, and Charminar, to which the secretary of education, Dr. I. V. Subba Rao, had directed me as being amongst the poorest. These three zones together had a population of about 800,000 and covered an area of about 19 square miles. Finally, within these three zones, I instructed the team to focus only on schools found in the "notified slums," according to the latest census and municipal documents, defined as areas that lacked amenities such as decent sanitation and clean water supply, adequate roads, and electricity.[6]

In addition to looking at urban Hyderabad, I also wanted to see what was happening in rural India. Again directed by the secretary of education, I sent my research teams four hours down the road to the Mahbubnagar district, one of the two worst performing of the 23 districts in Andhra Pradesh on a range of educational indicators, such as literacy rates, proportion of children in school, and retention of students. My team selected five subdistricts in Mahbubnagar, three of which were wholly rural, and two of which had some urban population in small towns. Again the focus was on these poor areas, through which we could usefully effect comparisons between both rural and "small-town" India with metropolitan India. Also in India, I conducted research in the notified slums of North Shahdara, East Delhi, reportedly one of the poorest areas of the capital city.

The studies were up and running in India. My teams were going down every street and alleyway, calling unannounced on every school they found, to collect its details and to see what was happening in the classrooms. I couldn't wait to see what they would find.

But what about Africa? Would I find the same things there? One of the first countries I visited for the research was Nigeria. I'd called universities and think tanks across sub-Saharan Africa, asking for research partners to help me in my work. The proposal from the University of Ibadan, Nigeria's premier university, in association with a Lagos-based think tank, the Institute for Public Policy Analysis, seemed particularly interesting. I couldn't wait to visit, to see whether I would also find private schools for the poor in that country.

3. A Puff of Logic, Nigeria

The Nigerian Ex–Chief Inspector

I first met Dennis Okoro in July 2003 at an education and development conference in London. Dennis was recently retired as chief inspector of schools for the Nigerian federal government. He was a charming, warm man with a soft, lilting voice and shiny bald head, who looked very much younger than his 67 years. Over a beer, I told him that I wanted to research private schools in poor areas of Lagos. He dismissed this idea straightaway: "There are no private schools for the poor. In Nigeria, private schools are only for the elite." The only problem here was that a month before, I visited Nigeria to meet with the University of Ibadan team; we went into the slums of Lagos and found private schools—everywhere, just as in India. (I'd been really excited by my find. The Ibadan team had been very surprised; they had been skeptical about finding any schools like the ones I'd found in India, and had in fact agreed to the research because they knew they would find very little. Now after our preliminary visits, we'd signed a contract and they were ready to get started on the detailed research.) It was a difficult situation to handle. One wants to be respectful of elders; above all, one doesn't want to appear arrogant—"I'm saying I know your country, educationally speaking, better than you do, although you were chief education inspector for 10 years, and I've only visited once."

So I pussyfooted around the issue: "I've found private schools in the slums of Hyderabad, won't they also be in Lagos?" No, he was adamant: "You might find some charities helping out, but no private schools. Public schools are for the poor." Sensing my disappointment, he then hit on the solution: "Ah! It's a problem of definition. In your country, you call your elite private schools 'public' schools, but *our* public schools are government schools. So it's a matter of terminology. They're not private, but *government* schools in the slums." *Quod erat demonstrandum.* For Mr. Okoro, the puzzle of these oxymoronic private schools for the poor "promptly vanished in a puff of logic." Steeped in our quaint British terminology, I'd been told that these schools I'd come across in the slums were "public" schools, and had assumed that this meant *private* schools. Elementary, my dear Watson.

I could see that there was no convincing him. I'd seen for myself something in his country and in other places too. He said they definitely weren't there, not in Nigeria and, by implication, not in any other country. So I dropped the issue and we went on to other matters, and further beers.

Makoko

A week after my conversation with Dennis Okoro, I was in a taxicab winding slowly through snarled traffic over the low, sweeping highway viaduct to Lagos Island and then to Victoria Island. I peered through the window, as so many visitors must do, at the shantytown sprawling out into the waters below. Wood huts on stilts stretched into the lagoon until they met the line of high pylons, where they abruptly stopped. Young men punted dugouts, skillfully maneuvering their long poles over and into the water; women paddled canoes full of produce down into the narrow canals between the raised houses; teenage boys stood on rocks in the water and cast their fine nets; large wooden boats, some with outboard motors, carried men out below the highway and beyond. Across the top of the shantytown was a thin drifting smog, giving all a surreal veneer, a dystopian Venice. Thompson Ayodele, the director of the Institute of Public Policy Analysis in Lagos, who had responded to my invitation to conduct the research and organized the University of Ibadan team, told me, "That's Makoko." This was exactly the kind of place that I wanted to visit, to find private schools. "You won't find private schools there!" he laughed, outraged at the idea. In any case, he added, "Too dangerous." In fact, he'd never visited, but said that it definitely wasn't safe for outsiders to venture. "There's no police there, anything goes," he said, with a finality that he felt should have been the end of the matter.

* * * *

The battered black Mercedes—a typical taxi from the budget hotel—crawled across Third Mainland Bridge into congested Herbert Macaulay Street and turned sharply into Makoko Street. It was the national holiday, October 1, 2003. Nigeria was celebrating its 43rd year of independence—if celebrating could be inferred from the breast-beating opinion pieces about widespread corruption in the national newspapers that I'd scanned at the hotel. I was in Lagos training the University of Ibadan team who would be collecting data on the proportion of students in public and private schools and to learn as much as possible about the nature of the low-cost private schools and how they compare with their public counterparts. Thompson and his team had decided we should focus on Lagos State only, for all the research indicators they'd read suggested it had problems enough to make it worth exploring in detail. An official report said that Lagos State, with 15 million people making it the sixth-largest global city, was "faced with a grave urban crisis," with over half the population living in poverty. They'd selected three "local government areas" for study, one randomly chosen from each of the three senatorial districts making up Lagos State. And they'd used official data to classify areas as "poor" or "nonpoor," with the former featuring overcrowded housing with poor drainage, poor sanitation, and lack of potable water, and prone to occasional flooding. I was only interested in finding out what was going on in these "poor" areas.[1]

My University of Ibadan team was led by Dr. Olanreyan Olaniyan (known to everyone as Lanre), a quiet, unassuming but gifted young economist, with a hugely warm and pleasing personality. He had recruited 40 graduate students from the education and economics faculties at the university. Following the methods developed in India, we trained them to go out and search for all the primary and secondary schools in the selected areas. Lanre had found government lists of public and recognized private schools, but we told the researchers they were on their own as far as unrecognized private schools were concerned. We told them to comb every street and alleyway in the urban areas, visit every village and settlement in the rural surrounding areas, looking for private schools. Be warned, we said, they won't necessarily have signboards advertising their existence: in Nigeria, there is a hefty tax on signboards, so school owners often prefer to go without. Consequently, they'd have to use their ingenuity and do detective work.

We instructed the researchers to call unannounced on the school and briefly interview the school manager or principal. Afterward, they were to ask if they could do a brief, unannounced tour of the school to look at what was going on in one classroom, and to check on school facilities. We'd role-played with our team to show them how to gain access to the schools by convincing school managers that it was worthwhile giving us their time. And then we'd taken the researchers out to some poor districts that we'd already reconnoitered to see whether they would find all the schools we had found, and to ensure that their interviews and observations matched what we had already found.

Finally, we were ready to go. But then came the national holiday, and there was only one place that I wanted to go to see for myself: Makoko. My taxi drove past fine, gated communities, outside of which security guards lazily dozed, down a reasonable suburban paved road. There was a water tap outside one of the iron gates; surrounding it, a dozen or so women and children waited their turn to fill up their assorted plastic buckets and metal bowls. Driving farther, we saw women sitting with baskets of tomatoes and peppers, yams and chilies, crowding the narrowing street. Makoko Street became Apollo Street; as it did, bustling market stalls now left barely enough space for one car to travel. As we moved slowly forward, people crowded around the car, letting us pass, but only just. Men sitting on doorsteps started calling, "*Oyinbo*" (white man). Children playfully joined in the chorus: "*Oyinbo, oyinbo, oyinbo!*"

My driver passed the rough metal gates at the entrance to two parallel and starkly imposing four-story concrete buildings. The signs indicated that this was, or rather, these were, the public primary schools, for, it transpired, there were three public schools here on the same site. The driver motioned to stop, but I told him to continue. He looked apprehensive and puzzled—"I thought we were coming to see the schools?"—but he didn't want to lose face, so he drove on. Over a canal, where hundreds of dugouts were tied loosely together, we ventured into a street so narrowed by the market traders that we had to inch forward, carefully parting the crowds as we moved. "*Oyinbo*," shouted the children; "*Oyinbo*," crowed the old men. "Mr. White," called out one young woman, looking up from dousing her small boy with a bucket of soapy water.

The paved road ended at a speed bump; beyond was just a track so muddy that it was impassable for our vehicle. My driver and I left the car there, in the safe hands of some friendly young men who had descended on us as soon as we stopped (who later, of course, demanded large, and accepted after protracted and angry negotiations smaller, sums of naira—the local currency—for their care). We picked our way carefully. The street was flooded from the previous night's rains. The open sewers along either side had spilled out into the road; I followed my driver, squelching my way from one side of the street to the other, avoiding the worst excesses of slime and mud, human excrement, and piled rubbish. But there was no way one could avoid it altogether. A young boy squatted in front of me, defecating in front of his home on an old newspaper; when he had finished, his mother collected the paper and threw it into the stinking drain.

I asked some teenage boys sitting on the low wall outside a general store if they knew of any private schools here. They said they did (my driver translating to ensure they had properly understood) and became my guides. We followed them as they moved carelessly along the planks that crossed the sewer; I moved cautiously. Down a narrow alleyway, we followed, past stinking fish markets where women worked, gutting and preparing the latest catch. And then there were the wood huts I had seen from the highway—made of flat timbers, with slivers of planks sunk into the black waters below. Beside the huts were raised, rickety wooden walkways out over the water and alongside the narrow canals. The boys moved easily; I moved slowly, testing my weight on each plank before I proceeded. Below was filthy black "water," swirling furiously in places, bubbling with some unknown organic matter. A pig wallowing in the stinking water looked up lazily as we passed. And a growing group of children joined us, playfully touching me, and shouting, "*Oyinbo.*"

At a narrow bridge across the dark canal, our guides negotiated with a young man in a canoe. And after some deliberations, we climbed down into it; the water looked even less inviting the closer we were to it. We glided down a narrow canal between the wood shacks and out into a wider waterway, a young boy effortlessly punting us. In the wider canal, women paddled by in their canoes full of produce—tomatoes and rape, spinach and yams, dried crayfish and larger fish. One canoe contained only water buckets; another had packets of cookies and soft drinks. A pied kingfisher flew by and balanced on a pole, looking for its prey in the murky waters. We glided past churches on stilts and stores on stilts, a thatched-roof building with "restaurant and bar" proudly displayed, but no

37

schools. Finally, we maneuvered expertly down into another narrow canal—where were these boys taking me? Of course I was a bit nervous; I self-consciously felt my wallet in my trouser pocket, bulging with a month's supply of dollars, there being no ATMs in Lagos (somehow I had thought it would be safer here than in the budget hotel); I'd better be a bit careful. I gingerly climbed out of the canoe and up onto the wood platform, where a dozen or so children were sitting, all now giggling at me in their midst. An old man, naked apart from tiny brown shorts, swatted at the children with a long cane, and they darted away, squealing with a mixture of pain and delight, only to return again moments later to crowd around me. I asked them their names. One tiny girl in a brilliantly clean pink dress—time and time again, I was brought to wonder how people's clothes could be kept so clean with so much filth around—told me her name was Sandra. She smiled beautifully and held on to me: "So where do you go to school?" "KPS," she said, and all around chanted, "KPS." What does that stand for? She cried out, "Kennedy Private School"—or at least that's what I thought I heard. I had found my first private school in the shantytown of Makoko. And suddenly it seemed that the teenage boys knew exactly where they were taking me. Would Sandra show me her school?

Down the gangplanks again, I moved more confidently now, above the black water swirling with mysterious life forms, the children accompanying me, holding my hand, telling me to be careful as I walk over plank sections that were rotten or falling apart. And there it was: a pink plastered building, with faded pictures of children's toys and animals, and the name of the school, not "Kennedy" but "Ken Ade" Private School emblazoned across the top of the wall.

It was closed for the national holiday, and the proprietor was officiating at a function some distance away; but that didn't ruin my excitement. One of the fishermen who had come with me had the proprietor's cell phone number; it was out of range at the moment, but this could be the way to find him later. After a while, my guides wanted to return, feeling uneasy there; and although everyone seemed friendly enough, I followed them back along Apollo Street, reluctantly, but satisfied that I had found my first private school in Makoko.

* * * *

The proprietor of Ken Ade Private School, Mr. Bawo Sabo Elieu Ayeseminikan ("Call me BSE," he told me when I eventually got through on the phone, which is somehow easier to remember) met me at the end of the muddy track when I returned a few days later, by the speed bump where the paved road ends. There was no holiday this time, but a national strike, with protests against a gasoline price hike promised around the country. At the hotel, the atmosphere at breakfast had been like a summer camp: all the workers had stayed away, partly in fear of intimidation; one besuited manager made scrambled eggs, and there were instant coffee, tea bags, and an urn of hot water so we could make our own beverages. I offered to do the dishes to show my solidarity with the management. No one must leave the hotel, I was told. It was likely to be dangerous across the city.

But I was anxious to get back to Makoko. On the phone, BSE told me that there should be no problem getting around in Makoko that day—he dismissed my fears and emboldened me. Finding a car that was willing to take me there was another matter, but eventually one driver agreed, and it was a dream driving swiftly through the uncharacteristically empty streets; he too clearly wanted to leave me at the public school—gates firmly locked shut on this day of strikes—on the outskirts of Makoko when it dawned on him where I wanted to go.

I followed BSE to his school. Inside the pink building, it was dark and very hot. Three classrooms were cordoned off with wooden partitions, while a fourth classroom was in a separate room behind; children sat at wood desks, while young teachers energetically taught. There was no strike in this or, it turned out, any of the other private schools in Makoko. We sat in his tiny office, while outside someone rigged up a generator and the fan began to whir. I wasn't sure if I'd rather have had the sultry heat or the deafening noise. Children crowded around the office: "Do you want to see the white man?" joked BSE. Some of the braver ones touched my hair; others shook my hand. He pointed out Sandra in one of the classrooms, and she hid her face, beaming shyly as I greeted her, the girl who had led me to this school.

BSE had three sites for Ken Ade Private School: the youngest children were housed in his church hall a few hundred yards up the road, learning on wood benches in front of blackboards; the middle children were in the pink building—actually the finest building in all of Makoko. And his eldest pupils were in a nearby building made of planks nailed to posts that supported a tin roof. (This building later burned down in the Great Fire of Makoko on December 6, 2004. Everyone you meet will give you the precise date, indeed precise dates are given for most key events.) BSE took me to see a site he had bought, so that he didn't have to be victim to landlords anymore and could invest in a school that he knew would always be his. He wanted to move one of his three schools to this site, and even build a junior secondary school. We walked down filthy, narrow alleyways, through water and mud, stepping delicately on the rocks and sodden sandbags that were placed there. In the open sewer were tiny fishes. The new site was partially flooded, but large enough for his dream school, with decrepit tin shacks on one side (I was surprised to see that a family lived in them) and beautiful purple flowers growing in the mud. We passed women smoking tiny crayfish, crammed on a thin mesh over a smoldering fire; one gathered handfuls and offered them to me to taste; I knew I shouldn't—for health reasons—but knew I should—to keep face with my new host. I chewed gingerly on one; it tasted surprisingly sweet; she stuffed the remainder into a plastic bag for me to take.

BSE had himself set up the school on April 16, 1990. He had started, like many, in a very small way, with a few children, with parents paying daily fees when they could afford to do so. Now he has about 200 children, from nursery school to sixth grade. The fees are about 2,200 naira ($17) per term, or about $4 per month, but 25 children attend for free. "If a child is orphaned, what can I do? I can't send her away," he tells me. His motives for setting up the school seemed to be a mixture of philanthropy and commerce—yes, he needed work and saw that there was demand for private schooling on the part of parents disillusioned with the state schools. But his heart also went out to the children in his community and from his church—how could he help them better themselves? There were the public schools at the end of the road, three schools on the same site—we both chuckled at this. How could anyone but a bureaucrat think of that? They weren't too far away, only about a kilometer from where he established his school, but even so, the distance may have been a problem for some of the parents. They particularly didn't want their girls going down those crowded streets where abductors might lurk. But mainly it was the educational standards in the public school that made parents want an alternative. When they encouraged BSE to set up the school nearly 15 years earlier, parents knew that the teachers were frequently on strike—in fairness to the teachers, protesting about nonpayment of their salaries.

I asked if I could meet some parents and visit some in their homes on stilts. The parents from the community were all poor—the men usually fished; the women traded in fish or sold other goods along the main streets. Their maximum earnings might amount to about $50 per month, but many were on lower incomes. Families were complicated here: Sandra lived with her mother, who was the second wife of the fisherman father of another child in the school, Godwin. Meanwhile, his mother lived a few doors down with her son James. In their home, Sandra told me that she really enjoyed reading. How many books did she have at home? I asked, looking around the crowded living room. She had her English reader, she told me, then butted in the conversation later: "Oh, and my agricultural science book." James said he had "at least four" books at home.

The parents told me without hesitation that there was no question of where they sent their children if they could afford it—to private school. Some had one or two of their children in the private school and one or two others in the public school—and they knew well, they told me, how differently children were treated in each. One woman said, "We see how children's books never get touched in the public school." One handsome young father, reading Shakespeare when we approached him outside his home on stilts, told me that in the private school, "the teachers are dependable." Another man ventured: "We pass the public school many days and see the children outside all of the time, doing nothing. But in the private schools, we see them everyday working hard."

I spent a lot of time observing the classes, in BSE's school and in every other private school I visited, unannounced. With the occasional exception, the teachers were teaching when I visited—in the rare case when a teacher was off sick, the principal had given the children work and was keeping an eye on their progress. Lucky was a typical teacher. He was 23, had just completed his high school diploma, and wanted to go to college to study economics. He couldn't afford to do that, so he continued living where he was brought up in Makoko and taught. He told me that he felt privileged to be a teacher: "When I am teaching, I am also learning. When I'm teaching children that the square on the hypotenuse is equal to the squares on the other two sides, I have to think deeply: why is that the case? And I find I learn all sorts of new things for myself." He was clearly enthusiastic about teaching and engaged all the children with him. His commitment and passion made him exactly the sort of teacher you would want for yourself or your own children. Or there was Remy, a bold, vivacious young woman, who commanded attention from all her children. She said that she enjoyed teaching so much in the private school because the class sizes were so small and she could give all the children individual attention. She loved being with children, she said.

Ken Ade Private School was one of the 26 private schools, BSE told me, in Makoko that were registered with the federation, the Association of Formidable Educational Development. BSE was its Makoko chapter coordinator. But there were also more schools that were "not registered," he told me—that is, it transpired, not registered *with the association:* government registration seemed irrelevant. BSE said that they wanted to create a national federation, although now it was only active in Lagos State. It was only for the low-fee private schools, like the ones in Makoko, and others that existed all over Lagos State, including the rural areas. Why was it formed? In 2000, he told me, there was a two-pronged attack to close down private schools like his. On one front was the posh private school association, the Association of Proprietors of Private Schools, which represented schools charging anything from 10 to 100 times what his school charged. APPS complained to the government about the low quality in schools like his, which prompted the government to move to close down the low-fee private schools. "We are still fighting that battle now," he said. "We are trying to give the people who are not so rich the privilege of having some decent education." With the association, they fought the closure, and with the change of government they were neglected for a bit. But then a few months earlier, the government of Lagos again issued an edict saying that they must be closed down. They were fighting it and had received a six-month stay of execution. Meanwhile, the association wrote to all the kings—as the local chiefs are called—in Lagos State telling them about the government's threat, saying 600,000 children would be pushed out of school and thousands of staff laid off if the government proceeded. "When you have a headache," said BSE, "the solution is not to cut off the head! If government has a problem with us, then we can work together to help us improve, not cut us off completely!" But there was no self-pity. "We find it impossible to meet all their regulations; we can't possibly afford them all." As we walked around the shantytown, he related that he had written to the Lagos education department saying that instead of hassling the private schools, why didn't it help them with a revolving loan fund? He had received, he said, no reply.

Over the next few days, I visited many of the association schools. There was a school in which French was the medium of instruction, with a principal from Benin serving migrant children from the surrounding Francophone countries who will return home for secondary school. It was the largest school, with 400 children; it was a two-story wood building (called a "story" building in Nigeria and elsewhere in West Africa) built on stilts. The oldest school, Legacy, founded in 1985, was also a "story" building, with an upper floor of planks that creaked and groaned as we walked on it, and through which we could see the classes below. When I visited at 5:00 p.m., a teacher was still teaching upstairs, voluntarily helping the senior children prepare for their examinations. The proprietor here had started the school by going door-to-door, encouraging parents to send their children to school—there being no accessible public school then, and he wanted his community to be literate. Then he started charging 10 kobo (that is, 10 hundredths of a naira) per day; later he worked on making parents pay weekly fees; as his numbers grew, he asked them to give what they could to help him run the place. As his school became established, he moved to charging by the month and then by the term. He, like everyone, found it really difficult to get the fees from parents, and he, like everyone else, offered free tuition to many of his children.

Were his teachers qualified? I asked. He began by telling me that he trained them himself; at the end of each term, they had workshops to increase the academic standard, and that was fine. Then he added: "We don't cherish qualifications, we cherish your output. Can you perform? That is the important thing, not whether you have certificates!" He told a story about how someone came for a job, with an "impressive BSc in mathematics," and he asked him: "OK, so my grandfather is 80 and in 8 years time he will be eight times your age. How old are you now?" I quickly butted in with what seemed the obvious answer, showing off my algebraic knowledge: "11."

Unfortunately, I fell straight into his trap, "That's what he said, but the answer is 3, because the question is how old are you *now*!" The story was meant to demonstrate something about common sense and problem solving not necessarily equating with good qualifications. I too had an "impressive BSc in mathematics," I thought. But the point was well taken—qualifications weren't everything.

I asked whether the teachers belonged to a union. "No union here," he said and laughed pleasurably. "No union, we work as a team, we cherish oneness, we have an end-of-term party, altogether, dancing, eating, and drinking." I noticed that most of the teachers were women, and mentioned this. "Why? You say why? Because the money that is being paid, the men cannot be here; salary for most men is higher, and most men don't like teaching, even here they want to be president, politicians, big men, lawyers," he said, dramatically emphasizing each possible option: "They don't want to teach, that's the way it is in this country!"

Throughout, as I traveled around the slum, it was clear that the school buildings were of poor quality—this criticism that I met so often when talking to the development experts back in England was certainly valid. But they were no worse than the buildings in which people lived. It was true, I saw, they didn't normally have toilets, but neither did the people's homes. The children felt at ease in them—the teachers were drawn from the community itself and knew all its problems as well as its vibrancy. The more I visited these schools, the more I realized how organic they were, part of the community they served, quite unlike the public schools outside.

One afternoon, BSE and I visited a public school. We arrived at 1:40 p.m. The private schools would be in session until 4:00 p.m.; the public schools were already closed, children playing boisterously in the muddy space between the high-rise buildings. I noticed that some were urinating in the corner—these children didn't appear to have functioning toilets either. The headmistress of one of the three schools was very friendly and welcoming, however, and invited me back the next day.

I return at 9:20 the next morning, slightly later than promised. Adekinle Anglican Primary School was the largest of the three primary schools closest to the road, taking up the daunting concrete blocks on both sides of the parade ground. (Many of the church schools were nationalized in the 1970s and 1980s, hence the Anglican title. They were classed as public schools, however, and received 100 percent of their funding from the state, although they still had some vestiges of private management, through the church.) The short, plump headmistress began ushering children into classrooms—supposedly the school had been operating since 8:00 a.m., but even so, many children seemed to be milling around. Possibly they were on break. In front of me, without trying to hide it in any way, the headmistress began to chase, then viciously beat with her cane, a small girl. She beat her to the ground and as the girl got up to limp away, she viciously laid into her again; the girl eventually escaped and made her way to the classroom, holding herself, weeping furiously; I've never seen anything like this in any of the private schools—yes, the teachers there sometimes had their canes, and I often worried about that, but they seemed playful with them, at most tapping the desks in front of the students to get their attention.

Shaken, I visited the classes with my host. She carried her cane with her, emphasizing every word she said with it; it was not only the children she made nervous as she thus gesticulated. Some teachers were teaching and appeared committed and pleasant, but in most classes, the children seemed to be doing little. Sometimes, this seemed to be because the teacher had completed the lesson, had written a few simple things on the board and the class had finished copying them. Then they sat in silence while the teacher sat at her desk and read the newspaper or stood outside chatting with her colleagues. The first grade classroom had 95 children in it, but it was three classes together—one teacher was sick, the other was on extended study or some other official leave. I wondered how often that happened, or whether today was just an exception. The children in this class were doing nothing; some were also sleeping; one girl was cleaning the windows. The one teacher was hanging around outside the classroom door. No one, certainly not the headmistress, appeared remotely embarrassed by any of this. I asked the children what their lesson was—when no one answered, the principal bellowed and barked at the children; it was a mathematics lesson she told me pleasantly, without any sense of incongruity, for no child had a single book open.

Of the three schools, this one could house 1,500 children. The headmistress told me that parents left the school en masse a few years earlier because of the teachers' strikes. But things were better

45

now, and children had returned. The school had a current enrollment of around 500, which was more than before, but enrollment growth was stagnant. It must be somewhat disheartening for teachers to go on strike and then find that the parents had made alternative, private arrangements. But the truth was actually more startling: no one here seemed to know that this alternative existed. For on the top floor of this imposing building, there were six empty classrooms, all complete with desks and chairs, waiting for children to return. Why don't the parents send their children here? I asked the headmistress, innocently. Her explanation was simple: "Parents in the slums don't value education. They're illiterate and ignorant. Some don't even know that education is free here. But most can't be bothered to send their children to school." I suggested that, perhaps, they were going to private schools instead? She laughed at my ignorance. "No, no, these are poor parents, they can't afford private school!"

I asked the teachers where they lived: many traveled for an hour or more to get to the school; some traveled over two hours. The principal also lived a considerable distance away. Two teachers lived outside Lagos State; Yoruba was not the mother tongue of one, even though the majority of the children were Yoruba. This didn't matter, she said, as the language of instruction was English. I mused how different it was in the private schools, where teachers were from the community; they knew the problems facing the children, for they themselves experienced such problems every day. And they could explain things in their mother tongue, if required, unlike the teachers at the public school.

I continued my visit to the other two schools on the same site—next was Ayetoro African Church Primary School. Some of the classes in the second primary school had only 12 or 15 children in them, although the class register showed 30 to 35. Why were so many absent? The principal told me: "You see, this is a riverine area, and when we have the rains like now, children have to stay home and clean their houses because they are flooded. So that's why today there are few children in school." When I told this to BSE afterward, he said, "But the children are here in the private school today!" He didn't need to tell me; I could see this difference for myself.

The principal of the final school, Makoko Anglican Primary School, was a lovely, dedicated lady, and I warmed to her considerably. She took me into classrooms, and I asked the children if they had brothers or sisters in private schools, remembering what parents had told me in Makoko itself. The principal interrupted: "No," she said, "these children are poor, they can't afford to go to private school." But I persevered; and the children said yes, yes, their siblings went to private schools. And they gave me names, like KPS, St. Williams' and Legacy, with which I'd become familiar. At this point, the headmistress admitted that she had never been into Makoko itself, had never seen where her children came from. When pressed, she said she didn't know whether there were any private schools there, but she was pretty sure there were not, and that the children were playing wicked games with their foreign visitor.

On the second floor of her school, two of the classrooms were empty; in the third were two middle-aged female teachers at their desks side by side near the door. They chatted with me pleasantly. Here, the third and fourth grades were housed together, with 60 children. Why were they in the same classroom? Because they didn't have enough desks for two classes, so they sat them together. On the third floor, three classrooms were empty and in the fourth were three classes together; with 90 children registered, I was told, although only 75 were present. The three teachers again sat at their desks neatly arranged along the window side, doing nothing apparently, while the children sat doing nothing either. Again, the reason given was that they had no desks and benches for the children.

I pointed out to the headmistress that in the six empty classrooms in the first primary school, just yards away from where we were standing, there were stacks of unused desks and benches. She said she didn't know that. Why didn't she have the desks brought over? "What goes on in the other government schools is not my business," she shrugged.

Coda

Almost two years after my first visit to Makoko, I arrived at the plush Secretariat buildings in Lagos, seeking an interview with the commissioner of education about the role of private schools in reaching "education for all." I'd got my research results in the interim, and they were quite astonishing: we'd found 32 private schools in the shantytown of Makoko, none recognized by the government, and estimated that around 70 percent of schoolchildren in Makoko

went to private school. In the poor areas of Lagos State more generally, we'd estimated that 75 percent of all schoolchildren were in
private schools, of which only some were registered with the government. In fact, more students were attending unregistered private
schools alone than were enrolled in the government sector. Based
on these findings, and after showing him photographs and video
footage of BSE and his school, I'd convinced television producer
Dick Bower that the work was of interest, and he'd received commis-
sions from BBC World and BBC 2's flagship news program *Newsnight*
to make documentaries in Makoko, illustrating the general themes
that were emerging.

It was fascinating to watch Dick's position change during the
course of his two weeks in Makoko. Before arriving there, he'd
been convinced that this would be a soft-focus story of one or two
committed people establishing schools against the odds, focusing
on a couple of cute children—like Sandra who had first led me to
Ken Ade Private School—and telling their story. I don't think Dick
had really believed that so many private schools existed, nor that
those who had set them up could be described as entrepreneurs
rather than social workers. But then as we'd wandered around
Makoko and bumped into one private school after another, I could
see that Dick realized there was more to this story than he had first
thought. But the real eye opener for him came when we interviewed
the commissioner of education for Lagos State and, with his permission, filmed in the government schools too. Far from being a soft-
focus film about the delightful antics of a few poor people, he realized
that he was onto a hard-hitting political story, about the denial
among people with power that something remarkable was happening among the poor. I'll return later to some of what he heard when
we interviewed the people in power. But waiting to get the interview
with the commissioner of education, something odd happened:

In the commissioner's narrow waiting room among the builders'
rubble and the rusting fridge marked "Property of the Ministry of
Education," sat a smart, distinguished-looking elderly gentleman,
who was also waiting for an interview with the commissioner. After
a while, he and I began chatting, and it turned out that he was
working for the British Aid agency Department for International
Development (DfID) on its project CUBE—cute—Capacity for Universal Basic Education. He was very keen to tell me about his work.

While the World Bank had made a soft loan of $101 million to this project, DfID had *given* about $20 million. He told me the basis of the project: "We need to listen to what the poor have to say, something that's never happened before—too many aid agencies just barge in and tell the poor what they require; we're different, we listen first to what they have to say. Only in that way can we create sustainable solutions." He told me that they had held frequent focus groups to discuss the poor's educational needs. "We even get the children to draw pictures of what they want in their schools." The children, he told me, had drawn pictures of merry-go-rounds and other children's playground equipment, "just like in the private schools; they want their schools to be just like the private schools!" he laughed—clearly referring to posh private schools. Then once all this listening had taken place, "We deliver a report to the community telling them what they have told us about what they want." All that then got translated, he told me, "'into sustainable solutions."

If he'd been listening to the poor in the locations where my teams had been working, he must know about what we'd been finding, I thought. So I told him of my research interest in private schools for the poor. "Ah," he said, "there is a confusion here. In England, you call elite private schools 'public schools,' but here by public schools we mean government, state schools. So in our country, private schools are for the rich, and middle classes, and public schools are for the poor. You got confused because of the language." For a moment I thought: what a coincidence, two senior Nigerians making the same claim about language being the source of my misunderstanding about private schools for the poor. Then suddenly, the penny dropped: this was not *another* senior Nigerian; this was the very same Dennis Okoro, the ex–chief inspector!

We joked about how we'd met before, even shared beers together, and how bad our memories were. It was more forgivable in a man of nearly 70 than someone in his early 40s, I contested. He gently excused me, "You must meet a lot of people on your travels." Anyway, I told him that I'd been working for two years in the private schools for the poor in Makoko, Badagry, and other poor places around Lagos State. He must have seen such schools in his work with DfID, if not before? He didn't actually say I was lying, but gently contradicted me by repeating his refrain: "No, private schools are for the rich, not the poor."

After the interview with the commissioner of education, Dick Bower, the BBC producer, hit on the idea of asking Dennis if he would be prepared to come to Makoko with us—not specifying any particular reason why. Dennis gamely agreed. He was only available the following afternoon—a Saturday, unfortunately, so children wouldn't be in school—but he had to be back in Abuja, Nigeria's capital, on Sunday. I'd been working with BSE all morning when Dennis and the BBC crew pulled up outside Ken Ade Private School in our battered old Volvo, hired from one of BSE's relatives who lived a few doors down. BSE and I walked over to greet him. As we stood in front of the school, I said: "So here is a private school for the poor. They exist!"

I could see he was put out. But he soon pulled himself together. Dennis put the challenge directly to BSE: "Why do you call it a private school? Do children pay fees?" "Yes," confirmed BSE. "Ah," said Dennis, "so it is not a private school for the poor." The conversation went back and forth, but the sum of his argument seemed to be this: The poor by definition cannot afford to pay fees for private schools. So if this was a fee-charging private school, it couldn't be for the poor. Public schools were free precisely because the poor could not afford to pay tuition, and parents who could afford private schooling could not be poor.

I got him to speak to some of the children who were milling around us, and they confirmed that they came from families of fishermen and traders. He agreed that there were pretty poor people around here; he agreed too, in a very deprived area. But he continued, trying a different tack. His argument now was something like this: The private school might be in this deprived area, even possibly attended by poor children, but it was not a private school *for* the poor because it was not in the poor's interest. It was not "pro-poor," a term I heard for the first time from him but now commonly used by development experts. A private school *for* the poor, by definition could not exist because the poor must not pay school fees. So it may be a private school, he conceded after all, but it is *for* the purpose of making money, that is all, not *for* the poor. Dennis then said, "Look, there is a way that private schools can be *for* the poor." He gave an example of how British Airways had wanted to help improve basic education in Nigeria. The company had found a very down-at-the-heels (public) school and refurbished it. It now had the most magnificent building and facilities—but still it was free, so it really was for the poor, but involved the private sector. "If Professor Tooley will fund your school," he told BSE, "then it can provide free places to the children. Then it really can be a private school *for* the poor." Then it can really be "pro-poor." I considered mentioning that Ken Ade Private School already provided free and subsidized tuition to its poorest students, but decided to leave Dennis with the last word.

We all—the BBC crew, BSE, Dennis, and I—traveled from the slum to our hotel, the Mainland Hotel, on its periphery. We ordered food and drink. We were in good spirits—Dennis is a very friendly person, and nothing that had passed between us while we stood outside the school could change the warmth we felt for each other. We talked generally about other matters. But then as we came to the end of our meal, he wanted to thank us formally and made a little speech. He told us that he had learned much today. He had never been to Makoko before, he admitted—indeed, he had thought when he heard the name that it was somewhere else entirely. But, he excused himself, no government education official will ever have gone beyond the public school on the outskirts of the shantytown, so no one would realize such private schools existed within. He then told us a parable: "The elders of a village warn their chief that they must make a clearing in the bush around his house because there are snakes aplenty, right there around his house, and he must beware. But he had never seen any, so he didn't believe that such creatures existed there. But then a villager had caught one, lying in wait by the chief's water hole to catch its prey. Cleverly ensnaring it, he had taken it to the chief. 'With my eyes I can see it. And with my hands I can touch it. Now I believe.'" Dennis finished: "And I've seen and touched this private school. It's good, yes it's always good to learn of something that you didn't know existed. I will tell everyone I meet about this from now on." I could have hugged him.

Only an Urban Phenomenon?

For Dennis Okoro—and he was by no means alone in this— denying the existence of private schools for the poor had a logical dimension. Private schools are for the rich because the poor, by definition, cannot afford to pay for private education. Therefore, it follows, private schools for the poor cannot exist. But there was also a practical dimension to his denial. The private schools are not necessarily easily visible. They're hard to find. In Makoko, you must go beyond the public schools on the outskirts, beyond the paved road into unknown and forbidding territory. If everyone tells you that there are no schools beyond, and it's a threatening place, why would you bother to go and look for yourself? To find the private schools, you really must get your boots dirty. Not everyone is prepared to do that.

Makoko is an urban slum. This in itself was significant for Dennis Okoro. OK, so these types of schools are in urban slums. "But," he said, "you won't find them in rural areas." To development experts, this is a hugely significant point. If private schools for the poor are only an urban phenomenon, they can't really play much of a role in meeting the educational needs of the poor because poverty is greatest in the rural areas. You might find a few private schools in urban slums. But they're nothing significant in terms of development because they don't reach the rural poor.

But I was looking in rural areas too. In Ghana, it was to be a major focus. Would I find anything there to further challenge Dennis's beliefs?

4. The Shifting Goalposts, Ghana

The Honourable Minister

Serendipity led me to choose Ghana as a country for my research because around the same time that I'd met Dennis Okoro at a conference in London, I was speaking at another conference on education and development, this one organized by the Italian Liberal Party in Milan. And at this event, I met the Ghanaian minister of education (and youth and sport), the Honourable Kwadwo Baah-Wiredu, a tall, handsome man in his early 50s, with a striking resemblance to the actor Richard Roundtree from *Shaft*. The conference was held in the beautiful ivy-covered manor house headquarters of the Liberal Party. My talk was scheduled for midday. At noon, the cool auditorium was packed full of gorgeous young women—I was very gratified to see the kind of audience the Italian Liberal Party could attract and braced myself for their admiring glances as I lectured on my findings about private schools for the poor in India, with brief references to what I'd also seen in Nigeria.

But it was not to be. Apparently there had been a late addition to the program. Leonardo, a star from AC Milan, one of Europe's top soccer teams, had been invited to speak on how his club was funding an education project somewhere in Africa. At the precise moment he finished his presentation and got up to leave, the auditorium emptied. The young women mobbed him on his way out. I gave my talk to the Honourable Minister, plus one or two other stalwarts who remained, including Andrew Coulson, now director of the Cato Institute's Center for Educational Freedom.

But we became friends over dinner, the Honourable Minister and I, a friendship that I'm glad to say we shared until his tragic and untimely death last year, and he invited me to Ghana to do the study. This was a rare opportunity—it would be very unusual to do the study where I had government support.

Soon after I met him, I traveled to Ghana. My first port of call was the Ministry of Education, where the Honourable Minister had told me to get the latest statistics on enrollment—public and private—to help me with my work. The director of statistics had apparently promised to have all the statistics ready. He was at a meeting somewhere in town when I arrived, so I waited in his office at the behest of his assistant, a balding and rather camp older man. A secretary was typing a report at one of the computers, touch-typing very slowly without looking at the screen. After a few minutes, she completed a paragraph then looked up at the screen. She had typed everything in capital rather than lowercase letters. She erased it all carefully and slowly retyped it all. But she still did not check her typing; her eyes were steadfastly focused on the page to be copied, ignoring the screen completely, except to check at the end when it was too late.

Hers was the only work going on in the room, and perhaps in the whole Ministry of Education. The entire place resembled a school during recess. Many men were wandering around on the balcony corridors, holding hands as Africans do, chatting, joking; others were eating and drinking, and some were sleeping. But this wasn't recess; it was 3:00 in the afternoon.

Eventually, the director of statistics returned. He hadn't prepared anything for me. He took a phone call, about an article he was writing for *Computer Africa* magazine, and talked for at least 20 minutes about how wrong it was for this editor to keep pressing him to have the paper ready. "Why not Thursday?" he said to me. "Why not Friday? Why today; today, always today?" After telling me this story, he then looked on the computer for the statistics I required. He searched for 15 minutes, while I sat quietly. Eventually, he learned that his assistant had the correct file; so he printed it out, transferring the single computer cable between the computers. Figures were only available up to 1994. That was nearly a decade before. Where were the later figures? "Oh, we haven't collated them yet. We have the figures, but they are not collated yet." I looked around his office as I waited: piles of paper, haphazardly strewn everywhere; piles on desks, on shelves, and on the floor; crumpled old folders; dusty desks and old computers; no other books apart from these myriad files.

From his office, I went to wait at the office of the Honourable Minister's secretary. She was very kind, very pleasant. But she had the brief I'd prepared for the minister in front of her, outlining my preliminary findings on private schools for the poor in India, and asking whether this could also be true of Ghana. She laughed at me; "In our country, private schools are for the rich,'" she said, baffled by the stupidity of this visiting white man.

It was a refrain that I was to hear time and again as I went around trying to find partners for the research. That wasn't the only frustration at getting started. I visited the superbly appointed, air-conditioned offices of the British aid agency DfID, a few blocks from the Ministry of Education, complete with lavish corporate images of poverty alleviation, to see if it could help me find research teams. Its education adviser, an affable Geordie,[1] Charles Kirkaldy, was friendly enough, but thought I was on a mission to nowhere. He told me he sometimes visited rural areas, passing government schools at 9:30 a.m. and seeing the teachers sitting under trees knitting while the children wandered around the school. But he tried to put me off looking for any private schools in these poor areas. "There's no money in the villages to pay for private school," he said.

He told me that DfID didn't put much into education, just $80 million or so over the past five years, all of which had gone to the government for improving primary schools—much of that was for improving their buildings. (I saw it as I traveled around later, plush new government primary school buildings proudly sporting the DfID logo. There were also European Union logos and logos for various other European government aid agencies.) But he was openly dismayed at the lack of accountability for how the DfID funds were spent. "We're spending a lot on capacity building in the ministry," he said, "trying to make it run better." But the Ghana Education Services was a "bureaucratic monster," he told me, and the money just got frittered away. I asked whether any of it benefited children's learning. He sighed and replied that he doubted it very much.

Although he thought my quest for low-cost private schools would be in vain, he gave me some names of possible research partners from Ghana's top universities. For a few days, I interviewed these prospective partners only to be quoted their *daily* rates of $500 or more. With salaries at the university the equivalent of $1,000 *per year*, this seemed rather excessive. They all also wanted dinner, or at least cocktails, in the luxury of the Golden Tulip Hotel, where DfID put up all its aid consultants for $200 a night. It seemed that international aid agencies had pushed prices for research consultancy sky-high. It was, in any case, more than my more modest budget could stand.

I'd given up hope of finding anyone reasonably priced to help and was about to leave the country, sadly abandoning it as a possible research base, when I heard of the Educational Assessment and Research Centre. It had done work for the U.S. Agency for International Development and came highly recommended as a rarity that charged realistic rates for its research. In its offices in a suburban house in the suburb of Legon, Accra, I met the deputy director, Emma Gyamera, a wonderfully warm woman, always ready to laugh and always smiling. I sat in her office and told her what I'd found in India and what seemed to be also true of Nigeria, and what I was looking for in Ghana. She blushed deeply, laughed, and rather embarrassed said: "In our country, it is the opposite, private education is for the rich. What you found in those countries doesn't happen here."

But I persevered—after all, I'd already found the modestly priced De Youngster's International School on my earlier visit, so I was convinced there were others. And the Honourable Minister himself had thought that I might be onto something. I hired a car and driver and went looking. First, I visited Madina, a low-income satellite town, north of the airport. Apparently, my driver Richard told me, it was named after Medina in Saudi Arabia and had a large Muslim community. On the way from the hotel, we circled what Richard proudly told me was "the largest roundabout in the whole of West Africa." He told me again on the way back.

We drove down bumpy, craterous tracks with open drainage ditches. The road abruptly disappeared at one point, an overflowing open sewer had apparently washed it away, so we parked the car. And we found Gina International School. We were introduced to the proprietor, Gina, who suffered from excessive sweating. It was very humid, true; we were all finding it difficult, but she had streams of perspiration pouring down her face, which she continually had to wipe with a handkerchief. She told me she established the school eight years before, starting with kindergarten; it now went up to fifth grade, with 300 students and fees of about $5 per month. There were 14 staff members, 8 of whom were men. Although in this predominantly Muslim area, it was a secular school. The children seemed lively and cheeky—when I greeted one class, "Good morning and how are you," one boy imitated my accent to much boisterous acclaim from his classmates.

We continued walking. My driver Richard told me that he also sent his child to private school. I asked him why. "Because the teachers are reliable in a private school. In a government school, they might turn up on one day, but then not another." The next school we approached had a sign proclaiming, "Elim Cluster of Schools" and beneath the legend "Exodus 15:27." Initially, of course, I assumed that it was a church school. Mama Janet L. A. Nugar soon got rid of that illusion. A fierce-looking woman in her late 50s, Janet was wearing one of those unruly permed wigs often sported by African women of her age; she also wore bold gold-rimmed spectacles, which added to her fierce appearance. But she was friendly enough, and when I told her that my luggage had not arrived and that was why I was not properly, formally dressed, she said, "Ah, Ghana!" choosing to place the blame firmly on her country rather than KLM, my carrier from Europe.

The name Elim was from the Bible, she agreed, but pointed me to her business card that said, "Proprietress." She had been inspired by the verse from the Bible, but her school had nothing to do with the church, but it was "properly run," she proudly said, "'as a business." She told me that in Ghana, everyone liked to name his or her business after some religious verse or sentiment. And it was true. As I left her, I saw down the same street Try Jesus Carpentry Store; No Problem is Too Great for God Fashion Centre; God Is Great Beauty Parlour. I didn't view these as being part of a church mission. But somehow I easily made that assumption with regard to schools. It's something that I was to realize was to put many people off the scent about the ubiquity of private schools for the poor—too often if people heard of them, they assumed they were affiliated with the church.

Her "cluster" of schools comprised daycare, nursery, primary, junior secondary, and senior secondary; she also ran two computer-learning centers. She had started the school chain 12 years before with the daycare center. She herself had been a trained government teacher, as had her headmaster; but she had then given up and joined the Ghana Prison Service, from where she took early retirement and decided to establish the school. All told she had 704 children. A handful received free tuition—and she knew each of them by name. But "I'm a business woman," she said, "I can't afford to give many."

How did parents compare her school with the government school? I asked. Well, I'd have to ask the parents, she said. "But parents do compare, they are looking for the best for their children, and they see our examination results and see they are always good, and realize that they had better pay more." And she added, "If a school is private, they know that the supervision of teachers is always keen; in a government school, they don't know that."

Later that day, my driver and I went out along the coast road, traveling for four or five hours, past Cape Coast to Elmina, with its terrible history of a Portuguese, then Dutch, then British, slaving station. We stayed at a comfortable hotel, and the next morning set off again. Miles beyond, in the remote district of Ahanta West, I asked Richard to turn down a rough track, signposted to a pig farm. We continued along this winding road in the low hills until we reached a small village built around the Catholic church. We asked a young woman at one of the ubiquitous shops fashioned out of a converted metal freight container, with a wood veranda, whether there was a private school there. No, she said. There was the public school by the church, which we could see from our car: it had marvelous spacious grounds and well-constructed buildings (built with aid from, among others, the Bill and Melinda Gates Foundation, I was told later). I probed her: but are you sure there is no private school? Well, she ventured, there is one, a small nursery; one, that's all. From my experience in India, nursery schools often continue on to primary school, once the children get older and parents ask the proprietor to extend provision, so I asked her for directions. A young man standing nearby turned out to be a parent at the school and took me there. And sure enough, this village did have a small private school, up to sixth grade, not just nursery grades. It was called Christian Hill, was in a makeshift wood building, and had well over 100 children. All around there were signs that read "Speak English." The children crowded around, delighting in their foreign visitor, and exploding with joyous laughter when shown their photographs on a digital camera.

From there, my driver took me down through the public school grounds, aiming for the next village on the coast. Down winding narrow dirt roads that usually had no motor traffic, we arrived at a steep bank, in an opening in the rocky promontory, to a beach, where fishing boats lay and men sat and mended nets. It was a beautiful, idyllic setting. I asked whether there was a private school here. No, I was told, the Catholic school was in the village a few miles away, I must have passed it . . .? No, I said, I was looking for *private* schools; isn't there one here, even a small one? Oh, well, yes, there was one, just over there. Past the village bulletin board advertising next week's soccer match, and over the village soccer field, haphazardly laid out on the bare soil, was a small two-room concrete-block building, with blocks outside by the sandpit and additional rooms under construction. It was another private school, going up to grade 2, with 80 students but ripe for expansion into higher grades as the children grew older. The school had no name, "because it is not yet complete," offered a villager called Isaac, who spoke very good English. In fact, several of the men did. Although when I gave them my business card, they scrutinized it upside down, suggesting no one could read as well as he could talk.

Two random villages, 100 percent success in finding private schools. So I returned to Accra and to Emma at the Educational Assessment and Research Centre, and told her that I was happy to go ahead with the project and see what we would find. We soon had a contract signed, and the research was under way. The research from then on wasn't straightforward. The greatest difficulty was convincing the researchers—all graduate students recruited from the University of Cape Coast—that I really was interested in finding the small, often-ramshackle private schools. It was almost as if they couldn't possibly think I was seriously interested in these nondescript buildings, that I must really be interested in the sounder government buildings and plusher private schools—just as the villagers themselves seemed to believe on my first visit. It was almost as if everyone was hung up with a sense of inferiority about the budget private schools, that they should really be hidden from outsiders. But I persisted, even going back in the field with the researchers a few times and finding five or six other private schools they'd missed.

We conducted the most detailed study in Ga, a largely rural district surrounding Accra, named such, not as I first thought as an abbreviation for "Greater Accra," but because it was home to the Ga people.

The district was classified by the Ghana Statistical Service as a low-income, periurban area—that is, a rural area surrounding the metropolitan city—one of the poorest districts in Ghana, despite (or possibly because of) its proximity to the capital. About 70 percent of its 500,000 people reportedly lived at or below the poverty line. Ga included poor fishing villages along the coast, subsistence farms inland, and large dormitory towns for workers serving the industries and businesses of Accra itself; most of the district lacked basic social amenities, such as potable water, sewage systems, electricity, and paved roads.[2]

During the course of the research, I was privileged to spend several days in one of the fishing villages, Bortianor, a small community set in the beautiful coconut groves that line the oceanfront. It was only a few hours from Accra, from the lavishness of the DfID offices and the Ministry of Education parking lot full of new four-by-fours. But it might as well have been a million miles away, for all the notice anyone seemed to take of what was happening there.

A Day in the Life

Ten-year-old Mary Tettey gets ready for school. It's 6:00 a.m.; the brilliant orange sun is rising over the horizon. She lives in the tiny village of Faana, wedged onto a narrow strip of sand not more than 30 feet wide, facing onto the golden sands of the ocean, with a shallow lagoon behind them. Her home is a compound of wood-frame huts with rough thatched walls and roofs. Her mother chases the ducks out of the living area where they've been rummaging around the cooking pots; they waddle onto the beach to settle down for the day in the dwindling shade beside an upturned fishing boat. Mary packs her bag with her exercise books and some dried fish wrapped in newspaper for her lunch. Every day except Tuesdays—the day of rest for the spirits of the ocean—her father will have been out on the ocean since 3:00 a.m., riding the waves in a 30-foot wooden fishing boat, with an outboard motor fixed into a little wood canopy on the starboard side, and "God is Great" and "Psalm 91, 1–2" carved into the wood on the port side. Each day he'll return by 9:30 a.m.; on the weekend, Mary will watch from the shore with her mother as the boats are steered through the gap in the surf into the lagoon. Then they'll pile the small fish into their baskets and return to their yard to smoke them, while the younger men in the village drag huge nets onto the beach to the rhythm of drums.

But today is a school day. Mary joins a dozen other children at their little beach on the lagoon side, where women are already washing pots, and they climb into the canoe that will take them to Bortianor, the main village. One of the schoolboys, barely taller than the wood pole itself, punts the canoe. It slides away from the shore and noses quietly through the reeds and lilies. A posse of terns combs the water searching for fish, while a black-tailed godwit, elegant on stiltlike legs, stalks the fringes of the lagoon.

It takes them 20 minutes to reach the head of the lagoon, where several fishing boats lie idle, and where the women will soon gather to welcome back their men of the main fishing fleet under circling vultures. The children disembark into the shallow water. On dry land, Mary puts on her sandals and sets off through the village, following the dirt paths between mud-and-thatch huts, with compounds lined with coconut palms and thatched fences. As she walks, Mary thinks of what she wants to do when she grows up. She wants to be a nurse because she loves to help the sick. Her favorite subject at school is integrated science; she worked hard on her homework for that subject the night before, knowing that it will help her in the future. As she gets farther from the lagoon, the huts become grander, huts made of planks or bamboo huts rendered with dark mud, with fig and mango trees in the yards, and cacti bristling at the compound edges. A cockerel crows, and chicks scamper across the path in front of her.

Mary reaches the center of the village where a sign points to the government school to the right. No children are there yet, but she can see the imposing plaster-coated block building at the head of the large playground. But she doesn't turn there. She walks past the sign and instead turns left, into a gap where there is no sign, and enters the compound of a ramshackle wood building. This is Supreme Academy, one of six private schools in the village. It's her school. It's 6:30 a.m. She's one of the first children to arrive, but one of the teachers is already there.

He's 21-year-old Erskine Feruta. He lives with his parents in a larger village a few miles down the coast. Every school day, he accompanies his parents in the company bus that takes them to a factory on the edge of Accra. It picks them up at 6:00 a.m. and

15 minutes later drops him at the main road, just past the workshop of the carpenter, a friend from his childhood who makes coffins in any shape you want, like fine fishing boats or monstrous fish, beds, or cakes even.

Erskine greets Mary, and together they sweep the schoolyard, getting everything ready for the new school day. Erskine is the only teacher in the school who doesn't live in the village itself. Last year, he had graduated from senior secondary school. He had wanted to go on to the Kwame Nkrumah University of Science and Technology in Kumasi, but couldn't afford it. So to try to save some money, he looked for work in his and neighboring villages, and found this vacancy at Supreme Academy. He loves being a teacher. He loves it that the children seem happy when they are around him. He feels proud when he can impart something new to his charges. And he reflects on the happy memories of his own school days and is continually astonished at his own achievement of now being a teacher, and no longer a pupil! And not only is he able to teach his own class, but he also teaches computer science to all the classes. Crammed into the tiny room that doubles as the proprietor's office, he shows them how to format a disk, what a computer monitor looks like, and all the basic computing skills of the Ghanaian national curriculum. He's sorry that so many children must cram into the classroom with only one computer because they rarely get to use it themselves. He's not unhappy with his wages. The 200,000 cedis per month, about $20, enable him to save toward his goal of higher education for himself.

Other children filter into the compound, and by 7:30 a.m., the schoolyard is buzzing with children. One of the last to arrive is Victoria, a beautiful child of 11, tall for her age, and already very elegant. Her family lives nearby, in a large block house they share with three other families. Victoria's father is a fisherman, and her mother is a fishmonger, who smokes the fish caught by her husband for the market and also runs a small store in the yard, selling canned goods and dried milk. Victoria's home is more or less adjacent to the government school compound. Her parents had started her schooling at Supreme Academy, the closest private school to them, in the nursery classes, but then had fallen on hard times. The owner of the fishing boat who had employed her father went out of business, and they could no longer afford the fees. So for a year, Victoria went to the government school. They had worried about her progress there. Before, she had been so bright and keen to learn; now she seemed listless. She didn't tell them what was happening in the school—somehow it wasn't her place to tell them. But most days, she knew that the teacher did very little; he arrived late in the morning, wrote a simple exercise on the blackboard, then went to sleep or read the newspaper, ignoring the children. Sometimes he didn't show up at all. Most days, she sat in the classroom, eager to learn, eager to do something. But it was impossible. As the other children ran riot around her, she'd given up.

Fortunately, her father, Joshua, in his late 30s, was hired by another fishing boat. And with income once more assured, he managed to send Victoria back to the private school. Indeed, having saved arduously for the last two years, he himself was now the proud lessee of a fishing boat and employed five other men from the village. He could see the problem in the government school with crystal clarity—the proximity of his house to the school meant he didn't need Victoria to tell him what was going on. Like Mary's father, he was out on the ocean by 3:30 a.m., to return home by 10:00 a.m., when he lit the fire in the blackened mud bowls of the kilns in readiness for smoking the day's catch. But often when he returned home from fishing, he could see the children still playing in the adjacent government schoolyard—even though the school day was supposed to start before 8:00 a.m.! Sometime later, as he helped his wife carry the fish on wood slats, buzzing with flies, across to the smoking kilns, he'd see some of the teachers saunter in, waving the children into their classrooms. But in only a few hours, he'd see the teachers pack up and leave, their work finished at midday, to enjoy a beer in the chop house on the corner, before flagging down the buses on the main road back to Accra. Nice work if you can get it! he thought. Joshua knew from his own experience now as a businessman and employer that the private school had to be different. There, the owner is totally dependent on fees from parents like him—if he removes his daughter, the proprietor will lose income, and that's the last thing he wants, since he needs the income to pay his teachers and make a profit. So he's bound to watch his teachers closely and to fire anyone who doesn't pull his or her weight, just as Joshua would do if one of his employees didn't show up. It's simple really. It's the way his own business works, and that of his wife, too. If she doesn't smoke the fish properly, her customers won't like her offering and won't return. Nothing complicated here. It's all so different in the government school, he can see that; "Government jobs," he mutters to himself, knowing exactly why it is so hard to discipline the teachers.

Joshua is proud that his daughter seems to be doing well again now that she's back in the private school. She has regained something of her old spirit and enthusiasm. He loves his daughter very much— his only child with his wife, although he has five children from another marriage across the village. She's so dear to his heart, so intelligent and bright. She will go far, he knows. One day, she will become a doctor or lawyer. That makes him very proud, to think he, a humble fisherman, with such an accomplished daughter.

His wife Margaret had easily persuaded him when she stated that education for girls was just as important as for boys nowadays. "Anything a man can do, a woman can do too, sometimes even better than a man," she had said, and he'd had to agree. And while he was out fishing, he knew that she'd been gossiping with the other village women, comparing notes about the respective merits of all the private schools in the village. In the end, none seemed better than Supreme Academy, where they knew from their previous experience that the teachers cared and taught well. Indeed, Margaret had persuaded her sister to move her children there only this last year.

Victoria's mother, Margaret, is preparing the baskets to take to the lagoon to pick up the fish, and sorting firewood in readiness for smoking the day's catch. From where she is gathering wood, she can see the fine buildings of the government school, newly improved thanks to the generosity of American benefactors. "What's the point of having such nice buildings, if learning doesn't go on?" she muses. She wishes that Supreme Academy had better buildings, however. Perhaps if the teaching improves at the government school, she can send her next child there.

Theophilus Quaye, the proprietor of Supreme Academy, has been working since about 7:00 a.m. in his small office that doubles as a classroom and computer room. He's 32 years old and proud of the business he has built from scratch in the last six years. Just seven years ago, he was unemployed and wondering what to do next. He'd been a teacher at a small private school in a nearby village but had lost his way in life and did not show up at school for a few days. The school owner had promptly fired him, despite his pleading that he would never do it again. Fed up with seeing him hanging around in the village, his pastor persuaded him to take a basic course in preprimary education. He then helped his friend Edwin establish a private school in the village, Brightest Academy, just across the main road from his mother's house. Seeing Edwin's success and encouraged by his new wife, Theophilus decided to open his own school. He saw that several hundred children in the village still did not attend school. In talking to Edwin, he realized that the main reason those children weren't in school wasn't because the parents didn't care about education, but because they thought the government school wasted their children's time. If a private school were available, they would clearly jump at the chance to enroll their children.

Theophilus persuaded his mother to let him start teaching on the veranda of their concrete-block house. He began with 14 children. At first he charged no fees, but then plucked up the courage to ask the parents to pay a small amount. A few said no and promptly withdrew their children; but most agreed, if they could pay daily when they could afford to do so.

His enrollment grew, and he borrowed money from people in the village to construct the wood building along the edge of his mother's 70- by 100-meter plot. He now rues that decision: he'd selected what he thought was the most affordable option (he didn't want debt hanging over his head too long), but the wood building turned out to be just as expensive as a concrete-block building, although he'd been convinced that it would be cheaper. If he'd only chosen concrete blocks from the beginning, he could then build a story building and expand upward to cope with the villagers' increasing demand. One day, he will have to raze his building and start again. His outstanding debt is 10 million cedis (around $1,100), which he'll finish paying off this year; then he can start his expansion plans. Anyway, parents keep sending their children to his school, apparently unconcerned about his wood building, which has not aged well in the salty wind, provided that his teachers care about their children, which he is proud they do.

Theophilus now has 367 children—up from last year's 311. He is not surprised that his numbers increased this year: the government school was finally free to parents, having charged about 30,000 cedis (around $3.30) per year previously. But the class sizes had doubled since then, and several parents, dismayed by this, had moved their children to Supreme Academy. They more than compensated for the few parents who had moved their children from his school to the government school to save money. At Supreme Academy, parents pay about 30,000 cedis per month, or 270,000 cedis ($29.70) per year. Many still pay daily—1,500 cedis (17 cents)—although he's gradually persuading parents to pay monthly or, if he is lucky, by the term. Twenty children attend for free, however; they are mainly children whose father died or disappeared, leaving a mother unable to afford the fees. Because of his expanding enrollment, this year he added two extra classrooms in another block building, which he rented from the family living on the adjacent site. His rent for each room is 100,000 cedis ($11.00) per month.

He's proud of his achievements; he knows that as he walks through his village, the villagers look up to him because he has become a distinguished figure. He's pleased that his school is now government registered—since October 12 last year. That had been a real struggle, keeping the inspectors at bay, as they threatened to close him down. But he'd been unable to become registered because such a school couldn't occupy the same site as the principal's home, which his clearly did. He'd tried to get a loan to buy the adjacent plot that was for sale but there was a Catch-22—no loan if your school is unregistered, the bank had said. Eventually, he had managed to persuade the inspectors to overlook the deficiency (the persuasion amounting to a one-time payment of about 4 million cedis, [around $440]) and was now the proud owner of a temporary three-year registration certificate.

At exactly 7:45 a.m., Theophilus goes into the school compound to lead the assembly as one of the older boys rings the bell. The children stand at attention as the flag is raised and sing the national anthem, followed by the hymn "Amazing Grace."

All his 11 teachers are present, as usual. No teacher appears ready to make the same mistake that he did, all those years ago. He's certainly told them what would happen if they did. All but Erskine live in the village itself and so have no distance to travel. The third-grade teacher is 24-year-old Gyimaclef Oladepo, who has taught in the school for three years. He studied automotive engineering at senior secondary school in Accra and wants to continue his studies to fulfill his life's ambition of becoming a marine engineer. So he is putting money aside from his monthly wages of 200,000 cedis ($22), although he thinks he's paid too little, recognizing that it's an uphill slog to save. If he can't save enough, he will remain a teacher, a job he really enjoys—apart from the financial aspect. He loves the respect he gets from the children and from the parents in the village, where he was born and now lives again. His mother is a trader in Accra and lives there now. His father disappeared about 15 years ago; he doesn't know his whereabouts. He was a "driver for a certain company," also from the village.

Another teacher is 21-year-old Julius, who is from the village itself. He also has taught here for three years, after senior secondary school. His father is a fisherman, his mother a fishmonger. He wants to be a professional teacher, to acquire his teacher-training certificate from the University of Education at Winneba. From there, he will be contractually obliged to work in a government school for two years, but then he wants to teach in a private school, perhaps even open one himself. Daniel is 26, although he looks much younger, a very small, slight young man. Like Julius, he attended junior secondary in the government school in the village, completing his basic education just two years ago: he'd started school very late because his parents—again, both fisherfolk—had needed him to work for them. He'd been glad to find employment in the school when he graduated.

Ebenezer is 30 years old. He has taught at Supreme Academy for four years. He's the second-grade teacher. He also studied automotive engineering at senior secondary school at the Accra Technical Training College. When he studied for his junior secondary certificate in the Bortianor government school, only three teachers had ever showed up, for the entire school of about 200 children. He wonders what might have happened if he'd been able to get "a good training." To be frank, he couldn't find any other suitable employment, which is why he became a teacher. But to his surprise, he loves teaching—it is an "offering job," he thinks, one where "you sacrifice yourself for the children." He knows his children would miss him if he were to leave. He earns 300,000 cedis (around $33) per month, higher than the others, he knows, but still very low pay. He has a wife and two children to support, 9-year-old Joyce and 18-month-old Jonathan. He's happy that Joyce is in his second-grade class at Supreme and that she is doing well. Being able to keep a close eye on his daughter is one of the perks of the job.

The teachers disburse with their children into their classrooms to begin their long school day. The teachers collect the fees from those who pay daily—they rarely have to send children away because if they haven't got the fees, they don't come to school. The school soon resounds with the noise of children doing lessons. Erskine leads his younger class in spelling: "banana, B-A-N-A-N-A, banana"; "watch, W-A-T-C-H, watch," reciting over and over.

At 1:00 p.m., the school breaks for lunch. Some mothers have set up stalls in the shade of a fig tree, where they sell snacks and drinks to those children who haven't brought their own. On the playground, the boys energetically kick a soccer ball around the dusty yard in the blazing sunshine, some barefoot, while the girls gather in the cooler shade of the trees and play jump rope with homemade ropes tied together from bits of thread. "Sunday, Monday, Tuesday . . ." they chant in English. Large groups play, the girls jumping on one leg, both legs, higher and higher over the rope. Two girls prefer to play separately, with one end of their rope tied to a post.

Another School

Just a hundred yards away, children are also playing in the school compound in a demarcated play area, equipped with new swings and merry-go-rounds. But here, it's not lunchtime. The government school operates a shift system, the morning shift runs from 7:30 to noon, and the afternoon shift from noon to 4:30. At 1:15 p.m., the afternoon shift should be in full swing. Instead, the children are playing outside when their foreign visitor arrives.

The deputy principal, Angie, meets me and gestures for me to sit on a wood chair that one of the children has spirited from a nearby classroom at her beckoning. We sit together on the raised concrete veranda of the long, neatly refurbished concrete building, which houses the six classrooms and offices under a tin roof. "You are welcome," she greets me. After some small talk, she asks, "So what are you going to bring for us?" I laugh, a little embarrassed, "I'm here just looking at schools." She doesn't look that impressed. She tells me that an American nongovernmental organization, Reach the Children, has been very active in supporting their school. Last year, it donated the playground equipment (she motions to where the children are noisily playing) and brought funds to help construct a new building (she points to the half-built structure running perpendicular to where we are sitting). A deep concrete foundation half as large as the present building has been laid, and the far wall has been erected, complete with wood window frames. A pile of cement bags lies against the completed wall. "Not only did they teach in our school, they even gave their physical labor too," she adds. "Many young volunteers, they came and they put up the building. We hope they come back soon and finish it for us. So what are you going to give for us?"

I muse: how odd that young Americans needed to assist with such physical labor, given the potential of the villagers themselves to do such tasks. However, I say nothing on this subject. Instead, I ask how the shift system is working in her school. She shrugs: "In this area, the parents don't care about education, and in the afternoon shift, the parents don't send their children very often. That's why there's not many here today."

Actually, there seem to be lots of children present. And in the nearby private school, there certainly was no problem with children being present, so that answer seemed unsatisfactory. Anyway, I ask her what has to be my central question: "Why are there so many . . . how can I put this? What puzzles me, is why are there so many private schools in the village, when the public school is free and you give free uniforms and free books?" She laughs, sharing her laughter with Eric, a teacher, who has just joined us. "That's not the kind of question I can answer. You must direct it to the District Circuit Office."

At this juncture, Lydia the principal arrives on the scene. Seeing me, she ushers the children from the play area back into their classrooms. She greets me warmly and relieves Angie of her welcoming duties. Lydia is a lovely lady, very friendly and articulate, and she is surprisingly candid about everything I ask. She tells me about some of the problems facing her school now. Free primary education is being slowly introduced across the country, and her school is in the vanguard. Since students no longer have to pay fees, she says, her school size has doubled, to 506, so she had to introduce the shift system. The junior secondary grades come for the whole day (behind us in a classroom with no teacher, 12 children from one of these grades are conscientiously working on their own). But the primary school must come in two shifts. Upper primary (grades 4–6) students come in the morning, whereas grades 1–3 come in the afternoon. They rotate the shifts from week to week. But it's caused big problems, she says. "Parents don't pay now, and so they are not bothered if their child comes to school or not. When they paid they were a bit bothered."

I tell her that I hear there is now a "capitation grant" to replace the small fees that parents previously paid. Does this work? I ask. She shakes her head. No, it's not enough to cover all the costs. She points to the concrete base on which we are sitting, and I see that it is cracked and falling apart at the end. "We don't have enough funds to repair that," she says.

I tell her of my surprise in finding six private schools in this village, even though the government school is now free. Why is that? I ask. She tells me that there are two reasons. First: "My school is full. I have 72 children in primary 1 and 65 in primary 2. I can't admit any more. So parents come wanting to send their child to my school, and I tell them I have no room. So they have to take their children to one of the private schools." I nod. Perhaps private schools are a second choice for some parents. Looking at the contrast between this rather well-appointed building—the crumbling veranda end is a minor complaint—and the tumbling shack of Supreme Academy that I've just left, I'd certainly think it was a viable reason for parental choice. The conversation drifts to other matters. She tells me that she lives in Accra and drives out to the school every day. Indeed, she says, all but 2 of her 18 teachers live in Accra, and everyone else comes by public transport. "That must be dreadful," I sympathize. I've been traveling from the city in a battered old taxi without air conditioning, and I know how wearing it feels, in the intense heat of the day, caught for ages in the snarled traffic of the Accra–Cape Coast highway. And that is in a personal vehicle. Imagine doing it every day, crowded into one of the decrepit minibuses that ply the route that takes two hours to get here and two hours back, all for four hours in the classroom! We both laugh at the difficulties of it all. "That's why some don't arrive until midmorning, because of the traffic," she sighs. "I try to get them to leave earlier, but they can't because most of them have their own families to get ready for school."

I then remind her that she had suggested that there were two reasons why parents sent their children to the private schools. What was the second reason? "Yes," she remembers. I nearly fall off my chair when she tells me, amazed by her candor: "It's supervision. Proprietors are very tough. If teachers don't show up and teach, the parents react. Private schools need to make a profit, with the profit they pay their teachers, and so they need as many students as they can get. So they are tough with their teachers and supervise them carefully. I can't do that with my teachers. I can't sack them. I can't even remove them from the voucher list [the payroll] if they are late or don't turn up. Only the District Office can. And it's very rare for a teacher to be sacked. So it's supervision that is the second reason why parents send their children to private schools." Possibly because she thinks she has said too much, she then continues: "But really, my teachers are good. I don't have any problems with my teachers." In my judgment, for what it's worth, I don't think that is true at all. But I don't say so.

We walk around the school together. I go into the first-grade class, in which the children are crowded—I don't count, but it certainly seems as though most of the 72 are present, 3 to a desk, waiting for something to happen—or perhaps waiting for their visitor to leave so that they can resume their playtime. I ask a group near the front where their teacher is. Only one seems to understand me; "She has gone home," a girl tells me.

The Remains of the Day

Just after I return to Supreme Academy, the heavens open. The black sky has been building up from the east; torrential rain falls. A teacher had been teaching cultural dancing to some of the children at the edge of the compound to prepare for a school festival; he repairs to one of the classrooms, where he continues to teach his children. The other teachers stoically try to continue, but the rain becomes increasingly heavy, first flooding the compound then flowing in rivulets into the classrooms through the doorways that are not raised on any concrete veranda to prevent this eventuality. Rain buckets in through the open windows and through gaps in the corrugated-iron roof. Everywhere—and everyone—becomes drenched.

Theophilus and I are standing in the shelter of the veranda of the block building that serves as the family home, classroom, computer room, and office. Some of the older children from the fifth and sixth grades have run across the compound to shelter on the veranda, where we all huddle together. From the other classes, the noise becomes deafening as the teachers have the younger children sing and exercise, to keep warm, Theophilus informs me. But as the pelting rain becomes heavier than I have ever seen, Theophilus signals for an evacuation. "The little ones are getting too cold," he says.

Several of the older children brave the elements and run across to the nursery and junior classrooms. They return with the teachers, carrying one or two, sometimes three, little children on their backs, bringing them over to the block building, where they pile onto the veranda and into the dark and crowded small office-cum-classroom-cum-computer room. Some little ones see me and burst into tears. In addition to the cold and the mighty storm, seeing a white man is too much of an adventure to bear for one day. Some of the older girls tease the younger ones; touching my arm, laughing at my "yellow" skin, as Theophilus translates. The noise is deafening. I can hardly think. The family goats join us, also escaping the elements.

When the rains subside—although they don't stop altogether—Theophilus and I walk through the flooded, muddy village to a small thatched chop bar by the lagoon's edge, also battered by the storm. We have a late lunch, chicken and fried rice, the staple food of my visit. Theophilus tells me how he hates being so at the mercy of the climate, hates having afternoons wasted like that. He's saving up to buy cement to improve his building so that they can be less dependent on the vagaries of the weather. He tells me that now that he's a registered school—which he'd hoped would solve his problems in this regard—he still can't get a loan to improve his building. He's obviously a high-risk customer for the banks in the city, and they're only offering him a loan at 8 percent per month, compounded. He can't afford that. We puzzle over ways of helping schools like his raise funds at more realistic rates. I tell him about the American nongovernmental organization that has helped the government school improve its building. "They're just trying to undermine the private schools," he says, matter-of-factly.

It's 4:00 p.m. Looking across the water, I see schoolchildren, some in the pink uniform of Supreme Academy, crowding into a canoe at the lagoon's edge. A small schoolboy, barely taller than the punt that he awkwardly but energetically maneuvers, pushes them into the lagoon to take them home to the satellite fishing village of Faana, on the distant shore.

A Million Miles Away

I visited the plush DfID offices in Accra again after I'd presented the initial research findings on the nature and extent of private schools for the poor to a conference set up in collaboration with the Ghanaian Ministry of Education. Emma's team from the Educational Assessment and Research Centre had found in Ghana a picture similar to the one my teams had found in Nigeria, and in Hyderabad, India, and interesting data were also emerging from Delhi and rural Mahbubnagar, India. Pauline Dixon and I had spent months going through the data as they came in from the in-country teams, aware that a remarkably consistent picture was emerging from disparate places. I gave a PowerPoint presentation showing the results of these four studies. See Tables 1 and 2.[3]

I pointed out to the audience that the studies showed the extraordinary reality that, in *poor* urban slums or shantytowns, and in poor rural locations adjoining metropolitan cities (termed "periurban"), *private schools for the poor made up the majority* of provision—in each case, we had found more private schools than government schools. And in all but one of the studies (East Delhi), the *majority* of school-children were enrolled in private schools—usually around two-thirds to three-quarters of all enrollment. The picture in Nigeria and Hyderabad was replicated in Ghana. The Delhi finding was anomalous but interesting. Although we found fully 65 percent of schools were private unaided, and that there were more private unrecognized schools than government schools (28 percent compared with 27 percent), these figures were not translated into greater enrollment in the private unaided schools. This may simply be because the private schools were much smaller in size than the government schools. However, it is possible that, as we were unable to physically count the number of children enrolled, there may have been considerable overreporting in the government schools.

In rural Mahbubnagar district, Andhra Pradesh, India, the team found that around three-fifths of schools were government run, only a small fraction were private aided, and well over one-third were private unaided. But breaking these figures into schools in the small towns and rural areas proper, I could see that small-town Andhra

Table 1.
NUMBER AND PROPORTION OF SCHOOLS, BY TYPE AND PUPIL ENROLLMENT

School Type	Hyderabad, India			Ga, Ghana			Lagos State, Nigeria			Mahbubnagar, India			Delhi, India		
	No. schools	% schools	% pupils	No. schools	% schools	% pupils	No. schools	% schools	% pupils	No. schools	% schools	% pupils	No. schools	% schools	% pupils
Government	320	34.9	24.0	197	25.3	35.6	185	34.3	26.0	384	62.4	47.8	71	26.8	60.4
Private aided	49	5.3	11.4	0	0.0	0.0	0	0.0	0.0	13	2.1	4.3	19	7.2	3.7
Private (unaided) unrecognized/unregistered	335	36.5	23.1	177	22.7	15.3	233	43.1	33.0	77	12.5	6.6	73	27.5	8.8
Private (unaided) recognized/registered	214	23.3	41.5	405	52.0	49.1	122	22.6	42.0	141	22.9	41.2	102	38.5	27.2
Total	918	100.0	100.0	779	100.0	100.0	540	100.0	100.0	615	100.0	100.0	265	100.0	100.0

SOURCE: Author's own data.

NOTE: Some percentage columns do not total 100 because of rounding.

Table 2.
SCHOOL FEES AND AFFORDABILITY, FOURTH GRADE

Area	School type (currency)	Mean monthly fees	Minimum monthly wage	Fees as percentage of minimum wage
Hyderabad, India	Unrecognized (rupees)	78.17	1,872	4.2
	Recognized (rupees)	102.55		5.5
Mahbubnagar, India	Unrecognized (rupees)	68.5	1,200	5.7
	Recognized (rupees)	93.51		7.8
Delhi, India	Unrecognized (rupees)	125.45	2,160	5.8
	Recognized (rupees)	227.60		10.5
Ga, Ghana	Unregistered (cedis)	33,066.00	268,800	12.3
	Registered (cedis)	55,225.00		20.5
Lagos State, Nigeria	Unregistered (naira)	748.25	5,500	13.6
	Registered (naira)	1,090.50		19.8

SOURCE: Author's own data.

Pradesh was rather similar to the metropolitan areas: Just as in urban Hyderabad, the vast majority of schools—nearly two-thirds—were private unaided in the small towns of Mahbubnagar. In the rural areas proper, however, government schools were in a majority—around fourth-fifths, with private unaided schools making up the remaining fifth. Despite the preponderance of government schools, there were slightly more children enrolled in the *private unaided* sector, although it was close to an even split.

Girls made up about half of all enrollments in the private schools in both African studies—apparently private schools were not biased against girls, nor did poor parents seem to prefer to send only their boys to private school. Private schools, both recognized and unrecognized, were no different from government schools in gender enrollment. In India, it was slightly more complicated. In Hyderabad, for instance, there were roughly equal numbers of boys and girls in both recognized and unrecognized private schools, again suggesting gender equality. However, there were more girls than boys in government schools (57 percent vis-à-vis 43 percent)—and hence, more girls than boys in school overall. That is, although private schools showed gender equality, it seemed that, if you were a boy *in school*,

75

you were more likely to attend a private school than a government school—it's just that more boys than girls were not in school at all.

Certainly, the private schools were not "fly-by-nights" either, as some critics contended, out to rip off the poor. In Ga, Ghana, we found the average opening date for a private unrecognized school was 1998—making the average school some 6 years old at the time of the census. For private recognized schools, the average year of establishment was 1995. In Hyderabad, the average year of establishment for unrecognized private unaided schools was 1996 (7 years old at the time of the survey in 2003), whereas recognized schools were on average established 10 years earlier, in 1986. In Lagos State, the equivalent figures were 1997 and 1991, respectively.

And the vast majority of the private schools my teams had found were run as businesses: In Ga, 82 percent of registered and 93 percent of unregistered schools reported they were owned and managed by one or more proprietors. In the Nigerian study, the figures were 92 percent of registered and 87 percent of unregistered private schools. The remaining small minority were run by charities or religious groups (churches and mosques). In Hyderabad, the figures were almost identical: 82 percent of recognized and 91 percent of unrecognized private unaided schools reported that they received no outside funding and totally depended on tuition for their income.

Finally, the schools were affordable to poor parents. In absolute terms, we found the fees to be very low. In Africa, private schools usually charge fees by the term—that is, three times a year. Translating these into monthly equivalents, the average fourth-grade primary fees ranged from around $3.30 in the unregistered schools of Ga to roughly $7.00 in the registered schools of Lagos State. Crucially, these fees are affordable to poor parents. In Hyderabad, India, average fees for fourth-grade primary students were even lower, at around $1.63 per month in unrecognized and $2.15 per month in recognized private schools. That is, the average fourth-grade fees at an unrecognized private school ranged between 4 percent and 6 percent of the monthly minimum wage. In recognized schools, they ranged from 6 percent to 11 percent of the minimum wage. In Africa, they were slightly higher, ranging from around 12 percent to 20 percent of minimum wages. But these figures are slightly misleading—they are higher because we had to use minimum wages set for Ghana and Nigeria as a whole, whereas wages are higher in the urban and periurban areas of the cities. Looking at typical low wages in the places we were researching, we also found that monthly school fees were typically 5 to 10 percent of what the breadwinner earned in a month.

I presented these facts and figures from the three studies to the Accra conference. And to put a human face on these bare statistics, I invited several proprietors of private schools serving poor communities in Ghana—including Theophilus Quaye from Supreme Academy in Bortianor—who gave presentations on their schools, their motivations for establishing them, and their successes and obstacles.

The Honourable Kwadwo Baah-Wiredu by now had been moved from the Ministry of Education to Finance, the number two position in government, and was busy on an anti-corruption drive, featured every day in the *Daily Graphic* during my visit. His replacement at the Ministry of Education, the Honourable Yaw Osafo-Maafo, seemed cautiously interested in what we'd found. He couldn't attend the conference, but sent his apologies and a highly positive speech, given by one of his deputies, highlighting the existence of private schools for the poor and their potential role in education for all. His deputy told me at lunchtime that she couldn't believe it when she'd been asked to give the speech, because she thought that "private schools" and "the poor" didn't belong in the same sentence. "I've had my eyes opened," she said.

The man in charge of education at DfID this time was an erstwhile colleague of mine from England, Don Taylor. I'd worked with him while at the University of Manchester, from where he'd taken early retirement to work as education adviser to DfID, first in Abuja, Nigeria, and now in Accra, Ghana. Don had attended the conference and had given a presentation himself. He's not against private schools' having a role in "education for all" as such, he tells the audience. (Indeed, it transpires that his wife is the director of studies at a private school in Roman Ridge, a posh area of Accra.) But he thinks that it's the middle classes who should be encouraged to use private education, so that government and aid funds can be redirected from richer to poorer, so that the poor can benefit from more investment in public schools.

The day after the conference, I met him at noon, and he took me from the plush DfID offices, in one of DfID's chauffeur-driven, brand-new air-conditioned Toyota four-by-fours, to lunch at the

Ivy, a tony air-conditioned café, frequented mainly by Europeans—possibly aid workers and the like. One could almost imagine oneself not in West Africa at all. He had a brie-and-tomato sandwich; I had chicken and rice. The odd thing about meeting government aid representatives in countries like Ghana is that they're not at all afraid to criticize the waste and inefficiency of their host government. Indeed, it seems that nothing is more important to share with you. But then as soon as you press them on the alternatives, like a greater role for private education, it's as if all they've said is irrelevant. There is no alternative, they repeat, to what the government is doing. It only has to be done better, with more aid. Don, it appears, was no exception.

He told me that DfID now gives Ghana more than £15 million (around $28.5 million) per year in education aid—not including Don's salary and office expenses, which come under the general administrative budget. He tells me of the huge problems of teacher recruitment, exacerbated by the arrangement whereby a teacher can attend the University of Education, Winneba, and earn the teacher-training certificate, at government expense, but is obliged to work in schools for only two years before becoming eligible to study for a degree at the University of Ghana, Legon, or other universities, again at government expense for another three years. Teachers obtain these degrees and then leave education altogether, or even leave the country to work elsewhere. It was a huge problem, said Don, that led to teacher shortages, all manufactured by this combined government and aid generosity.

Then he told me of the new funding scheme that was part of the gradual introduction of free primary education around the country. At 30,000 cedis ($3.30) per year per child, it was designed to replace the similar amount that parents paid in school fees at the government schools. Soon, no school would be permitted to charge parents *anything*, everything from parent-teacher association fees, books, exam papers, and so forth would soon be provided free of charge. "So then we really will have free primary education," he said, proudly. I didn't probe him on why it had to be for the rich as well as the poor. But in any case, he volunteered the observation that it wasn't working at all well in the pilot areas. Many public schools were now short of money because in truth, public school fees were usually higher than 30,000 cedis per year, so the per pupil grant didn't fully replace what parents were previously willing to pay. Some public schools were even saying, Don laughed, that they wanted to become private schools, so that they could charge fees again.

And he told me how two-thirds of all government employees, some 230,000 people, worked for the Ghana Education Service, which brought huge bureaucratic inefficiencies. Moreover, there were problems of imbalances in education, with spending tilted toward higher education and the rich, not the poor.

Problems, problems, problems with public education. So I cautiously pressed him on what he'd heard reported at the conference about the ubiquity of private schools for the poor in Ghana and their potential role in helping the poor. Why couldn't DfID channel some of its huge aid budget toward these private schools, I asked him: perhaps it could finance a revolving loan fund to help schools like Supreme Academy repair its roof? He chose his words carefully. Yes, I had made quite a persuasive case about the private schools, schools that he hadn't realized existed. Yes, they were in rural as well as urban areas. Yes, they seemed to be doing a good job. But there could be no place for aid funds for them because they were proprietor driven: "We can't plough aid money into for-profit businesses." And that was the end of the matter as far as he was concerned.

I mused on how the denial seemed to have moved on since I first visited Ghana to do the research. The goalposts had shifted. Now the denial was not about the existence of private schools for the poor—you couldn't get away with that, given the mounting evidence. Now the denial was about their *significance,* and about their role. They couldn't be part of any "education for all" strategy because they were for-profit. Public education can be the only vehicle for international assistance.

Overnight, I flew out of Ghana. As I landed in Amsterdam to wait for my connection to Newcastle, I knew that another school day was beginning in Bortianor. Mary, Victoria, and the hundreds of other children at the private schools were busy by now with their schoolwork. Their classes were small enough for them to get individual attention from their teachers, who lived in the village or its vicinity and knew their charges' hopes and difficulties intimately. But they were studying in a building that would be flooded by the rains again in a day or two's time. But no aid could be made available

to help, not even through loans, because the proprietors were motivated, among other things, by profit—profit that seemed wholly
beneficial as far as Victoria's parents were concerned because it
ensured that the proprietor would keep an eye on his teachers.
Meanwhile, in the government school, I guess that children were
awaiting the arrival of their teachers from the plusher suburbs of
Accra, caught in the snarled traffic on the Cape Coast highway,
reluctant conscripts to the poor fishing village. No matter, the children could patiently wait, playing on the swings and roundabouts
thoughtfully provided by their American donors.

5. The Logically Impossible, China

The Red Flag

In China, I met the most graphic instance of denial of the existence of private schools for the poor—a denial so strong that I thought I had finally met my match. I was invited to speak at an international conference on globalization and private education at Beijing Normal University in April 2004. I spoke about my findings in other countries, huge numbers of private schools for the poor in India, Nigeria, and Ghana, and tentatively wondered aloud if similar schools existed here, in China. My hosts were polite, didn't want me to lose face, and were certainly interested in what was happening in other, poor countries. But their response was clear enough. They were interested in private education because it served the well-off and could help in China's technological and economic boom. Not only were they uninterested in private schools for the poor, they were adamant that they did not exist in China. Indeed, it seemed almost insulting to compare China with poor countries, my hosts implied. I could see why whenever I looked around Beijing, with its burgeoning sky-scrapers and multilane highways everywhere—it looked much richer than London, for instance. So how dare I suggest that this rich state couldn't provide for its poor, educationally?

"In China," Dr. Philip Hou, a sympathetic academic from the University of Hong Kong, told me over noodles and beer one evening, "there is the Confucian ethic, so government schoolteachers work harder than in other, poorer countries. There is no problem with absenteeism as in the other countries you've looked at." "Besides," he continued, when we had relaxed together, "communism has made things different in China: schools, especially primary schools, are organs of state control, and so they won't be given up lightly by the state." None of this seemed conducive to the existence of private schools for the poor in China, I agreed. I was nearly persuaded that I had finally met my nemesis in a strong, centralizing state and a keen work ethic.

Nearly persuaded, but he could see that I was not quite convinced. Finally, he told me that his friend Liu Binwen worked for the British aid agency DfID in Gansu province, one of the most impoverished regions of China, in the northwest: "He'll know exactly what is happening on the ground. He'll tell you." He'll tell me, in other words, that what I am studying elsewhere does not exist in China. I took Liu's phone number and arranged to meet with him the next day. It turned out that we had met before. We had worked together briefly in 2000 when I was on the International Finance Corporation consultancy project, where I was evaluating a chain of private schools for the middle classes, South Ocean Schools, that was looking for investment; the Chinese government had temporarily assigned him to help me.

Liu is very boyish, with a huge grin that frequently melts into laughter, and great fun to be with. We got on well before, and we were getting on well again now. We met in my hotel lobby, and he told me that DfID had put 11 million pounds into a project on *school development plans* in Gansu province. I did a double take here. In England, school development plans are all about listing the school's curriculum, aims and objectives, information technology requirements, and so on in one document. But spending millions on these "school development plans"—SDPs, he calls them—seems an odd priority for one of the poorest areas of China. But no, I haven't misheard him, and he is at pains to tell me how important this work is. After all, he says, school development plans are the key to our success in England, embedding schools firmly in their local communities, so they must be the way forward for China too. Seeing that I was not fully convinced of their indispensability, he reassured me that DfID was also spending money upgrading facilities in public schools, as well as introducing SDPs because—and this is where my interest picked up—facilities in many public schools, especially rural ones, had not been up to scratch.

This interested me greatly because the hint that circumstances had not been so good before in public schools (and hence might still not be great in other places that weren't blessed by DfID's munificence) raised the possibility that what I'd seen in other countries—inadequate public schools leading parents to abandon them for the private sector—might also be present in China. Why wouldn't poor parents in rural China also seek out something better for themselves if public schools were not good enough?

I asked him about the quality of the public schools in Gansu, and he replied that there are excellent public schools in every county town—like Linxia, the base for the DfID project. But, I pressed him, not everyone can go to these schools in the towns. He agreed, there were some terrible public schools in the remoter rural areas—hence the need for the DfID project. So, I persevered with this line of questioning: "Where does an aspirational peasant—," "farmer," he corrected me, "—where does an aspirational *farmer* send his children?" Liu said, "To the upgraded public schools." But where did they send them before the schools were upgraded? Did they go to private schools? He didn't think this was possible. "No, there are no private schools in the rural areas."

I ordered more beers. As we talk, I looked over his shoulder to the two large fish tanks in the lobby. There were six or seven very large colorful fish in each and a host of guppies. Very pretty, I thought. Then I noticed one of the larger fish pursuing a smaller fish, only to swallow it whole. Then I realized the larger fish were continually pursuing and eating the smaller fish. It dawned on me: the smaller fish were the food for the larger fish! I chuckled to myself, this was China, very practical. And I recalled that when Liu and I had met earlier on the International Finance Corporation project, we were taken around a posh private school in the finer suburbs of Beijing, where ducks swam in a small pond in its court-yard. The hosts had proudly showed off this feature. A 10-year-old pupil, however, confided in us: "The ducks are for you. When you are gone, we shall eat them." This was China, I had thought. Very practical. And this was China, I thought now, clearly the end of the road for my search for private schools for the poor.

But, as Liu Binwen began to relax over beers, and I told him about what we had found in other countries, he became intrigued. And, conspiratorially, he leaned over and whispered that, in fact, 15 years previously, while working for the Ministry of Education, he had done a somewhat similar project. The ministry had been worried by the phenomenon of *Si Shu*, "private schools operating in intellec-tuals' houses," he translated, even though private education was illegal then. So he was asked to do a secret study in his home province of Hubei. Just like we were doing in other countries in Africa and in India, he and his team explored every village, and gaining the confidence of the villagers, found, just as we were find-ing, in every village, at least one of these private schools! They found that children attended these schools because they couldn't afford to attend the government schools, which were much more expensive then. His confidential report went to the highest officials, who were apparently indignant. We laughed about their reaction. And he wondered what had happened to that report . . . he would see if he could get me a copy. Literally hundreds of those small private schools, he laughed, even though they were illegal, with thousands of children enrolled.

So, I asked, surely such schools existed today? Now he was not so adamant. He doubted it, but to be honest, he'd never asked, never looked for them. State schools were less expensive now, in any case (although they weren't free), so that major reason was gone. But wait. He picked up his cell phone and called several contacts in Gansu. The response was always the same. There were many private kindergartens, but no private schools. "Sorry, James," he said, "there aren't any." I still had some hope, however. For elsewhere in the world, I'd found that this was precisely how many private schools got started. An entrepreneur, usually a woman, opens a kindergarten, but then the pressure from parents arises: "Where can I send my child now that she is older? She is happy in your school, you have taught her well. Please will you open a grade 1 for my child?" Later, "Why not a grade 2?" And a primary school is born, without anyone intending it. I told him this experience from Africa and India. No, he said, that won't happen here, because it was easy to open a kindergarten but very difficult to open a primary school. Even the government acknowledged that there were thousands of private kindergartens. But the government was equally as adamant: there were no private primary schools in these areas; the few that existed there were in the cities, only for the rich. I told him that was where we would find our private schools, hidden behind the façade of a kindergarten! He said it wouldn't be true.

Anyway, he proposed to help me in my quest. He was genuinely intrigued: if I could provide a few funds, which I readily agreed to, he could explore some the next time he was in Gansu—which was the following week. He wouldn't promise that he would find anything, but he could certainly look for me. We arranged to meet the following day to finalize the financial arrangements.

The next day, Liu phoned me at my hotel. Grinning still, I imagined, he told me that his boss, an Englishman working for DfID, told him that he shouldn't help me with my project, as "this would confuse the DfID." Those were his exact words. In any case, Liu reassured me, there really were no private schools in Gansu province. Not one, he had asked everybody, and everybody agreed. DfID, he repeated, was working to help improve the public schools; there weren't any private schools. Could we meet to discuss this again? I asked, hoping to persuade him to change his mind. Unfortunately, no, his trip to Gansu had been moved up, and he had to leave that very afternoon, so sadly there was no opportunity. I put the phone down, and took a deep breath.

The way Liu mentioned DfID was a red flag to this bull. A few weeks earlier, while I was in Hyderabad, India, the secretary of education in the Andhra Pradesh government, with whom I was working very closely, had confided in me that the DfID office in Delhi had written to him. The gist of the letter, he said, was that they had heard he was working with me, and that he should "be careful." What? I had been astounded: what on earth did they mean? He had laughed it off. "I don't take orders from anyone!" he had said, "and I'm always careful." The battle lines were drawn. If DfID didn't want me "confusing things" in Gansu, then very definitely I would go to Gansu.

Gansu

I had to rush back to England after the conference, so I couldn't go immediately. But on my return, serendipity played its role. I gave a lecture about private education to international graduate students at Newcastle University, many of whom were from China. I briefly touched on the recent work on private schools for the poor. Lu Xiang, one of the students, came to see me afterward, saying he would like me to be his PhD supervisor. Great, I said. "I want to study private schools for the poor in China." Really? Did he think they existed? Yes, he was sure. He had heard of one, and there must be others. Where was he from? Lanzhou, the capital of Gansu!

I did my homework on Gansu. One of China's five northwestern provinces, Gansu was also one of the country's least developed. Its 25.6 million people lived in an area about the size of Texas. Gansu ranked 30th among China's 31 provinces and autonomous regions in terms of gross domestic product per capita. The average rural per capita income was only 1,500 yuan ($186.57), making it the 28th poorest of the 31 provinces and autonomous regions. About half of Gansu's rural population lived below the poverty line of 1,000 yuan ($124.38) per year, compared with only 3 percent nationwide, while nearly 2 million people lived under the absolute poverty line of 637 yuan ($79.23) per year.[1] It sounded like a great place to do my research.

I flew to Lanzhou via Beijing on September 18, 2004. Lu Xiang had flown ahead to prepare the groundwork—including getting a team ready to conduct the research. Our first meeting was with a Mr. Wang, a senior education official from Linxia, the county town where DfID was working, who had made the long journey into the city especially. The meeting was disappointing. Mr. Wang said that there were only three private schools in his entire region, and, of course, none were for the poor. He told me something I'd heard so many times from education officials the world over: "our minorities"—his region had 18 minority groups, Xiang told me—"don't value education, so they will not invest in schools, they don't care about their children." But this time, I braced myself that it might be true; perhaps Lu Xiang had become rather carried away with wanting to please his professor; that would be very Chinese, I thought. And who was I to say that there really were private schools for the poor in rural China, against all the advice to the contrary?

Anyway, afterward we had a sumptuous banquet lunch together in a private room in a nice enough restaurant, with a large group of people interested in this foreigner, the sine qua non of doing any work in China, it turned out. On the meticulous agenda that Xiang prepared for me, this meal was listed as "Eating Lamb with Hands in Nan Chang Road"—the novelty of eating Gansu lamb being that you ate it with your fingers, not chopsticks. The only dish that might not be welcomed back home was "vegetables cooked in lamb's blood." Around the circular table, Mr. Wang initiated the toasts, with strong Chinese liquor in tiny glasses—and because I was the guest, everyone took a turn to toast me. We both stood up, said gang bei, literally "bottoms up," knocked back the spirit, and ritually displayed our empty glasses to all around the table to prove that we had really done the required. I found that if I drank copious amounts of the hot tea liberally provided with the meal, I could just about get through the toasting without getting too drunk. The toasts were full of affection and mutual flattery. Mr. Wang then sang a wonderful song of the minority people in Linxia region, in a weird falsetto voice, about how the rivers and the trees welcome you, Professor Tooley, from Newcastle (you put in your own words of greeting, Xiang explained) to Gansu, and hope that you will prosper here. No doubt affected by the alcohol, I sang them a song I had heard played on the accordion while in Beijing: "Doe, a Deer." Then we had our pictures taken. Mr. Wang told me that in China they said *qie zi*, pronounced "chee-zee," the Chinese word for "eggplant," because it made your mouth smile widely. I told him them that we said "cheese," to the same effect.

The next morning, Xiang arrived with a brand-new four-wheel-drive vehicle and a driver, another Mr. Wang, both procured with the influence of Xiang's mother. We set off for one of the poorest regions in Gansu, Zhang County, where Xiang told me he had heard of a village private school. The fine new toll road from Lanzhou to Xi'an had road signs in English as well as Chinese and impressive mile-long tunnels bored through the arid brown, terraced mountains. After two hours, we exited at Ding Xi, "potato town of China," as the English rendition read on its welcoming sign; then the road deteriorated. Through the utilitarian town center, the street was still wide and was lined with endless rows of potato vendors huddled under tarpaulins. Immediately outside the town, it narrowed to a potholed and incredibly dusty track, which left the wonderfully fertile and verdant valleys of the tributaries of the Yellow River, climbing through hairpin bends into the dry mountains that were terraced right up to the summits, sculpted by man to support the potato, bean, cabbage, and broccoli crops. By the roadside were many small tent encampments surrounded by beehives, housing itinerant farmers collecting honey to sell in the towns.

After driving three hours, we arrived in a village just outside the county town of Zhang County, one of the poorest districts of this poor region, the district that Xiang had heard had a private school for the poor. We stopped to ask people by the roadside if they knew of any private school. They told us of a private kindergarten, but when we found it, it was just that, only a preschool, not also a primary school as I had assumed it might be. The proprietor told us there were no private schools as such, neither here nor in any of the other villages, nor in the town of Zhang County itself. And the same story greeted us as we arrived in town—we were directed to several private kindergartens by helpful onlookers, but all told the same story. Perhaps Liu Binwen was right after all, I mused. Why don't the kindergartens become primary schools? I asked Xiang to ask the women who were running them: "The government runs primary schools, we're not allowed to," they told him. Or "People here don't have much money; they are too poor for private schools." By the time I went to bed in the Spartan government hotel on the main street by the local government offices, I felt very down. I had extended myself too far. Why did I assume that there would be private schools here, in one of the poorest districts of one of the poorest regions of China? I slept only fitfully.

In the morning, though, I met Xiang for breakfast, and he was the bearer of good news. He had risen well before dawn and had gone to the market just opposite our hotel where villagers from even the remotest parts of the district came to sell their produce. He had asked around and had finally located the names of four private schools in the villages! The quest was on again.

We drove out of the county town, into the bright autumn sunshine, to try to find Xu Wan Jia, the first of the villages that Xiang had been told contained a private school. Although we had rough directions, we traveled backward and forward along the now well-kept paved road, asking anyone—farmers tilling the soil with donkey plows, women walking along carrying water—where this private school might be. Because of our altitude, at 10,000 feet or more, the air was very thin, and I ran out of breath very quickly; Xiang got a headache. But the dialect was hard for Xiang to understand—and I began to fear that this might have been a problem in the market too. Perhaps we had come all this way because of a linguistic misunderstanding? (Thoughts of what Dennis Okoro had said in Nigeria obviously echoed in my mind.) We tried asking in the public schools that were present in every major village along the paved road, but no one seemed to know where Xu Wan Jia was—not even the village, let alone any private school therein. Many of the public schools had plaques besides their entrance gates, proudly announcing that they were recipients of foreign aid. I saw the gold stars and blue background of the European Union flag everywhere. The Japanese government was also well represented. The public school teachers, while being extremely friendly and welcoming, said that no private schools were out here—wouldn't it be better to try in Lanzhou, the capital?

Eventually, thinking that we might have to give up, we asked a woman bent double in the fields, weeding her crops, and she seemed to know the village (although again, Xiang laughed in frustration as she was difficult to understand, and I wondered again whether she had really understood the nature of our quest). Anyway, she would lead us to where the road to the village left the main road.

The red-cheeked lady went to fetch her baby boy, and we drove off in the car together. She guided us off the main road, and Driver Wang maneuvered us skillfully down a narrow dirt track and onto the wide riverbed below that doubled as a road, because at that time of year, the river was a feeble brook. But he was adamant; our vehicle couldn't take us any farther, although I protested irrationally that I couldn't see why. Anyway, the woman went off to see if she could find someone to take us farther. We waited. After an hour, she returned with her husband in one of the three-wheel trucks, appearing to be adapted from motorcycles, which were ubiquitous in rural China.

I was offered a share of the seat in the enclosed cab with the driver, but fearing that this would be too noisy, opted to travel in the truck's open back with Xiang. As soon as we left the riverbed and began ascending into the mountains on a track only wide enough for the three-wheeler, we found we couldn't sit down, the vehicle rattled so much with the deep staccato throb of the two-stroke engine. The views were superb, as we wound our way through hairpin bends, alongside terraced potato fields, bumping about in the back, exhilarated, higher and higher into the mountains. At times, we stopped precariously on tiny raised lay-bys, to let other similar vehicles pass. After 90 minutes, we finally arrived at the village, Xu Wan Jia, nestled into the mountains, with its neat brick and red-tile buildings. The village existed. And then, finally, down narrow dirt streets, barely wide enough for the three-wheeler, we arrived at the private school, nestled deep inside the village. I felt an extraordinary sense of elation.

Xu Wan Jia Private Primary School inhabited the proprietor's courtyard home, with his office doubling as his residence and the classrooms taken over from his family. The proprietor and principal, Mr. Xing Ming Xin, was absolutely thrilled to have visitors; he couldn't quite believe that anyone had come that far to see him. As was the custom here (we'd already experienced this in the public schools in the valley the day before), he searched crazily in drawers and cupboards, and had others searching too, until he found a brand-new unopened packet of Lanzhou cigarettes, reserved for any such occasion—clearly rare—which he opened and offered to me (although he didn't smoke himself, until I offered him one of mine that I had bought that morning in Zhang County, realizing the custom from the previous day). He insisted we take off our shoes and sit comfortably on the raised earthen area that, I was told, was the shared family bed. I settled comfortably on blankets and pillows, feeling very warm and cozy. It turned out a fire was lit underneath. It was incredibly comfortable, quite unlike interviewing in tropical countries, where the heat was normally overwhelming.

And so I interviewed the principal of probably the most remote private school I had ever found, then and still. Xiang wrote all my questions in his notebook and translated; when he encountered difficulties, he wrote the Chinese characters in his book, and the two of them argued over their meaning. The school, he told us, had 86 students, precisely 43 boys and 43 girls. So why did he open the school? He said that he had been aware that the public school test scores were very low, and the villagers didn't want all their children to be illiterate; they wanted him to help bring up the standard of education. He was the only person then in the village with a high school diploma, so he was under pressure to do so. He finally opened his school in 1996, and has since, he said, offered a higher standard of education than in the public school. Why did he say this? He said he worked hard and honestly to ensure that his good reputation was maintained. He and his wife also ensured that the students had food and drink, which didn't happen in the public schools. The children took the public examinations in fifth grade—he had had five cohorts of students tested up to now, and their scores were always better than those in the public school. They went to the county to take these exams.

Was this why parents sent their children to his school rather than the public school? He replied that it was one reason. But there were two others. The nearest public school was over an hour's walk away. Children could walk that far at this time of year. But when it rained or snowed, the route was impassable. For most of the year, he told me, the public school was simply inaccessible to the children here. And when I asked the children themselves why they came to this school rather than the public school, all said that it was because of the inaccessibility of the public school.

But second was the issue of expense. Tuition in his school was 60 yuan (about $7.50) per semester; on top of that was 25 yuan ($3.13) per semester for textbooks and exercise books. The nearest public school charged 75 yuan ($9.38) per semester, plus roughly the same charges for textbooks and exercise books. So his school was less expensive than the public school, even though it received none of the public school's government funding!

Getting fees from parents, all of whom were, needless to say in this remote village, peasant farmers, was a struggle. His biggest problem, however, was finding anyone able and willing to teach because people with high school diplomas didn't want to come to a village such as his. Even young people from the village who had gained their high school diplomas didn't want to return. So this year, because of teacher shortages, he had to "delete" the fourth and fifth grades, teaching only the first three grades with two other remaining teachers. They were both men with high school diplomas. They were each paid about 200 yuan (about $25) per month. So I calculated in my notebook while Xiang translated other questions, if he had 86 students paying 75 yuan ($9.38) per semester, his income was about 6,450 yuan ($806.25) per semester, or 1,075 yuan ($134.38) per month. So he probably took home slightly more than the other teachers and spent the remainder on school facilities, heating, chalk, books, food, and drink. Not a hugely profitable business, but none-theless enough to keep it all running, if only he could find other teachers.

What did he do before becoming a principal? Mr. Xing, translated Xiang, was "doing fieldwork"—that is, he was a peasant farmer in this village. His wife now did the fieldwork while he ran the school. They kept pigs (later I met them, sharing the same shack as the open-hole latrine) and bees for honey, and grew maize, potatoes, spinach, and beans. I didn't see any chickens, which surprised me.

I asked whether there were other private schools like his? He didn't know, apologizing that he only rarely left his village. He thought there might be one or two, but not more: "Other people have different hobbies. This is my hobby, to run a school. It would be impossible for me to give up this occupation for any other!"

When our interview was over and we had visited the school and spoken to the extremely shy and nervous children—all with very ruddy cheeks and a multitude of different-colored and irregularly fashioned clothes: no uniform here—the wonderful rural hospitality kicked in. No, we couldn't leave yet. He herded us back to the warmth of the bed, insisting we remove our shoes again, and his wife nervously and shyly served us "pie," broken-up, very greasy fried pastry, cooked in an oil called *you bin*, a culinary delight here, Xiang told me, but one which I found exceedingly bitter, rather too bitter to enjoy. A jar of honey was brought in, and Mr. Xing took a spoon and liberally spread it over the pastry. This was a real delicacy, said Xiang; I felt very guilty when Xiang told me that it would probably provide them with enough income for a month or more. But there was no stopping this hospitality. Mr. Xing then made us honey tea, over a tiny stove the size of a small teacup. In a filthy metal dish he heated up tea leaves and water, and then spoonfuls of honey were liberally applied. Relatives and villagers came to visit and share in banter and cigarettes while the children gazed in through the curtained windows.

And for the next three days, we visited similar private schools, finding five in total. Only one was in a less remote village—meaning that we could reach it by car, although that still required an hour's driving off the paved road. This one was founded by an ex-villager who had made some money through business in Sichuan province, giving something back to his community. It had one classroom, in which the head and only teacher instructed all age groups together. A tiny boy sat next to his big sister at the same desk. The children paid no fees; it was only for those who were too poor to attend public school. But all the others were in the remoter villages like Xu Wan Jia.

On our second day, we found ourselves back in the town of Zhang County by midafternoon. Rather than try to find other schools, which would take hours, Xiang suggested we go to the Education Bureau, as a courtesy call, to begin the process of getting permission to do an in-depth study, and also to see if there was a list of private schools. The Education Bureau in Zhang County was just off the main street, close to the hotel, and seemed a superior-quality government office compared with those I was used to in India and Africa; but it was no more helpful. After waiting for awhile to see someone who might be responsible for private education, we were told that we first must go to the Government Office for "Helping the Poor"

(Xiang's translation) to gain permission before the list of private schools could be released to us. Fortunately, this was the imposing public building set back across the road right next to the hotel. We climbed the stairs to the fourth floor, to the "Office for Helping the Poor." While cooling off outside, it was very warm inside; benefiting from the heat of paraffin heaters, two senior staff were reading daily newspapers. Along the wall, two brand-new computers, a printer, and fax machine sat, unpacked, and unused. The office contained no books, no files, just the unused computers and newspapers.

The man and woman were friendly and helpful, making us hot tea in paper cups, but said there were no private schools in Zhang County, rural or urban. In any case, they couldn't give us the permission required from the Education Bureau; in fact, they didn't see why we need its permission at all. They called in the "Helping the Poor" bureau chief, a very young, very smiley, and pleasant official. He concurred that there were no private schools. In any case, he couldn't give permission; we'd have to talk to the regional office in Ding Xi first, and if they gave permission, he might then consider it. Xiang cajoled him for some time, even gently stroking his arm as appeared to be acceptable here in rural Gansu, but he left the office without agreeing, purportedly to ask his supervisors. When he returned, he was not smiling: what we needed was not regional permission from Ding Xi, he reported, but permission from the province itself, in the capital Lanzhou. His advice, however, was to simply return to the Education Bureau anyway, as they might let us have the information now that we had visited him.

Feeling relatively buoyant still, we headed back to the bureau, where we were told to wait while the dean of the office finished his meetings. We waited an hour. Finally, we were told that the dean of the office was not in today after all. Anyway, the junior official who had kept us waiting said that there were no private schools, so why did we want a list that didn't exist? While we were waiting, I wandered around the spacious open office and stood admiring a map of Zhang County. When Xiang joined me, the junior official had coolly motioned for us to sit down. Outside, Xiang informed me that, on the map's legend, there was a symbol for private school and there were two marked on the map, both of which we had already visited! Clearly, the local government knew at least some of these private schools. Equally as clearly, they didn't seem to want us to know about them.

The final private school we visited was the one that had initially drawn us to Zhang County—for apparently some journalists had visited and publicized its existence, and that was how Xiang had heard of it. We drove a few hours from the town, over mountain roads where our vehicle served to thresh the villagers' corn as we went—they would lay it out in the road for any vehicle or animal to pass over. Harvesting was under way everywhere. Villagers were also threshing their corn in their courtyards and fields, horses and donkeys moving slowly around in a circle pulling a heavy weight behind, often guided by a young child. Ahead of us, children herded ducks, pigs, and chickens in the road. Again, at a relatively prosperous-looking village on the paved road, we negotiated the hire of a three-wheeler for the final leg of the journey. We left again up a riverbed, then over more mountains, crawled along a valley floor where the track merged with a fast-flowing stream, and entered a gorge, with imposingly high rocky sides only as wide as the track itself. Then we headed through verdant pastureland on the other side through more villages, past a nice looking public school (one with no foreign signs indicating support), and, finally after another hour of moving slowly over the bumpy, meandering track, we reached the village hosting Xin Ming—People's Hearts—Primary School.

Zhan Wang Xiu (the proprietress) greeted us warmly and ushered us into her tiny living room, again making us take off our shoes to sit comfortably on the earthenware bed. Although the late afternoon was cool, no fire warmed the bed this time. There was also no light; although the village apparently had electricity, there was no supply tonight. The classrooms were also very dark—we peered in and saw children working hard at their desks. The living room was wallpapered with newspaper. And she told us her story. Zhan Wang Xiu and her husband started the school in 1998. Now it had 52 students—38 girls and 14 boys. There were three teachers—the husband and wife and their 18-year-old son, whom they had persuaded to stay in the village and teach with them.

Why did they start the school? Their village was very poor, she said, and the public school was over an hour away (we saw later when we returned that children could walk the route almost as quickly as we could drive it). The villagers especially do not pay attention to their girls, who cannot attend the public school because their parents don't want them to travel that far or because they cannot afford the school fees. So the aim was to start a school mainly for these girls. She had seen how the girls "got cheated"—Xiang's translation; I suppose she meant "harassed"—when they traveled on foot or on the three-wheelers to the school and wanted to spare them from this. The best way to eliminate poverty, she said, was to reduce women's illiteracy, not to build a road (for which the local government, far from the village, was apparently agitating).

She told a complicated story of how she and her husband were once public school teachers; she was hospitalized for a while, and her husband wanted to look after her; he lost his job too as a result. Returning to being peasant farmers, they realized that their true vocation lay in teaching and so decided to start the school. Every day they were happy, she says, because the children were around them. But before they started the school, the adults in the village wanted evening classes in literacy for themselves. Once the county saw the success of these classes, she said, they were given permission to open the school. They put all their own money into the school, which they set up in their own home after moving their own parents into another house in the village to make room for the classrooms. They charged 18 yuan (about $2.25) per term, but if three children were from one family, the third attended for free. (It was noticeable how little purchase China's "one-child" policy seemed to have in the remote villages.) She said that 60 children in her village were still illiterate, and she wanted her school to expand. Some village children did go to the public school that we had passed, but its fees were 75 yuan ($9.38) per term, plus textbooks—too exorbitant for most of the villagers.

Again, her big problem is finding teachers. Once they employed a woman teacher, at 800 yuan ($100) per *year*, but she decided that the salary wasn't enough so she left for a job in Zhang County town. Their fifth-grade students were now facing graduation, but they needed teachers. So they asked their eldest son, who had passed high school, to come and help, and he agreed. He seemed happy enough. They didn't pay him, except in kind, she joked, and he— coming to join us on the family bed—laughed too. They wanted to help him to go to university, but "What can I do?" she said. So he stayed to help the poor in their village. He has worked there for two years now. And he just received a prize from the government as the best third-grade teacher.

Her husband, Chen Wang, arrived at nightfall. He taught all day and then left to work in the fields. "The fields still need us," he joked. His warm greeting touched me deeply. He implored us to stay the night; I was really disappointed, but Xiang said we couldn't, as our driver was waiting on the main road and we needed to be in Lanzhou the next day. But we must stay for dinner? Reluctantly, we told him we couldn't; boarded our hired three-wheeler, which fortunately had a headlight; and went slowly down through the dark, negotiating the gorge, to driver Wang, who met us by the roadside and was very agitated because he thought something bad had befallen us in the mountains.

Nemesis

We arrived back in Lanzhou in time for lunch, then went to the Provincial Education Bureau to gain permission to do the study. The head of the Education Bureau was not in his office when we arrived; but when told by phone that a foreigner was waiting to see him, he said he would be there in 30 minutes. He actually arrived within 10 minutes, gave us scalding hot tea in paper cups, was very friendly, but told us, apologetically, that he had to follow the regulations, and so we must talk to the director of international cooperation and exchange first, a Mr. Ming Ding. Then he would happily do all he could to help our interesting project.

Sitting at the computer, Mr. Ming's assistant Mr. Zheng was rather put out that we arrived without an appointment; in any case, Mr. Ming was away and was far too busy to see us. He greeted me in impeccable English—as the interview progressed, I was very pleased that I realized his English was excellent, for otherwise I would have tried to speak with my student Xiang behind his back. Unfortunately for his story, Mr. Ming then arrived and greeted me in a very friendly fashion, waving aside Zheng's scruples. He invited me into his office, all smiles. "Let them talk, I'm here now, they've come a long way!" Xiang translated. Zheng joined us with his notepad.

Xiang introduced me and the project. Through him, I tell Mr. Ming that many people believed that private schools were only for the elite, but my research in India and Africa had shown private schools for the poor, and so forth. Was the same true for China, I wondered? To answer this question, I told him, we went to the mountains in Zhang County. "Who gave you permission?" interjected Mr. Ming, as he jerked forward in his seat at this point in the translation, deeply concerned. "Who did you report to there?" I reassured him that it was not a research visit, just a tourist visit to see if the research was possible, and we did pay courtesy calls, as was the truth, to the Education Bureau and other bureaus. So I continued, but the atmosphere had changed now, and Xiang's voice became more hesitant and nervous. So, I continued, we found five private schools for the poor, and now that we knew the phenomenon existed, we were seeking permission to do a wider study.

Mr. Ming was silent for a while. Then he leaned forward and said that he had some questions and comments. First, what are the aims and objectives of your project? I asked Xiang to explain them again. Ming looked very puzzled. Zheng then asked in Chinese, who was funding it? I told him of the John Templeton Foundation. He asked of its aims and objectives, and I tried my best to describe an American philanthropic foundation. Then Ming took over the questioning again. He spoke slowly and coolly: "We will need to be convinced that there is a research project to be done. In your case, it is hard to see how this is possible because the People's Republic of China has achieved universal basic education. This means that public education serves all the poor as well as the rich. So there are no private schools for the poor, because the People's Republic has provided all the poor with public schools. So what you propose to research does not only not exist, it is also a *logical impossibility.*"

I felt suddenly immersed in George Orwell's *1984*. Black was white, and white was black. What I'd seen did not exist because it was logically impossible. I had not expected anything like this. My mouth got dry, my body tensed. And as English-speaking Zheng was sitting there, I could not ask Xiang what on earth we should do next.

He continued: "Of course we are pleased to welcome research that helps the poor. We are not saying that everything is perfect in the public schools that the People's Republic has provided for all. A good example of research"—I couldn't believe that I was going to hear this again—"is the DfID's Gansu Basic Education Project, which is providing SDPs, school development plans, which are a valuable way of helping the poor, and we are grateful to the British government for sponsoring this important and worthwhile project. Why don't you find a good project to do, like school development plans, rather than your strange ideas?"

Suddenly, I thought I better understood DfID's motives for setting up its project. When I'd been traveling in the mountains, it became even more preposterous that what the poor needed was school development plans in the public schools! What a terrible crying waste of 11 million pounds, I'd thought. Now, I saw DfID sitting with bureaucrats like these, thrashing ideas around and finding the only thing that was harmless and unthreatening to the Chinese government. Who would complain if it were known internationally that the only thing lacking in Chinese schools for the poor was school development plans? That was much less threatening than the news that villagers were too poor to send their children to public schools, or that the public schools were too inaccessible, especially for girls. Perhaps that was it?

At this point, (English-speaking) Zheng was called out of the room, so I asked Xiang if he had told Mr. Ming that we had seen the private schools for ourselves in the villages. Yes, yes. Shouldn't we remind him? No, no.

Mr. Ming slowly continued, while Xiang translated: "We have a close relationship with DfID, and we are very pleased to host the SDP project. Indeed, when your prime minister, Tony Blair, visited China he was very pleased to meet with delegates of the Gansu Basic Education Project. Now if you were to show to DfID that your ideas made a worthwhile, practical project, then we would obviously take this seriously, because we respect their judgment. But as it stands, I don't see that you have a viable research project. Of course, you may apply for permission and we will consider it carefully."

We closed the meeting politely, with me apologizing profusely. I was crestfallen. I realized how stupid I had been in not realizing that my work might be threatening to the Chinese government. But the cat was out of the bag. What to do? Xiang, however, told me not to worry. He pointed out that we hadn't yet asked for permission. We only visited to ask how *we might go about* getting permission! So we hadn't actually been refused. The way was still open for us to conduct the research. But how? I certainly didn't want to put Xiang and the team he had assembled at risk. He said they would not be and not to worry, they would get permission. And a few weeks later, much to my surprise, once I was safely back in England, and after several sumptuous banquets to get to know bureau chiefs better, they did.

The Reality: Private Schools for the Poor in Rural China

So we conducted the research in Gansu province. Xiang hired a dedicated team from the Gansu Marketing Research Company, a specialized research organization with a network of researchers across the province. We used a large team (48 research supervisors and 310 researchers), distributed across all 14 regions of Gansu. We gave all researchers and supervisors a two-day training session. Just as in the other studies, the aim, we told them, was to locate *all* private primary and secondary schools in rural Gansu. For comparison purposes, researchers were also asked to locate a public school "nearby" each located private school, defined as being within a maximum of one day's travel for the researchers, who were traveling mainly on foot. The researchers were allocated to areas that they knew reasonably well. They could ask for lists of private schools from the local education bureau, but were warned that such lists might not be forthcoming, nor complete. In addition, they should ask local residents, in markets or on the street, whether other schools existed, unacknowledged by local authorities.

Because we were using such a large team, quality control was especially important. All questionnaires from the school had to be imprinted with the official school stamp and contact telephone number. Researchers were required to photograph each school to prove that they had visited it—I have a large album of all these schools now. All schools were subsequently telephoned, if possible by the supervisors, to check whether the researchers had in fact conducted the survey and observation.

What did we find? In total, there were 586 private schools located in the villages, serving village populations.[2] These were our "private schools for the poor." Of course, this figure is a lower bound, as we cannot be sure we found all the schools that were not on the provincial list of schools: officially, Gansu province has only 26 primary schools, all of which are based in the cities and larger towns, not in villages.[3]

The researchers also identified 309 government schools that were in villages "nearby" the private schools. (The number is smaller than the private school total because in some areas, the researchers found no "nearby" public schools.) These were only a very small fraction of the total in Gansu—there are 15,635 primary schools alone. The researchers told us that in the major towns and the larger crowded, bustling villages, they would find a public school, often a fine two-story building, sporting, as we too had found, a plaque marking it as a recipient of some foreign aid. To find the private schools, researchers had to abandon public transport and either walk or hitch a ride on one of the three-wheelers to travel up the even steeper mountain paths to the small clusters of houses that made up smaller, more remote villages. And there, nestled on mountain ridges, were stone or brick houses converted to schools, with the proprietor or headmaster living with his family in one or two of its rooms. Sometimes the school was purpose-built, constructed by the villagers themselves. Over and over again, researchers followed these trails high into the arid mountains to discover the private schools.

In the 586 private schools for the poor, it was reported, nearly 60,000 children were enrolled, an average of about 100 children per school. The largest school had 540 students, whereas the smallest had 5. There was a slightly higher percentage of girls in the private than in the public schools. Unlike the other country studies, private schools for the poor in China did not cater to a huge proportion of the school population—we estimated around 2 percent of school-children were in private schools. However, the fact that they were there at all, apparently completely unknown to the regional officials, seemed itself remarkable enough.

What fees did these schools charge? It is significant that during the time we were conducting the research, public schools charged fees—this was an anomaly that the Chinese government had been taken to task over by the United Nations special rapporteur on the right to education. The vast majority of the schools charged fees, by the semester (i.e., twice annually). The mean semester fees in private schools ranged from 68.79 renminbi ($8.56) in first grade to 78.66 renminbi ($9.78) in sixth grade. In public schools, the mean fees were slightly higher for most grades.

Who managed the private schools? Around two-thirds of private schools were managed by a group of villagers, whereas individual proprietors managed around one-third. And why did private school managers establish their schools? The most commonly reported reason was the inaccessibility of the public schools—reported by three-quarters of the total. It was clear from follow-up interviews with school managers that the public schools were too far from their villages—sometimes requiring children to walk five or six hours to get there—so this was the major reason for setting up a private school in the village itself.

The Extra Mile

In short, despite the denial of those in power, private schools for the poor exist in large numbers in rural China. They are set up by villagers and proprietors to cater to children whose needs are not being met by the public schools—mainly because they are simply too far away from the remote mountain villages. But officials from the government and the aid agencies denied their existence. Perhaps those from the aid agencies genuinely didn't know they existed. The private schools are hard to find. Go to the very remote villages, along paved or poorly maintained dirt roads, and you'll find a public school. And if you're an outsider, having taken the already long, arduous, and breathtakingly beautiful journey through the mountains there, why would you assume that there is anything beyond, educationally speaking? Especially when everyone, from officials to the public school teachers, said that there was not? To find the private schools, you must go the extra mile—or even an extra day's travel. Not everyone is prepared to do that.

For the officials, the reasons may be the same, or it may also be because of the sensitivity of China's purported position as having achieved universal public primary education. By the time I visited Gansu, the Chinese government had been roughly criticized, by among others the UN special rapporteur on the right to education, for still charging school fees at the primary level.[4] If it then had to admit that some children were in private schools because they were too poor to attend public schools, or because no convenient public school was provided for them, then this would add weight to the criticisms.

Anyway, taking these criticisms to heart, the Chinese government recently announced moves to bring in free public education, starting in the poor rural areas in western China, including Gansu.[5] The development experts regard free public education as something of a panacea; it is required before a country can be considered as properly developed—indeed, a necessary path to that development. It's all part of what everyone knows.

But is free primary education really the universal remedy held up by the development experts, or could it bring its own problems? This was another part of the accepted wisdom that I was being forced to confront as I made my journey. Before I'd even gone to China, I'd visited Kenya, which had introduced free primary education in January 2003, only months before I'd secured the project funding to do my research. What I'd found there on my first visit made me realize that I must do the research there too. The Kenyan findings were to astonish even me, despite what I was already seeing in India, Nigeria, and Ghana.

6. A Kenyan Conundrum—and Its Solution

The Man to Meet

Television anchor Peter Jennings asked former U.S. president Bill Clinton on ABC's *Primetime* which one living person he would most like to meet. He chose the current president of Kenya "because he has abolished school fees." By doing that, Clinton said, "he would affect more lives than any president had done or would ever do by the end of this year." The upshot was that President Kibaki invited Bill Clinton to Nairobi to see for himself how free primary education was being implemented.[1]

While chancellor of the exchequer, British Prime Minister Gordon Brown also went to Kenya as part of his "Discover Africa" tour.[2] The BBC filmed him in a public school, Olympic, on the outskirts of Kibera, reportedly the largest slum in Africa. Schoolchildren surrounded him, singing the praises of free education introduced by the new National Rainbow Coalition government in January 2003. He told the gathered multitude that British parents gave their full support to their taxpayers' money being used to support free primary education. "Our new resolution," he announced, "for every country must be universal free education—the best and most empowering investment we could ever make." Official sources acclaimed that an extra 1.3 million children—up 22 percent, from 5.9 million to 7.2 million—were now enrolled in primary school in Kenya because of free primary education. The capital of Kenya itself, Nairobi, boasted a 48 percent increase in primary school enrollment. And because the World Bank gave the Kenyan government $55 million, the largest grant to any social sector, to finance free primary education, the pressure was on to match this international generosity in other countries. All the new children in primary school, Brown was adamant, have been saved from ignorance by the benevolence of the international community—which must give $7 billion to $8 billion more per year so that other countries can emulate Kenya's success.

On the face of it, Clinton's choice sounded like a good one. The poor, by definition, have few resources; having to fork out for schooling is bound to hurt them harder than anyone else. So providing them with free schooling would seem to be a good thing. After all, it's what we take for granted in Britain and America too. If it's good enough for us, it must also be good enough for those in poor countries, surely?

Everyone seems to agree. Jeffrey Sachs, special adviser to the United Nations and author of the bestseller *The End of Poverty*, with a foreword by pop star Bono, has "eliminating school fees" at the top of his list of "Quick Wins" for development, funded through increased international donor aid.[3] The United Nations Development Programme says that requiring "poor households to pay for schooling (private or public) is not conducive to achieving universal primary education." In countries where primary school fees have been removed, "children have flooded into schools." Oxfam International is just as clear: "The case for abolishing user fees for primary education is largely accepted." So is Save the Children: requiring parents to pay fees makes the difference "between a child's attendance at school or their removal from the education system." Abolishing school fees is especially needed for girls: poor parents "overwhelmingly choose to invest in their sons rather than their daughters" when deciding on which to send to school. And getting rid of school fees releases the pent-up demand for education. Countries held up as great examples of how this has worked include Malawi, Tanzania, Uganda, and Kenya, where abolishing school fees "almost overnight" has led to a huge increase in primary school enrollment.

The Conundrum

So it's all relatively straightforward and uncontroversial. School fees are bound to put the poor off sending their children to school; getting rid of them is the right idea and has no obvious disadvantages of its own.

This might be the end of the story. Except that while reading these tales of success, I came across a conundrum that went along with that success, which seemed to sorely perplex the development experts. I found that Dr. Pauline Rose of the University of Sussex expressed this puzzle particularly well. Yes, she agreed, abolishing fees in government schools in Uganda and Malawi had led to millions more children in school. But, she noted, curiously, *private schools for the poor had* "mushroomed" at apparently the very same time that these free primary education policies were being enacted! Rose pointed to one study from remote rural Uganda that showed that fully 40 percent of primary school pupils attended private schools, with private school enrollment much higher in the towns and cities. This mass enrollment in private schools puzzled her: "If children were previously out of school," she mused, "in countries such as Malawi and Uganda because of inability to pay fees and enrollment increased dramatically following their abolition, how is it possible that these same poor families can now afford to pay fees in private schools instead?"[4]

My research in Kenya gave some pointers for solving this conundrum. My study started there in October 2003, some 10 months after free primary education had been introduced in government primary schools. Indeed, the solution to the conundrum seemed rather simple, if one only bothered to go and look.

Kibera

Former president Bill Clinton wasn't the only one to notice that Kenya had introduced free primary education. Early in 2003, when deciding which countries to focus on for the research, James Stanfield, one of my research associates at Newcastle, suggested that we look at Kenya. He'd seen BBC footage of crowds of children flocking to the newly-free-of-tuition state schools, with the commentator praising this great success story. "What's really going on there?" he asked. "Is it really as good as it seems?" And so I decided to visit to see if our contacts there could help us with the project.

As usual, it seemed unpromising at first. When I arrived at the airport, I was met by my host James Shikwati, who had recently established the Inter-Region Economic Network in Nairobi, which was to become one of Africa's foremost free-market think tanks. James is a very bright, articulate young man in his early 30s, someone who very much believes that free enterprise can help solve Africa's problems, and he is committed to fighting excessive state intervention in all sorts of areas of the economy. I had communicated with him a few weeks before my visit, telling him of my finding private schools for the poor in India, my preliminary investigations in Nigeria and Ghana, and my interest in finding whether the same was true of Kenya. He had been very sympathetic to the idea and had promised to ask around and assist me in my quest in whatever way he could.

I arrived at Nairobi International Airport to be greeted by his bombshell: "I think I should tell you," he began, a bit embarrassed, "there aren't any private schools for the poor here." Although accustomed to this kind of remark, hearing it from someone of James's caliber had me a little worried—if anyone should know about their existence, it should be someone like James, who was aware of how the private sector was helping the poor in other areas. But no, "I've asked everyone who knows anything about education," he said, sensing my unease, "and I'm sorry, they're not here." He'd asked teachers, sympathetic academics, and some friends who worked in the Ministry of Education. Everyone told him the same thing: "Private schools here, you see, are mainly for the elite and middle classes." Perhaps again he was right? I said we'd go and look anyway. That wasn't the only mild frustration on my arrival in Kenya. Again, my baggage didn't arrive at the airport, and I was left for several days without a change of clothes. (A few days later, still with no baggage, I went shopping for essentials, including trousers. "I have a short leg," I helpfully told the attractive young shop assistant, idly leaning forward rocking her tummy on the counter. "Only one?" she inquired.)

The next morning, however, things brightened up. I had suggested that we must at least go and look in one poor area; James's driver, Alfas, was acquainted with the slum of Kibera, not too far away from James's office. "You never know, we might find something," I said. We should check, just in case all the people James had spoken to were wrong. Alfas parked the car at the top of a bumpy road by the government offices—"Hopefully, if we leave it here, everyone will think it's a government official on business," said James. So we walked into the slum. Apparently, over half a million people lived here, crowded into an area the size of Manhattan's Central Park. Corrugated-iron-roofed huts crowded alongside the narrow muddy track that was the main thoroughfare into the settlement. The mud was deep and suspiciously colored—it was one of Nairobi's two rainy seasons, and everyone was walking on a narrow spit of slightly drier path weaving along the edge of the track, but our feet were already deep in the mud, or whatever it was. Along the track ran an open sewer and piled along its sides were all kinds of trash and household effluent.

It's striking how much activity there was everywhere—the street was lined with small wooden shops, selling everything from kitchenware to television sets. There were even little windowless shacks with the list of the videos being shown and their times—little video theaters. There were hairdressers where women sat and had their hair braided. There were little restaurants where the proprietor sat by an old oil drum, cooking meat. It all seemed thriving, busy, very entrepreneurial. And then by a line of women collecting water from a tap, we found our first school.

It was next to the Baptist church, with its signboard proclaiming "Makina Baptist Primary School." As we entered through the rickety wooden gate, a pleasant, tall male teacher greeted us and took us down an alley with two-story tin buildings on either side, to a cupboard-size office, where Jane Yavetsi, the proprietor, warmly welcomed us. She was well built, full of smiles, and very pleased to meet us. And her school it turned out, just like similar schools elsewhere, had nothing to do with the church, but simply used the name for marketing purposes—"Church schools have a very good reputation in Kenya," Jane told me, "so it's a good name to have for our school." But her school received no subsidy from anyone, neither church nor state; it simply rented the land next to the church. And so we found the first of what turned out to be many private schools in the slums of Kibera.

Jane was keen to tell me her story, as we sat on old school chairs crowded into her office. "Free education is a big problem to me," she said. Since the government abolished fees in the state schools, "parents have opted for free education." She used to have about 500 children in her school; now she had only 300. She was in a real fix, she said, and couldn't afford the rent. It was true, a substantial number of her parents had opted to stay with her, rather than move their children to the free public school. She explained: "Children have to walk two kilometers to outside the slum; there is no public school in the slum itself. But parents are worried about their children, especially girls, because there are child abductors around." So that was one reason why 300 parents stayed, even though the public schools were now free. She was sure that if her ex-parents could see some slight improvement, they would return and make her school viable again. The wealthier of her poor parents had taken their children away, she said, the ones who paid their fees on time. "So what I can do now?" she asked.

Her school fees were about 200 Kenyan shillings per month, or about $2.60. But for the poorest children, including 50 orphans, she herself offered, and had always offered since she established the school 10 years before, free education. She chuckled at the irony of her having done all along what the government was now getting so much credit for doing—offering free education, at least to the poorest of the poor. In the last decade, she told me, she had experienced so many difficulties. But now she felt very crestfallen, that she might be unable to surmount this particular difficulty. "When free education came, I am really being hit very hard."

Why did she establish a school? "Even my grandfather was a teacher, it is in my family's blood," she responded. She loved being a teacher, but also enjoyed the role of helping families, being "upfront" in her community, being noticed. She enjoyed "the best of all worlds," she said, running a business and being respected in the community, at least, that was, until free primary education came along and shattered her dreams. She herself had not been trained as a teacher. Of her teachers, six were men, seven were women; some were trained, but she believed that they had talent even if they had failed the exams or had not even taken them. Government teachers, she said, were paid much, much more than her teachers— she didn't want to say how much, because, she laughed, "the comparison will make me cry!" A big problem with the government teachers, she said, was that they frequently went on strike. This was one reason why parents were willing to pay for private education, even if there was a free alternative.

I visited the classrooms, creeping carefully on the rickety boards of the upstairs rooms, which were pretty dark and not full of children—but this was the first day of the term. James Shikwati told me that he wouldn't have expected any children at all in schools on the first day of the term, as teaching didn't normally get under way until at least the second week. But that was in the government schools. Here, teaching was going on, right on the first day. I talked to the children after they stood to greet me and said, "Welcome, you are welcome." I asked a boy in the upper classes why his parents sent him to this school when government schools were now free. "In government schools," he said, "there are too many children and too few teachers."

We left Jane, promising to return later. Immediately next door was another school, Makina Self-Help School, but we didn't call there because we didn't want to offend Jane's hospitality. We continued walking down the muddy street. Waterfalls tumbled from rocky heights, carrying along with the heavy overnight rainfall the detritus of the slums to the humanity below. We arrived at a narrow-gauge railway line, weaving through the slums, to a small gorge etched out of the rocks. Crowds of people were using the railroad track as a major thoroughfare, relieved from the mud as they moved along the steel line and wood sleepers. It was the old Uganda Railway, James told me, built by the British to connect the coast at Mombasa with Lake Victoria, where a steamer could take people across to Kampala, Uganda's capital. I was about to ask if it was still in use when the deep throbbing that had been in the background for some time answered my question: a diesel locomotive appeared out of the gorge, pulling an immense train of freight cars. As it approached, people dove off the track into the mud, as the train seemed to plow its way through the crowd. The moment the train passed, they all crowded back on the track and resumed their business.

While the train passed, we asked if anyone knew of any private schools. Of course, we were told. There were private schools in every direction. *Private* schools? We ensured that people had heard us correctly. Of course, there were no government schools here in Kibera! James Shikwati took it all in his stride. OK, so I was wrong, he joked, very wrong. We crossed the railway line, turned left, and clambered up the steep bank to the top of the gorge. And five minutes later, we found three other private schools. We stopped first at Huruma Secondary School, across the tracks from Starlight Educational Centre. Huruma was the longest-established private school in Kibera, we were told. We met the principal, a jolly rotund man, who was in the office as parents were lining up to pay for their children's education. Free education did not affect enrollment in this school, he told us, because education was not free at the secondary level. But even his sister primary school had no problem now—some students did leave in January when free primary education was introduced but were now returning, and there were more children now than at the end of last year! Why was that? we asked. "You ask my parents," he chuckled. The sister's primary school was farther down the railroad tracks. Painted in bold white capital letters on the blue corrugated-iron shack walls was the legend:

The Huruma Kibera School.
Free *Education for*:

- Orphans
- Poor Families
- Refugees.

Welcome.

An arrow pointed to the entrance, down an alley between the shacks.

We made our way out of the slum. Its exits seemed to be fine locations for young entrepreneurs, who would wash and shine your shoes for a "few bob" (that is, a few Kenyan shillings; Kenyans used the same slang for their money as the British used to for theirs) as you prepared to go about your business in the city proper. And James pointed to one of the grand houses bordering the slum, with beautiful and extensive gardens, flush with jacaranda trees, pale purple in season. Here lived the notorious ex-president of Kenya, Moi. And running parallel to the railway line a few hundred meters away on higher ground was a high brick wall; on one side the crowded slums, on the other the spacious and attractive municipal golf course.

Back in the office, James told me how astounded he was that something was on his doorstep that he never knew about—but, more important, that those who should have known were also in the dark! Why did no one tell him, especially those that should have known better? I, on the other hand, felt vindicated. We could do the research here and see what we could uncover about private education and the poor in urban Kenya, and how free primary education had affected it all.

Kakamega

We did the research proper on private schools for the poor in the slums of Nairobi; but I also wanted to see if the same phenomenon also existed in rural Kenya. When I returned to Kenya in August 2004, my opportunity came. I went with James Shikwati's elder brother Juma to the province of Western, where James and his family came from. We flew—a new experience for Juma—from Nairobi to Kisumu. He struggled manfully with his seat belt before I intervened to show him how: "Will we really need this? Is it going to be so bumpy?" he asked, looking squeamish. He studied the safety card for sometime after the flight attendant had taken us perfunctorily through it, and asked me how exactly we should leave by the emergency exit when required. And as we flew, he delighted in looking at the clouds. They *were* extraordinarily beautiful, with deep chasms between their cauliflower heads and what looked for all the world like a lakeshore in the distance, with the dark-blue line of the water, clouds reflected below and standing in their whiteness above. But it was all cloud illusion. As we broke through to see the earth below, Juma said, "I can now tell my children I have seen how God looks down upon us." Later he told his brother of his flying experience: "There were potholes. Potholes, in the air, which made it all very bumpy. They called them air pockets."

I also experienced a new form of transport, with as much delight. This was the *boda-boda* bicycle, so named because it originally took people's goods illicitly across the Uganda-Kenya border—there being no duty on goods taken by bicycle. "Border-border" became transmuted to *boda-boda*. Since then, *boda-bodas* have emerged as a major public transport system in Kenya, particularly Western province. You sit on a comfortable seat fitted with footrests and hand rests, above the back wheel of an otherwise ordinary bicycle, behind a fit young man who energetically cycles you where you want to go. Except that when you reach a hill, you get off to walk alongside him.

By *boda-boda* to the bus station, then on to the town of Kakamega in a *matatu* (minibus-taxi), and then to Juma's village, Lubao. Juma lives in a mud-and-wood building with a half-acre plot on which he grows bananas and other staples and keeps his cow. We arrived at nightfall. As his wife prepared some food for us, Juma took me across the village to the local private school, Victory Academy. It was run by Lydia, who was breastfeeding her baby in the dark corner of a classroom that doubled as her home as we arrived. Her possessions were all around, but when school was in session she bundled them away during the day and unpacked every evening. It was nearly 7:00 p.m. and getting dark. In the gloaming, she unlocked and unbolted each classroom door and showed us rooms with wonderful displays for the young children of animal pictures and alphabet friezes.

Lydia told me a familiar story: She had started a nursery four years earlier, but then the parents came to her when their children transferred to first grade in the public primary school and said that her children were far ahead of the other children and now nowhere nearly as happy as they had been. So why couldn't she teach first grade too? So she had started first grade, moved the children up to second grade, and had hoped to expand further as the children grew up with her. She currently had about 50 children, paying fees of about 200 Kenyan shillings (about $2.60) per month. She had no view on the effect of free primary education—her school population had stayed the same, she said, nothing much had changed.

We left her, to have *chai*—sweet, milky tea—and sandwiches that Juma's wife had prepared for us. The sun was setting, golden on the horizon. The crickets chirped, and in the middle distance was the noise of older children playing, joyously, exuberantly outside, while babies coughed gently in the next room; there were flickering candles and the smell of paraffin lights; at the end of the drive, the old men and younger men and women stood and chatted.

In the morning, after an excellent breakfast of tiny bananas, paw-paw, juice, and *chai*, we hired a car and went looking for private schools. We found plenty; there was no shortage here in the rural areas. Typical of the schools was one just outside Mukumu, where the hospital sign by the roadside advertised: "Hospital Mortuary: Cold Rooms Available." Here we found Wema Academy. *Wema* means "goodness" in Kiswahili, the proprietor, Stella, told me; it was taken from the hymn "Surely Goodness and Mercy Shall Follow Me." The school occupied a very pleasant site by the main road; it had a couple of block buildings with tin roofs, but most were made of mud-rendered wood. Apparently, the school was originally a residential site—a terrace of rooms for individual families to rent—but Stella had persuaded the owners to lease it to her as a school. The owner family lived on the adjacent plot.

Stella served us *chai* from a flask in her office. Why did she found the school? I asked her. She was clear: "In order to make an income for my family," she said, surprisingly boldly, but also added, "and to help the children in the neighborhood." The school currently had 120 students, from "baby class," nursery up to fourth grade. Fees were comparable with those I'd seen elsewhere. She told me that "the growth of the school has been less, as there are bureaucratic obstacles." Government officials were harassing her, and she has only one way of dealing with these officials—she wouldn't say how, but presumably meant through bribery. One problem the officials brought up was that a school should be on owned property, with proper deeds, but she rented the buildings. This was not good enough. Another problem was the size of the playground, which should be the size of a soccer field, but hers was only half that. It seemed a perfectly adequate size, however. (A cow was grazing there.) They also harassed her about the classroom sizes, she said. They were supposed to be at least eight feet by eight feet; hers were smaller. "But my class size is also smaller than in the public schools; I have less children so I don't need such a large classroom." But the inspectors wouldn't listen: "You can't tell them that the class is small, but the students are few," she told me, "they don't listen; they have their rules and keep to them." She said that none of the public schools around had the right-sized playground, or classrooms, yet they were not even inspected, let alone harassed. "Anything private, the government officers harass it. If it is a public school, no one cares how many toilets are there. But in a private school, they harass you!"

Stella also said that her school had been approved for registration, and she had a letter from the district education officer to prove this, but for the last two years the District Education Board "has been busy and has not discussed new private schools."

Had she been affected by free primary education? I asked. She was more forthcoming than Lydia had been, but her response carried the same message: nothing really had changed after free education because "there is overpopulation in the public schools." None of her parents had wanted to move their children to the free primary schools; "They know that their children are not getting a good deal in those schools." Indeed, she added, other private schools were opening now, even after the introduction of free primary education, whereas hers had been the only one in the district last year.

Far more important than any effect of free primary education was how to improve the learning of the children under her care. We continued our discussions over *chai*. Stella said that she wanted to introduce the Montessori method into her classrooms, and she asked

me my views on the pros and cons of various curricula. It was
wonderful to be sitting with her talking about education and the
improvement of young lives.

Back in Nairobi, I interviewed prospective academics to become
advisers to my research. The contrast to my conversation with Stella
was stark and unfavorable. One young academic from the University
of Nairobi was exactly the type of person I didn't want. "What do
you mean, private schools for the poor? Private schools are for the
rich," she began, and I felt that we were going to make little headway.
She seemed to dislike my arrogance at coming to Kenya; likewise,
I didn't warm overmuch to her. Finally, oddly, she changed her
tune, once I'd convinced her that I'd been to the slums and rural
areas and had seen for myself: yes, low-cost private schools do
exist, she now agreed, "and before free education, they served an
important function, when it comes to access; but the question is,
after access, what happens, it's the quality that matters."

But how did we know what their quality was like? I told her that
was a research question, one I wanted to answer now, which was
my reason for being in Kenya. No, they knew they were poor quality
already, without any research, she told me: "They don't satisfy any
of the regulations. When the learning environment is not good,
they will be harassed by the inspector and should be closed down.
Buildings must be made of an appropriate material." Why was
learning in a brick building better than learning in a mud building?
I asked. "Ah, I can't answer that," she said. And schools should
operate in owned, not rented, buildings, she said: "The legal framework is that every school must have a title deed." But she was
adamant: private schools could exploit anyone because they didn't
mind what they delivered. I pointed out, "But the parents mind."
She shook her head, laughing with embarrassment: "Ah, the parents." She clearly didn't have a particularly high view of their capaci-
ties to choose.

Private Schools Serving the Poor in Kibera

So what did we find in the slums of Nairobi? It is estimated that
about 60 percent of the population live in "unplanned informal
settlements," slums like Kibera. A household survey conducted in
2004 suggests that nearly three-quarters of Nairobi's population lives
"below the poverty line."[5] In the slums, there are no public services—

114

no publicly provided water, sewage, health, and, of course, no public education. But clearly, there were private schools. How many? James Shikwati assembled a team of researchers, graduate students from Nairobi universities. We trained the team in methods of finding and gaining access to schools, and in the use of an interview schedule for school managers. We found a great map of Kibera, created by a German aid agency, which showed how the Uganda railway snaked through the slum, and sent researchers out with copies to systematically sweep the whole area. As usual, we were only looking for primary and secondary schools, excluding "nonformal education" places, and schools serving only nursery students. The researchers were also asked to visit any government schools that the local residents said served Kibera.

The researchers found 76 private primary and secondary schools in the slum of Kibera (plus 59 nursery-only schools, which we didn't examine further). This was quite remarkable—so many private schools where even sympathetic observers, like James Shikwati and his informers, had reported there were none. These schools served 12,132 children (excluding those in the nursery streams, which many of the primary and secondary schools also had). About a third of the schools were managed by women. And—a clear potential answer to the conundrum that private schools, for whatever reason, seemed to have emerged only after free public education was introduced— we found 1996 to be the average year the private schools were established. These schools clearly had not simply "mushroomed" only recently.

The researchers also visited five government schools that reportedly served the Kibera community, located on the outskirts of the slum area. In these schools, reported enrollment was 9,126— although many of these children came from the middle-class suburbs, not the slums. These visits enabled us to make several interesting comparisons between the public and private schools serving Kibera. First, Jane was right about the relative wages in public and private schools. Our researchers found that average salaries were three to five times higher in the government schools than in the private schools. And her suggestion about relative class size was also borne out by our evidence. The public schools had much higher pupil–teacher ratios than the private schools: in the private schools, the average pupil–teacher ratio was 21 to 1—and this was also the average class size, since there were no extra "floating" teachers for specialist subjects. In the public schools, the average pupil–teacher ratio was nearly three times higher, at 60 to 1. But that included several teachers who were specialists in different areas, and so the average class size was even larger.

Again, there wasn't a big difference in the proportion of boys and girls in public and private schools—contrary to what might have been expected from the pronouncements of the development experts: In the private schools, there were roughly equal numbers of boys and girls (51 percent and 49 percent, respectively)—nothing like the gross gender inequality that we'd been led to expect. The figure was more or less identical in the public schools (49 percent boys and 51 percent girls).

All but 2 of the 76 private schools charged fees—the exceptions were both run by religious organizations. The average monthly fees in the rest ranged from 149 Kenyan shillings ($1.94) for nursery classes to 256 Kenyan shillings ($3.33) per month for eighth grade. We compared these figures with the "absolute poverty" line for Kenya as a whole, which was set at a monthly income of 3,174 Kenyan shillings ($41.33), excluding rent. The average fees per child would thus range from 4.7 percent to 8.1 percent of this minimum income level—which seemed to be pretty affordable, even for the poorest of the poor.

Free Primary Education Did Not Lead to an Increase in Enrollment

The excitement about free primary education, as we saw from former president Bill Clinton's comments, was that it reportedly led to a massive increase in enrollment—an additional 1.3 million primary school children across Kenya, with a reported increase of over 48 percent in Nairobi alone. This was the crucial point that I wanted our research to explore. However, these headline figures don't take into account what is happening in the private schools in the slums—because no one seems to have either been aware of their existence or thought they were worth bothering about. What difference would it make to these headline figures if changes in enrollment in these private schools were also taken into account?

My researchers asked managers, in both private and public schools, how free primary education had affected their *primary school* enrollment. They also asked if managers knew of any private schools that had closed altogether because of free primary education. What I found completely contradicted the accepted wisdom of the development experts, and provided a ready solution to their conundrum.

True, free primary education had dramatically increased the number of students enrolled in all five government primary schools reportedly serving Kibera. The total increase was 3,296 students, or 57 percent, an even higher growth rate than that reported for Nairobi. This might have been anticipated given that government schools on the periphery of slum areas would be expected to have enjoyed larger enrollment gains than schools farther away. It was, in any case, a dramatic increase, part of the reported increase in enrollment of 1.3 million nationwide.

However, taking into account what was happening in the private schools in the slums, a totally different picture emerged. Just as Jane had pointed out from her own school, in the vast majority of the private schools, free primary enrollment had led to a net decline in enrollment. This was not the case in all schools—around 30 percent of the schools reported that enrollment either had stayed roughly the same or had declined initially but since recovered, or even, like Huruma Kibera School, had actually increased. Adding the decline in the majority of schools, then subtracting the increase in the others, gave a *net decrease in private-sector enrollment of 6,571—far greater than the growth in public school enrollment.* That is, far from leading to a massive increase in the number of children in school, as the official figures acclaimed, there seemed to have been a large decrease.

However, this was not the end of the story. We were given the names of 33 private schools that school managers told us had closed since the introduction of free primary education. We went searching for the owners of these former private schools. After much detective work, we located and interviewed 32 of them. We also uncovered an additional three private schools that had closed since free primary education was introduced, the names of which existing school managers had not given us. Not all these 35 private schools had closed because of free primary education, however. In fact, two of the schools had relocated and were still open, whereas six had closed because of demolition work from the building of a bypass through Kibera. And two had closed, the managers candidly told us, because of mismanagement or lack of funds, unconnected with free primary education. However, in the 25 schools that had closed specifically because of free primary education, a total of *4,600 children* were reported to have been enrolled in the primary grades.

Pulling all this information together, I arrived at an estimate of the net decrease in the number of students enrolled from Kibera as a result of the introduction of free primary education. In private schools as a whole, I estimated that enrollment had declined by 11,171 since the introduction of free primary education. Set against the increase in government schools of 3,296, this meant an overall net *decrease* in enrollment of 7,875 primary school children since the introduction of free primary education. That is, my estimate indicated that about 8,000 *fewer* students from Kibera were enrolled in primary schools than before the introduction of free primary education. This was quite astonishing.

Of course, the figure could be inaccurate. After all, it was based on the increases and declines in school enrollment *reported* by school managers. These may be incorrect simply because the managers may have remembered incorrectly. Or they may have felt some incentive to exaggerate their decline in student enrollment if they felt it would lead to financial or other assistance. It also assumed that all children who had left Kibera private primary schools could only have gone to the five primary government schools bordering Kibera, but they may have enrolled at other government schools once those bordering Kibera reached capacity. And children may also have relocated to other towns or rural areas, perhaps through natural movement of families in and out of the slum areas—but we had no way of quantifying this "natural" movement unconnected with free primary education.

Another question was why private schools were closing if relatively few children were transferring to government schools. One reason suggested by private school managers was that, as private schools ran on very tight budgets, the loss of even a few children might make them unviable financially and hence force them to close. And when we interviewed parents, they gave the impression that it was the more prosperous slum dwellers who could afford to send their children to government schools, given their "hidden costs"—reported to include requirements for school uniforms, parent-teacher association fees, and so forth. These more prosperous parents may have been the ones who could afford to pay fees on time in the private schools, and the private school managers may have felt their loss particularly acutely.

My team asked managers of private schools that were now closed for their views on what had happened to the children who had left their schools. They were not very optimistic. William Onyando, who had run Upendo Primary until he was forced to close because of free primary education, told us, "Some children joined other private schools and city council schools but others are still at home because of limited chances in the present schools." Stephen Juma Kulisher, the former proprietor of Jesus Gospel Church School, said, "The needy children remained at home; others went to the local private school and some to the local government school." Oscar Osir of the now-closed Sinai Academy told us, "Some joined the city council schools but others did not since they were orphaned and needed special treatment which the city council schools do not provide."

The suggestion that some of the displaced children enrolled at other private schools in Kibera may help explain why a few of the remaining private schools experienced an increase in enrollment, but this cannot account for all the missing children. Some of the comments above suggest that some adversely affected by the introduction of free primary education were orphans who previously enjoyed free education at a local private school. Following the closure of these schools, such children may have been unable to find a free place at another local private school or couldn't afford the "hidden costs" of enrolling at a government school, or couldn't afford transportation costs to schools farther away, if local government schools were already oversubscribed.

Whatever reasonable objections there are to the data I found, they clearly pointed to the need for a more sober assessment of the net effect of free primary education on enrollment. They dramatically showed that one ignores enrollment in private schools for the poor at one's peril. And they demonstrated that the strategy of free primary education succeeded above all in "crowding out" private schools that were already serving the poor.

At best, even if the reported figures were exaggerated by *a factor of four*, it would still mean that the net effect of free primary education was *the same number of children enrolled in primary streams*—the increase in government enrollment merely reflecting a transfer from private to government schools. Far from being a huge success story for aid in Africa, at best, the free primary education that has been so held up as something to be emulated by others may have led only to a straight transfer of children from private schools in the slums to the public schools on the periphery. Worse than that, it has destroyed a not insignificant number of private businesses that gainfully employed workers without the need for international aid funding—just the sort of self-sustaining economic activity that is responsible for the rise of nations out of poverty.

Indeed, the failure of free primary education to actually increase enrollment was not lost on the public school administrators themselves, as I learned from Mr. Gitau, the charming and handsome deputy principal of Toi Primary, one of the public schools on the periphery of Kibera. I called on him while doing the research—although as usual when visiting government schools, I didn't immediately mention my interest in the private schools in the slums. He told me that his school enrollment had increased by over 700 since free primary education—although he had no new teachers to cope with the influx, so things were now becoming impossible. "My class sizes are 75 to 100," he said, "How can a teacher mark all those books?" But then, almost conspiratorially, he leaned forward and asked: "Did you know? These are not children who hadn't been at school before. They all were in private schools in the slums before!" Really? "Yes, it's just like moving from one store to another. But if they could pay before, then why can't they pay now? What is the sense in the government doing that? If only they had spoken to people like us, neutral observers, perhaps they wouldn't have done anything so silly."

But by this time in my journey, I already knew what the response of the development experts would be to my findings. Even if the "best-case" scenario was true, and there had simply been a shift from private to public school enrollment, then it was obviously all to the good because the quality of the private schools in the slums was purportedly so low. It was an argument that I'd begun to hear from many of the development experts I spoke to. And it was something I'd heard on television. Shortly after returning from one of my research visits to Kenya, I saw a report on the BBC lunchtime news. A young female reporter had visited Kibera to explore some of the problems with free primary education to reinforce the need for more British aid. It was around the time that the then British prime minister Tony Blair was embarking on his mission to save Africa, hence the BBC's interest. The young woman visited a private school in the slum, one I had got to know well from the research. The camera played tenderly on gaps in the crumbling mud-and-timber walls and delighted in the dust storm blowing through, choking the children (the dry seasons also have their problems, much as the rainy ones). The reporter spoke of how the "unqualified, poorly paid" teachers were doing their best. "But," she concluded, "no one believes that these schools can offer quality education."

If You Go to a Market . . .

But is it really so grim? After all, my research had shown that significant numbers of parents had tried free primary education in the public schools but had decided to move their children back to the private schools. Surely, they weren't doing something so counterintuitive if they thought that the private schools really were hopeless? My research assistant from Newcastle, James Stanfield, and I decided to interview groups of parents in four schools that had reported parents' returning their children, having moved them first to the government schools. These parents at least were clear that they had behaved rationally moving back to private school.

In each discussion, parents eagerly told us how the education being offered in the slum private schools was higher quality than in the neighboring government schools—however much the buildings' appearances might suggest the contrary. Not one parent expressed the opposite view.

One mother told us: "I have two children who joined this school since their nursery level and they are still in this school today. I see them doing good in subjects. Their time and subjects are well planned; they spend time well and are taught all subjects. . . . For those reasons this private school has impressed me a lot. I have saved money and cut many costs of my maintenance in order to bring children in this private school. Even though people might question why I send children in private school while there are free [government] schools, I am concerned with high-quality subject teaching offered in this private school."

We asked parents to elaborate on what particular features made the private schools preferable. One mother told us: "People thought education is free; it may be free but children do not learn. This

121

makes the quality of education poor and that is why many parents have brought their children back here. People got their children out of the private schools to the public schools because of free education. . . . However, the children do not learn; all they do is play." Other parents agreed. A father told us: "While most of the teachers in government school are just resting and doing their own things, in private school our teachers are very much busy doing their best, because they know we pay them by ourselves. If they don't do well they can get the message from the headmistress, of which we cannot allow because we produce ourselves the money, we get it through our own sweat, we cannot allow to throw it away, because you can't even take the money from the trees, you have to work harder to find it so the teacher must also work harder on our children so that he earns his own living."

A mother agreed: "You will never see [in a private school] a teacher working on something else like sewing a sweater while she is supposed to be in class."

But how did parents know the quality in the private schools was better than in government schools? We asked them for details. Parents, it turned out, actively compared children in the government schools with children in the private schools in their neighborhoods. One mother commented: "If you make a comparison between a child attending private school and one who is in government school by asking them some questions from their subjects you will find the one in private school is doing very good, while the one from government school is poor. Even when you compare their examinations scores you will be able to see private school pupil is performing well while that from government is poor." Another gave a similar story: "I am living next to parents who send their children to a government school, and I always compare their children with mine who are attending private school. I always find private schools teach better than government schools from these comparisons. Government school children are always smart dressed in good uniforms but when you ask them some questions, you will realize that they know nothing. Those attending a private school are usually not smartly dressed, but they are good in school subjects."

Finally, parents were learning from the experience of those who had moved between the two systems. One mother told us that she had a sister who used to be a pupil in Olympic, the government school bordering Kibera: "She told me that there is a difference in the teaching. In Olympic, teachers do not concentrate on the pupils and so her performance started going down. She told me when she moved to the private school, the teacher teaches well; let's say it was an English class; the teacher teaches well and spends enough time with the children but when she was in the government school, the teacher does not spend much time with them; as long as she has seen she has taught *something*, she walks out of class."

But it wasn't just the perceived higher standards in the private schools that attracted parents. Parents also told us of the ways in which private school managers were sensitive to the plight of parents who could not afford to pay their fees on time, a point in favor of sending children to private schools. One mother remarked: "I am thankful to the head teacher [of the private school] very much for being very considerate to parents. You will never see a child not in school because of delay paying school fees. In those cases, the head teacher will write to the parent to ask them to meet with her to discuss when the fees can be paid." A father concurred, "Here, with the little money we earn we can pay bit by bit." And then there was the concern about the "hidden" costs of the supposedly free education in government schools. One of the main requirements was school uniforms—and it was argued by parents that, in their view, government schools were using the inability of poor parents to meet uniform requirements in full to turn them away. One mother pointed out, "In a private school, a child is allowed to attend school with only one uniform while in the government school he must have two uniforms before he is allowed to attend school." Another agreed: "Even if learning there [in the government schools] is free, school uniform is expensive and you have to buy full school uniform at once. I prefer to pay fees and buy the school uniform bit by bit."

One mother enumerated what she saw as the costs that she would incur if she sent her child to a government school: "I went there [to a government school] to see [and] they told me I had to have 11,000 Kenyan shillings [$143.23] cash in hand." Partly, she reported, this charge was for the building maintenance fund. She continued that once you'd "bought a school uniform," you still had to buy "the school sweater, which costs 600 Kenyan shillings [$7.81], and you have to make sure you have two sweaters, which is 1,200 Kenyan shillings [$15.62]. Good leather shoes and socks two pairs. You have to have two of everything." In short, the mother argued about government schooling, "I don't think it's free."

One father summed it all rather neatly as to why he still preferred private schooling for his daughter rather than what was provided free in the public school: "If you go to a market and are offered free fruit and vegetables, they will be rotten. If you want fresh fruit and vegetables, you have to pay for them."

Education Free, for All; or Education Free-for-All?

After all this, the introduction of free primary education in Kenya didn't seem like such a success story. What I found in Kibera—and I also did parallel research in the slums of Kawangware and Mukuru in Nairobi, with more or less identical results—surely didn't point to free primary education as being the panacea that the development experts made it out to be. Far from leading to an increase in enrollment, at best it might have led to a simple transfer of children from private schools in the slums—where they appeared cared for in small classes by teachers who were accountable to parents—to the government schools on the periphery, where parents believed their children were left pretty much to their own devices.

Interestingly, I found that some development agencies appeared aware of the problems in public schools after free primary education. But they put it all down to introducing free primary education *too quickly*. I read a report from Save the Children, for instance, which noted that, following the introduction of free primary education in Uganda and Malawi, there were "some disturbing signs of quality declines." They were in "no doubt that such declines have taken place," but argued that "we should be clear on the reasons for this." The reasons? "In both countries user fees were abolished swiftly without sufficient funds being made available to meet the shortfall. This problem was compounded by the immense success of the abolition of user fees in terms of attendance."[6] A report from Action Aid took the same line. It agreed that "quality problems encountered in education systems . . . that have eliminated fees are real and urgent." Again, however, this implied the need for "substantial increases in donor support" to properly plan and finance the introduction of free primary education.

In other words, it was all the fault of donors for not providing sufficient funding to these countries. Give additional massive amounts in aid and free primary education can be made to work properly. But it seemed to me that it couldn't really be that simple. After all, free primary education was introduced decades ago in both India and Nigeria: in Nigeria, the Universal Free Primary Education Act was enacted on September 6, 1976, nearly 30 years before my research. In India, the National Policy on Education of 1986, nearly 20 years before my research, proclaimed free and compulsory primary education, which was soon introduced in many states, including Andhra Pradesh, and finally made law with the Constitutional 93rd Amendment of 2001. And in Ghana, free primary education—their Free Compulsory Universal Basic Education—was being introduced very slowly indeed, from 1996, financed with huge doses of foreign aid, including $100 million from the U.S. Agency for International Development, $85 million from DfID, and $50 million from the World Bank. But none of this seemed to have stopped a mass exodus of poor children from public to private schools.

The Conundrum Solved

I was now in a position to answer the conundrum, which was, as Pauline Rose had put it, "If children were previously out of school . . . because of inability to pay fees and enrollment increased dramatically following their abolition, how is it possible that these same poor families can now afford to pay fees in private schools instead?"

My research in Kenya suggested that these poor families had *always* been able to afford private schools. Before free primary education, they were *already* in private schools. The real conundrum for me was why the development experts hadn't already figured this out.

I was to get more puzzled the more I read their work. They seemed to agree with what I was finding about problems in public schools, but they didn't then consider what poor parents were choosing— the private alternative—as a possible way forward. Were they, too, like the academic I'd interviewed from the University of Nairobi, less than impressed by poor parents' abilities as education consumers?

7. Poor Ignoramuses

The Bad and the Very Ugly

When the BBC film crew came with me to Nigeria to make a documentary of the private schools for the poor in Makoko, I interviewed Mrs. Mary Taimo Ige Iji, the chief educational administrator for Mainland, Lagos—the local government area under which the shantytown of Makoko falls. We had traveled in convoy to the three government schools on the edge of Makoko—we in our battered old Volvo hired from a friend of BSE's in Apollo Street, Makoko; she with a team of five assistants in her brand-new white Mercedes. We had assumed that she would know where she was going—in her office she had proudly said that she personally inspected all the schools in her local government area. In the event, her car waited by the side of the road for us to catch up, so as to follow us to Makoko. It seemed that they had never been there before, not even to the public schools on the outskirts of the shantytown, let alone inside the shantytown itself.

We interviewed her on the balcony of the top floor of the first public school. I found her a rather fierce and domineering woman and was nervous that my questions might have offended her. But I needn't have worried. Her answers conveyed absolutely that she knew I could only be playing devil's advocate asking about possible virtues of low-cost private schools: no one could possibly think any differently from what she was saying.

I asked her why poor parents apparently—how could I put this, *strangely*—seemed to prefer to send their children to private schools in the shantytown, rather than to this rather nice public school building. (Actually, *she* had said it was a rather nice building—I found its architecture austere, imposingly grim, and Stalinist. But I went along with her characterization for the interview.) She didn't mince her words.

"There are many reasons. Parents don't have the information that the public schools are free; some of them they chose private schools because they are near their homes." So much by way of introduction. "But the most important point is fake status symbol, in quotes 'fake status symbol'"—she said this, without any sense of irony, standing above her Mercedes. In fact, at about this moment in the interview she moved to rest her arm on the balustrade, probably coincidentally, but it did have the effect of blocking out the car beneath from camera view. Relaxing now, getting into the swing, she continued: Poor parents "want to be seen as rich parents, *caring* parents, who take their children to 'fee-paying' schools supposedly better." But these poor parents, as we all know, are completely fooled. Poor parents, she said, are "ignoramuses."

I tried not to flinch as she spat out her contempt for the people I'd been working with. Why? I asked. Because the private schools, far from being any good, "are very poor in facilities, because there is no way you can compare these poor, ill-equipped private schools with government schools where all the teachers are qualified, fully qualified." The private schools, she said, are in "three categories— the good, the bad, and the very ugly." It was clear in which category the private schools in the shantytown fit: ". . . these poorly, ill-equipped unapprovable private schools, 'mushroom' schools, they are causing a lot of damage, a lot of damage," she continued. "At the end of it the children will come out half-baked, they are not useful to themselves, they end up in occupations like their parents are doing, they don't progress further, so that's two generations, three generations, wasted."

She couldn't have been clearer. Private schools for the poor were bad—"very ugly"—because of poor facilities and untrained teachers. Children came out half-baked; generations were wasted. Mary Taimo Ige Iji turned out not to be alone in her views. Her views were the common refrain about private schools serving the poor, that they were schools of "last resort" and must inevitably be offering a low-quality experience (it would be hard to call it an "education") because the facilities were so bad.

Certainly, the conditions of the schools I visited on my journey sometimes looked miserable. Buildings looked rough, and schools were usually poorly equipped; the teachers, it was true, were largely untrained. I pointed out these obvious criticisms to a young teacher in Ghana, the daughter of the proprietor of Shining Star Private School, which was little more than a corrugated-iron roof on rickety poles at the side of the main road out of Accra. The government school, just a few hundred yards away, was housed in a smart building, newly refurbished by the British aid agency DfID. "Education is not about buildings," she scolded me. "What matters is what is in the teacher's heart. In our hearts, we love the children and do our best for them." She left open, when probed, what the teachers in the government school felt in their hearts toward the poor children.

But was she right? What was the actual quality of the private schools for the poor? Could the human spirit rise above these meager surroundings and still provide something of educational value? And in any case, what was the quality of the alternative—the public schools to which parents could send their children, but which many were abandoning? Parents from Makoko who we interviewed for the BBC film were adamant in their reasons why they sent their children to private school. Perched at the end of a wood walkway above the stinking lagoon, the fisherman father of Sandra, the girl who had first introduced me to Ken Ade Private School in Makoko, told us, "In the public school they do not teach very well and that is why everybody, including me, prefers the private to public school, because they want their children trained for the future." Sandra's mother agreed: "In the private school, the teachers are better and when they teach, the children will be able to get immediately what they are saying. That's why I prefer to send my children to private school." And another articulate father put it like this: "Going to the public school here in Nigeria, particularly in this area in Lagos State, is just like saying wasting the time of day . . . because they don't teach them anything. The difference is clear, the private school and the children of private school and the children of public school, the difference is so great that the children of private school can speak very well, they know what they are doing but there in the public, *the children are abandoned*."

Certainly, when we visited the public schools on the edge of Makoko with the BBC crew we got a sense of that abandonment. I've already listed some of the things I first saw in those public schools in Chapter 3. But much to my surprise, we caught footage of something else, something I'd seen many times, but which I never believed we'd capture on camera. A young male teacher was sleeping, sprawled at his desk, while a girl in his class tried to teach her peers from a tatty textbook. Picture the scene: The BBC cameraman, producer, and director arrive in the classroom. The children shoot up, boisterously as always to greet their visitors. They sing out, "Welcome to you, BBC crew." Still the teacher sleeps. A pupil, embarrassed, tries to wake the teacher. Still he sleeps.

A bit unkindly, the BBC broadcast this bit of the film dubbed over with the voice of Professor Olakunle Lawal, the honorable commissioner for education, Lagos State, a very distinguished gentleman, with a PhD from Oxford University (it was while waiting to interview him that I had met Dennis Okoro, the ex–chief inspector). Giving his view on the past problems but current well-being of the teaching profession in Nigeria, he told us eloquently that, in the past, "teachers were not well motivated because of the challenges attached to their conditions of service. At times you had *haphazard* payment of salaries, and at times *outright non*payment for some. However, in the last six years things have changed considerably. This public school is very good now, you have well-trained manpower." That was a tad mischievous, putting his voice over the image of the sleeping teacher. Adding insult to injury, they also had Mary Taimo Ige Iji criticizing teachers in the private schools for the poor, and contrasting them with the public school workforce:

> Well in the private schools the teachers are not qualified, while they are there they are not paid regularly.... They can be fired anytime so they are not dedicated and most important they are not qualified. But in government schools the teachers are very disciplined and they are trained teachers. They can be fired for misconduct but it rarely happens.

I felt sorry for the teacher who prompted all this. Had I not seen so many like him, I would have discouraged the BBC from using his image. But it just seemed to capture so well the problems I'd seen in the public schools for the poor.

But was I alone in thinking that standards in the public schools were pretty appalling? On my journey, I devoured as much as I could of the writings of the development experts. Reassuringly—if reassuring is the right word for the anger and disgust I felt—I found that all the development experts I read seemed to agree that there were dire problems in the public schools—as personified by the sleeping teacher. Public education, they agreed, *was* a disaster. But then their conclusions on what to do about the problem seemed just baffling to me.

Public Education for the Poor Is a Disaster ...

All the development experts I read seemed to agree. I've already noted the PROBE Report's findings for northern India, summarized too by Amartya Sen, that teaching was occurring in only half the classrooms visited at random—with some teachers doing exactly what we reported in the BBC film, sleeping at their desks or in the staff room. Others were drinking and making merry. These voices are not alone. I could not find a single dissenting voice in what I read as I traveled. And whenever I spoke personally with any development agency officials in country, they were always eager to tell me of the failings of public education. Here's a summary of what I was told, what I read, and what I saw for myself.

Absentee Teachers

Public schools are letting down the poor, first, because of their teachers. The most serious problem, said the development experts, is teacher absenteeism. I read the most recent United Nations Educational, Scientific, and Cultural Organization (UNESCO) report on how to reach "education for all," which was clear that "random surveys in many countries confirm that teacher absenteeism remains a persistent problem."[1] The most up-to-date report from the United Nations Development Programme agreed that in India and Pakistan, "poor households cited teacher absenteeism in public schools as their main reason for choosing private ones." An academic article on teacher absenteeism reported that in two districts in Kenya, teachers were absent nearly 30 percent of the time and that children would expect not to be taught by public school teachers for over 40 percent of their time in the classroom.

Indeed, it appeared that, so much taken for granted was teacher absenteeism, UNESCO was able to make the following mind-boggling distinction when considering "corruption": "A distinction should be made between graft and corruption: graft is a relatively minor form of rule-breaking often stemming from need, as when a teacher sometimes misses classes to earn extra income because salaries are too low or irregular. Corruption is more severe." What could this mean, I thought, other than teachers' missing classes—hence leaving poor children stranded, "abandoned" as the Nigerian father put it—was now so common as to be considered acceptable? What kind of apology for bad teachers was this?

I read about corruption concerning the allocation of resources to schools too. UNESCO reported a study from Zambia that found "not even 10 percent of books procured had reached classrooms," but had instead been filched by officials at various levels of the hierarchy. And for teachers and principals, corruption turned out to be just part of their normal day-to-day work life. A World Bank report said that both schoolteachers and principals "solicit bribes to admit students or give better grades," or perhaps even worse, "teach poorly" during lesson time so as "to increase the demand for private tuition after hours." In general, "corruption is rife, and political patronage is a way of life."

And even if officials wanted to do something about problems of teacher absenteeism, what I read pointed to severe difficulties. An academic article from Calcutta, India, reported that teachers as "members of major teacher associations are usually immune from any penal action. If a school inspector tries to take action against a teacher the association 'gets after him.'"

I suppose it was reassuring that these experts agreed with what I found whenever I spoke to government officials. In the District Office of Ga, Ghana, I had met with the enthusiastic and very friendly Samuel Ntow, who was in charge of basic education. Completely unprompted, our conversation had drifted to his concerns about public education: "The problem we face with the public schools is *supervision.*" In the government schools, he said, there was a "paternal" atmosphere, the head knew his teachers well and so wouldn't criticize them, and certainly wouldn't do anything to rock the boat in the cozy environment of the school. The District Office couldn't monitor them, as it had limited staff and, in any case, only two vehicles, one of which was used exclusively by the director of education, who most of the time, he told me, was away at some development conference or seminar. She was away doing exactly that on the day I met Samuel Ntow. "So there is no effective supervision— the heads," he expanded, "are too familiar with their teachers, so don't do this effectively. The public schools have no ability to fire their teachers; the best they can do is transfer them." This is completely different in the private schools, he volunteered: "If you don't do well, they can fire you, work out how many days pay you are owed and fire you, or pay you at the end of the month and tell you to leave. We don't have that power in the government schools." He told me the story of a public school principal whom they found last year sleeping at school at 9:00 a.m. on a classroom bench; he was drunk and no other teachers were present. "Eventually, we managed to get him transferred. That's all. There was nothing else we could do." It's always the same story, he says, "If teachers or principals are caught in child abuse or alcoholism, then all we can do is transfer them elsewhere. And then they continue with their abuse."

And I heard so many stories in the public schools I visited that made me reel—with incomprehension as well as anger. One government school in Bandlaguda in the Old City of Hyderabad, where I was testing the children for comparisons between public and private schools, contained hundreds of children, all sitting on the floor (there being no desks or chairs). The children were eager to greet me, eager to hear what I had to say, bright-eyed, and really excited about taking these tests for me, that someone was paying them attention. But their enthusiasm for learning normally came to naught. For in their school, only two of the seven sanctioned teachers were present, including the "teacher in charge." And that would be pretty normal, the teacher in charge, a wonderfully dedicated and sincere man, told me. Two of the five missing teachers had been moved "temporarily" to other schools by the deputy district education officer, where no teachers were showing up at all. The other three teachers were away on in-service teacher training for a week—after they had just had one week's holiday. The teacher in charge showed me the teacher register; I saw clearly how seldom the teachers were actually present in school. He also showed me the page of "CLs." He assumed that this was something I knew about, but I had to probe him to learn that it meant "casual leave": In addition to all the school, national, and state holidays, the teachers unions have also negotiated an extra 22 days of casual leave, plus 5 more days of "optional leave," plus a certain number of sick leave days! And all the teachers take them. The school must be open for 220 days per year, but teachers must teach for only 193 days, minus whatever sick leave they are entitled to. "The union has wrapped it all for itself," said the teacher in charge. "How can the children learn if the teachers are so often absent?" Seeing the children sitting on the floor, wanting so badly to learn, nearly broke my heart.

And at another government school in rural Mahbubnagar, in the village of Thanda, I'd arrived with my team leader, Gomathi, during school hours to find only one teacher present. He was reading his newspaper while the children sat idly on the classroom floor; some ran around outside. The other two teachers were on "casual leave," he told us, hurriedly putting down his newspaper and gathering the children into rows on the floor. One of these women, he told me, was on casual leave because her husband had just died. I gave my condolences. Unfortunately, Gomathi told me as we drove away, this was precisely the same excuse he had used when she had visited the school three months' before!

Distant Teachers

According to the literature I was reading, government school teachers have another problem when it comes to poor children: they don't particularly enjoy teaching them. The World Bank had even coined a name for this problem—"social distance"—that is, government teachers and principals coming in from richer areas of the city to teach in poor communities have little understanding of or respect for their charges. The World Bank report said poor parents commented that teachers "have their noses up in the air and neglect us," and that they "really have a way of making you feel like you are a piece of rubbish."[2] In the study from Calcutta, I read that teachers and principals blamed poor home-learning environments and lack of parental concern as the reasons for poor parents' taking their children out of school to undertake jobs. Parents, however, disagreed vehemently. They said that they took their children out of school because of the low quality of state schooling.

"Social distance" was something I encountered time and time again on my journey. I found it in the Makoko public schools where the majority of teachers had never even been inside the shantytown where most of their pupils lived, but drove for a couple of hours from the posher suburbs of Lagos; one even came from a different state altogether and didn't speak the language of her pupils. None knew that there were private schools just across the slum boundary. The same was true in the fishing village of Bortianor, Ghana, where the vast majority of the public school teachers traveled from the nice suburbs of Accra. And perhaps most strikingly, I found it in the public school that looked down from its Olympian heights upon the slum of Kibera.

Behind the headmistress's desk was a blackboard listing details of the school. It showed an enrollment of 2,255 students, made up of 1,445 "slum dwellers" and 810 "middle class." That was her classification, not mine. The headmistress was unabashedly candid about the horrors of having slum children in her otherwise pleasant surroundings. "They don't even know how to use the toilet!" she complained and gave a mocking demonstration of how they used the toilet seat. "They only know how to squat!" she ridiculed. She told me, "Children from the slum are exposed to a lot of dirty social language; they can even say anything about the teacher, the teacher has big buttocks, and everyone gossips." And then she starts repeating things the children say to one another: "Your mother and father were [fornicating] in the streets" or "I didn't sleep last night, I heard my mother and father doing it, and they were doing it again this afternoon." The slum dwellers, she said, "'all live together in one room, so these children are exposed to so many bad things, and they spread these things like a virus around." Things were so bad in the school now, she said, that she was thinking of moving her own two children to a private school. Prompted by this, I asked her what she thought of the private schools in the slums; she told me that they didn't exist in the slums.

When I thanked her for letting the children in her school from the slum take my tests, I thought I must have misheard her. "Yes, they should have been cleaning," she said matter-of-factly. Learning? I thought I must have heard. No, the children from the slums should have been cleaning the school, and we had taken them away from that task. Whenever I visited the slum schools after that, I tried to see the children as if through the public school headmistress's eyes. But I couldn't. They seemed well behaved, clean and tidy, eager to learn, nothing like the ogres she painted them out to be.

And I found social distance in rural India, where in one public school a pair of female teachers arrived at 11:30 a.m., more than two hours after school had started. Why were they late today? I innocently asked. "There's only one bus from the town. It reaches the main road at 11:00 a.m., and then the teachers have to walk three kilometers." These teachers, through no fault of their own, were posted to a rural school. They understandably didn't want to move. There was only one bus, which didn't even go as far as the village. So that's the time they arrived *every morning*.

All this seemed in sharp contrast—it's worth repeating this—to what I observed in the private schools for the poor, where teachers, whatever faults and inadequacies they might have had, were drawn from the communities themselves. In the private schools, there never seemed to be a problem with teachers' arriving late for their lessons because of transport; they simply had to walk around the corner to their classrooms. And if they were late for whatever reason, the school owner would be pretty keen to find out why and ensure it didn't happen again.

Poor Conditions

To add to absent teachers and social distance, public schools, the development experts I read also agreed, had grossly inadequate conditions. One government school in Bihar, India, highlighted by the World Bank report, revealed "horrific" conditions:[3] "The playground is full of muck and slime. The overflowing drains could easily drown a small child. Mosquitoes are swarming. There is no toilet. Neighbours complain of children using any convenient place to relieve themselves, and teachers complain of neighbours using the playground as a toilet in the morning." The same study found that half the schools visited had no drinking water available. Similarly, a survey in Calcutta found that of 11 government primary schools, only 2 had safe drinking water and only 5 had a playground. Listing major problems in their schools, principals included the lack of electricity, space, and furniture. Teaching in these government schools, it was observed, was being carried out "amidst din and chaos."

I'd seen so many public schools like that on my travels. One in Kosofe Local Government Area in Lagos State was called Comprehensive High and Junior Schools, Alapere. The junior school was a complete mess; that is all one could say (apart from the head's office, which was reasonably well apportioned). The buildings were decrepit, fashioned out of crumbling old breeze blocks with tin roofs supported by wooden frames. A few months before, a rainstorm had ripped the roof off one. The hall was completely destroyed, and the wind blew apart half of one of the buildings. The government, the principal told me, had said there were no funds to rebuild. Ruefully, he also told me that Nigeria got 18 billion naira (about $140 million) from the World Bank for universal basic education. "Where is this money?" he asked. None of it was apparent in his school. It was all like the parable of the festival cow, he said: The chief wants to celebrate and so gives a cow for the celebrations. The butchers take their cut, as it were, so we now have the full cow minus the butchers' cut. Then the cooks take over, and they take their cut too, so we now have the full cow minus the butchers' cut, minus the cooks' cut. The waiters then take their cut, so now we are left with the full cow minus the butchers' cut, the cooks', and the waiters'. "That's like the education budget," he said: "We hear there are funds in the budget, but we don't see it in our community. We don't know where the money goes." The government had also apparently outlawed parent-teacher associations, the head told me, because education had to be free, so he couldn't even raise money from parents to help improve matters. Free education apparently meant there had to be no resources at all.

The buildings that were still standing were not much better. Classes of 80 to 100 children were crammed in, with smashed up desks, broken walls, and shattered ceilings. On the blackboard of one, the form captain had scrawled some motivational words: "Reflections on Life: take life easy. Life is full of ups and downs. Life is full of joy and sorry. Life is full of successes and failures. Life is full of hardships and enjoyment. . . . A man must work hard to achieve success in life." It was almost impossible to imagine what one could achieve there. In other classrooms, huge holes were gouged in the blackboards so that you could see into—and of course hear—the neighboring classroom. This was the work of frustrated and bored children, like prisoners scratching away at the walls to break out.

The secondary school, if anything, was even worse. Its roofs too had been ripped off by the rain and wind. It had a huge classroom block, open plan you might call it, with only blackboards dividing the classes from each other. There were 125 students per class; the noise was deafening; the incentive to learn—or to teach—nil. The senior block, where children 15 years and older sat and tried to learn, had 150 children per class, no walls, again classes divided only by blackboards. The heat under the tin roofs was deadening; there were no fans to cool the children, nor even any electricity.

I'd also found the same in India. I visited one lower primary school off the main road of Kishanbagh, in the Old City of Hyderabad, to check on how students were progressing with the tests for the comparative survey of achievement. It was near a stinking pool peppered with snow-white egrets. Cattle and goats wallowed in the waters. From outside, the school looked fine—it was a large, properly constructed concrete building with a decent-size playground. But the roof was leaking, and so there was a big puddle in the first room where I was taken—the room where the fourth-grade students were taking my tests. The children were sitting on the bare floor, cramped on one side to avoid the puddles; the room was full of mosquitoes, which the children nonchalantly swatted away from their faces but which would have driven me mad in a few more minutes.

I thought angrily, why on earth did the researcher allow the tests to be taken in this bare, filthy, infested room? After visiting the rest of the school, I realized it was the best room. There were four others—all large and spacious, but all filthy. There were 40 or so children in two of them. All were flooded, all were swarming with mosquitoes. In one, the teacher had lit a tiny remnant of mosquito coil, bravely trying to do his best to make the classroom habitable. A pack of these coils cost 23 rupees (about 51 cents). The school had no funds to buy them, he told me, so he had resorted to bringing his own from home. The other two classrooms were empty. Why? Because the government hadn't provided two of the teachers, so these classes were doubling up with the other classes, so at least they had a teacher, doing mixed-grade teaching.

Indeed, the development experts seemed to agree that conditions were so bad in government schools, that they were to blame for school dropouts, not parental poverty or lack of concern for education, or child labor. A report from the British development agency DfID put it succinctly: "Many children, particularly those from the poorest households, drop out of school or fail to enroll as a direct result of poor quality schooling. Parents will be unwilling to invest in their children's education unless they are convinced of its quality and value."

Low Standards

With poor conditions and lack of teacher commitment in public schools, it would be no surprise if pupil outcomes were poor. The evidence I read as I traveled confirmed these fears: The World Bank reported a study from Tanzania showing that "the vast majority of students learned *almost nothing* that was tested in their seven years of schooling."[4] A DfID report said that in sub-Saharan Africa, "up to 60 percent of children leave primary school functionally illiterate. This is a waste of human potential, and also a waste of scarce resources." In Bangladesh, it was reported, fully "four out of five children who had completed five years of primary education failed to attain a minimum learning level." The Calcutta study article said that "economically hard up parents soon discover that attendance in schools for one year—and even two years—has not meant any substantial improvement in the general level of awareness of their children or in the content of their learning. Such a realisation has sometimes led to the decision that it would make better sense to withdraw the children from school and to put them to work in fields or workshops, hereby adding immediately to the household income."

Failure Even to Reach the Poor

All the problems above were reported for those children "lucky" enough to be in government schools. But this, I read, was just the tip of the iceberg. For national governments, the development reports concluded, had singularly failed to ensure that all their citizens received an education. The United Nations Development Programme reported that 115 million (that is 17 percent of the 680 million children of primary school age in developing countries) did not attend school. Three-fifths were girls. In India, 40 million children were not in primary school. A report from Save the Children said that an estimated 56 million children in South Asia were out of school and that states "continue to struggle in the universal provision of an education which is of a sufficient quality." The World Bank said that "many governments are falling short on their obligations, especially to poor people."[5]

In Short, a Disaster

The development experts I read appeared unanimous about the problems of public education for the poor. The World Bank called it "government failure," with "services so defective that their opportunity costs outweigh their benefits for most poor people." Action Aid didn't mince its words either. Government basic education "in many of the world's poorest countries" is "a moral outrage, and a gross violation of human rights."[6]

... But the Only Solution Is More and Better Public Education

The only possible reaction to this litany is anger. That's what I felt the more government schools I visited on my journey, and the more development experts' conclusions I read. Of course, the disappointment and frustration of these development experts were palpable, too. So what should be done? This is where my reading left me frankly baffled. The proposed solution, in exactly the same sources, was, well . . . more of the same. Of course, the development experts didn't put it like that—this time, there would be the *right kind* of public education, as opposed to the *wrong kind* that had been such a disaster for the poor. This time they'd get it right—usually by throwing additional billions of dollars at the problem. But the same governments and the same development agencies would still have to be entrusted to do this. Why did they believe that they would get it right this time? It was not as if they'd been starved of resources in the past. It was not as if they hadn't already published ream after ream of papers on improving the system, on abolishing corruption, on ways of really delivering resources to the poor, concluding that the poor really must be served this time. Somehow, this time, it would be put right. All I could think, the more I read, was how?

Action Aid set out this position unambiguously.[7] Despite public education's being a "moral outrage" and a "gross violation of human rights," the solution was clear: "in many—if not most—developing countries, the state remained the most effective, and often the *only*, agent capable of mobilizing the technical and financial resources to bring education to all." The "appropriate response" to "state failure" was not to look elsewhere, but instead was "to strengthen state capacity." The World Bank just as strongly concurred: Although "public provision has often failed to create universally available and effective schooling," this "does *not* imply that the solution is a radically different approach."

The solution for the development experts was clear. More and better *public* education was required. The World Bank, however, cautioned us not to expect too much, too soon: "The challenge is formidable, because making services work for poor people involves changing not only service delivery arrangements but also public sector institutions. It also involves changing the way much foreign aid is transferred." Above all, the poor *"should be patient."* This need for fortitude appeared so important that they repeated the phrase:

"There is no silver bullet. . . . Even if we know what is to be done, it may be difficult to get it done. Despite the urgent needs of the world's poor people, and the many ways services have failed them, quick results will be hard to come by. Many of the changes involve fundamental shifts in power—something that cannot happen overnight. Making services work for poor people *requires patience."*

To soften the blow, the World Bank report wrapped it all up with a joke about a French general, a gardener, and a tree. (It's not so funny that it's worth repeating.) But was it really a joking matter for poor people? *Why* should they be patient?

Of course, they might have to be patient if there were really no alternative. But the question that shouted out for an answer the more I traveled, the more I saw, the more I read, was, what about the alternative of *private* education? If public education is so dismal, and it is so difficult and time-consuming to reform it, to make it better for poor people, why should the poor wait for these "fundamental shifts in power" before they can get decent services? Why should they wait for changes in the way foreign aid is transferred? Why should they wait until their governments get their acts together? Why wasn't anyone else thinking that private schools might be part of a quicker, easier, more effective solution? The longer I spent on my journey, the odder it seemed that none of the development experts considered private education a possible alternative.

Actually, they did give some reasons. The World Bank summarized the position clearly: "The picture painted so far may lead some to conclude that government should give up and leave everything to the private sector." No, no, no! "That would be wrong. . . . The extreme position is clearly not desirable." Why not? "For *various good reasons,*" the World Bank concluded, "society has decided that [education] will be provided not through a market transaction but through the government taking responsibility." And these reasons remain, whatever the disaster public education brings for the poor.

I'll come back to some of these "good reasons" later. But the simplest reason that emerged time and again from the development experts is pretty easy to grasp: private education is no solution because when it comes to services for the poor, the quality is *even lower* than that found in government schools. I took time out from my field trip and read up on what the development experts were now saying about the quality of private schools for the poor. It didn't make for happy reading.

Save the Children from the Development Experts

However bad the government schools are, the private schools for the poor *are even worse*. As I read the work of the development experts, it became clear that Mary Taimo Ige Iji, the Nigerian education administrator, was not alone in her assessment of the low quality of private education for the poor. But by extension, it seemed, the development experts must also share Mary's views that poor parents are "ignoramuses"—for how else could they explain poor parents' choices? Of course, they didn't put it like that; they were far too polite or perhaps politically astute to do so. But the more I read, the more convinced I became that there was no other explanation for the dim view they took of poor parents' choices.

I read a couple of reports by the development charity Save the Children. It was quite clear: in Pakistan and Nepal, poor parents' demand for private schools was "not due primarily to a shortage of government schools," but was based on the perceived *low quality* of the government schools.[8] They even reported what poor parents identified as the inadequacies of the public schools, which came as no surprise given what I'd already read: "irregularity, negligence and indiscipline of the teachers, large class sizes and a lower standard of English learning." Conversely, Save the Children also listed what parents told them was "better"—they put the word in "scare quotes"—about low-cost private schools: they had greater contact hours and much smaller class sizes than public schools, allowing for individual pupil attention, and teacher attendance was regular.

But these parental preferences be damned! Save the Children knows best: the "assumption that the quality of private schooling is higher than that provided by government schools" is simply not true for the private schools that poor parents can afford: "A significant number of families are therefore paying for private education delivery which is offering an extremely low standard of education," lower than that in the public schools. Poor parents *"may perceive* private schools to be superior to those in the public sector," but these parents are, let's not mince words as Save the Children tries to, *ignoramuses*, because "the new generation of private schools which cater to poorer children in urban and rural areas commonly employ a high proportion of untrained teachers and offer a poor service."

I read and reread these sentences in Save the Children's reports to make sure I hadn't misunderstood them. I hadn't. Let's spell it out: poor parents say private schools are better than public schools and can catalog the reasons why. The development experts at Save the Children say they are wrong. Did they have any evidence for this? The only evidence they offered was that in their case study, in private schools "almost none of the teachers have teacher training qualifications and, furthermore, little interest in obtaining these."

Hmm. I mused that perhaps it was true that teacher-training qualifications made for better education. But surely you can't just assume this, when set against the weight of parental preferences that judge that it did not? Poor parents, after all, with limited resources and much to lose by sending their children to private school, must be pretty *stupid* to make that difficult and expensive choice if the private schools really are of inferior quality to the public schools they are abandoning. Perhaps poor parents think that untrained teachers are more committed, have better subject knowledge, or at least turn up regularly? None of these possibilities appeared to be explored by Save the Children.

I read the same refrain with the same bewilderment whenever I turned to other writings of the development experts. It was there in former British prime minister Tony Blair's Commission for Africa report. The *only* mention of private education is the following short paragraph:

> Non-state sectors, including faith-based organisations, civil society, the private sector and communities, have historically provided much education in Africa. Some of these are excellent, but others (often aiming at those who cannot afford the fees common in state schools) are without adequate state regulation *and are of a low quality.*

Looking up the references given for this sweeping assertion of poor quality in low-cost private schools, I found only one. It was from Pauline Rose at the University of Sussex, whose conundrum I've already discussed. The Commission for Africa certainly had read her conclusions correctly: poor parents, she wrote, need to "be protected from the poor quality private provision which is becoming increasingly prevalent." Poor parents must be saved from the private

143

schools, which they are forced to attend "by default (or despair) rather than by design." Again, let's not mince words: for Rose and the Commission for Africa, it had to be that poor parents were ignoramuses, who must be saved from the consequences of their hopeless choices. I couldn't read them in any other way.

But, bafflingly, going back to her report, it seemed that Rose didn't have any real evidence for her assertion; at least nothing more than the observation that in Uganda for instance, "teachers are often less qualified, and more poorly paid" in the private than the public schools, so "the quality of education received is debatable." It was just the same assumption again that high educational standards need trained and well-paid teachers. Again, was it *true*? If high wages and teacher training lead to the kind of government teachers whose absenteeism and general neglect is a well-documented cause of concern, then perhaps—just perhaps—lower-paid and untrained teachers who at least turn up and teach will lead to better outcomes? It didn't seem that anyone else was willing to countenance this possibility.

I followed up the work of Dr. Rose to see if she came up with anything more substantial later—I really wanted to know if there was evidence out there that would show that poor parents were misguided. If they were, I wanted to help expose this as much as anyone. It didn't seem reasonable, unless poor parents really were ignoramuses, but I could be wrong and if so, this would have huge consequences for the poor. Rose was one of the authors of a study commissioned by the British aid agency DfID, specifically looking at low-cost private schools in Nigeria.

Well, actually, that wasn't what they called them. They called them "nonstate providers," complete with its own new acronym—NSPs—to add to the development alphabet soup. That in itself struck me as odd. Why would anyone want to invent a cumbersome phrase like that when a perfectly respectable phrase already existed, and was already in use by ordinary people? So I tried it out in the slums of Lagos. Nonstate providers? No one had a clue what I was talking about. They were quite comfortable with the notion of "private school" in English, however. For that fit in with how they described them in their own languages. In Nigeria, the Yoruban word for school is *ile-iwe*—literally house of learning. A private school is *ile-iwe aladani*, literally "self-assisted school," and *aladani* is precisely the word used to describe anything private. A public school is *ile iwe ijoba*. I asked for the literal translation of nonstate school. It would be *ile iwe ti kinse ti ijoba*. But no one ever uses this language; they are quite happy, thank you very much, with private school.

Or in the Nigerian language of Igbo, a school is *ulo akwukwo*, again literally "a place of learning." A private school is *ulo akwukwo akankpa*, with *akankpa* literally meaning "personal or belonging to me," the word used precisely to describe "private." The same was true in Ghana: in the Ga language, a school is *nii kasemhoe* (again, "place of learning"). A private school is *nii kasemhoe ankrankrong*, literally meaning "school of an individual."

Bringing in a new phrase to describe an old phenomenon struck me as odd. It seemed to be cultural imperialism of the worst kind, I figured, when the language of the poor was not considered good enough to describe their own activities and experiences.

Anyway, looking at nonstate providers in Nigeria, Rose and her coauthor concluded that although the "unapproved" private schools serving the poor had "grown in response to state failure to provide primary schooling which is both accessible and of appropriate quality," it did not mean that the education offered in the private sector was any good. No, she wrote, the private unapproved schools offered a "low quality of education," "below a desirable level"; they were "a low cost, low quality substitute" for public education.

OK, these were strong assertions, damning the efforts of all those, like BSE, I had met in Makoko who said they were trying to help their fellow Nigerians. These were powerful accusations, given by a respected university academic and taken on board in good faith by the British government aid agency. So how did she know?

It seemed she didn't. And she couldn't possibly know it, given that the DfID commissioned study "derives from interviews with key informants undertaken *over a period of one week*." The italicized phrase leaped out at me. Can you really make such damning accusations on the basis of one week of interviews? There was at least one point in the study where Rose herself didn't feel she could: "It was difficult in the time available to assess the quality of service delivered in unapproved schools compared with government schools, but it is evident that the class size is considerably smaller and discipline in the classroom is apparent." And again: "It was not possible to obtain the perceptions of communities served by these schools. As such, some of the points made *need to be treated with caution, and deserve more in-depth investigation.*" So why then tell us so categorically that the private schools were low quality? The more I read, the more nonplussed I became.

True, she did list a few concrete things she had found. To the usual list of untrained and low-paid teachers, working in, to an outsider, low-quality buildings, was added the complaint that the private school proprietors were motivated by the need "to make a profit." Almost on its own, this seemed to imply that private unrecognized schools were unlikely to be able to provide "an education of an appropriate standard." But did Rose similarly believe that the need "to make a profit" meant that her computer manufacturer couldn't provide a laptop that worked in the field or that the airline that flew her to Nigeria might possibly have dumped her over France, en route from London, in order to save on fuel? It seemed that she was judging the private school proprietors by a different standard. Private school proprietors, she wrote, were "more concerned with making money than the quality of education provided." Curiously enough, there was a parenthetical qualification: *"other than to the extent that this influences enrolment in their schools."* But couldn't she have used this insight in a different way? Instead of damning the private schools, couldn't it suggest a key motivation for the proprietors to ensure that the quality of education provided was at least high enough to satisfy parents, linking the desire to make a profit with the desire to maintain or raise standards in education? Indeed, Rose also noted, "Proprietors of private schools are concerned about ensuring that they receive a return on their investment, so monitor the teachers closely." Isn't that a positive? Isn't that precisely what poor parents had told me was one of their key reasons for preferring a for-profit private school: the close monitoring of teachers, which was so sadly lacking in the government alternative, where their children were abandoned? None of this seemed to occur to Rose when she came to write her damning conclusions—but then, by her own admission, she had not taken the time to speak with the "communities served by these schools."

I couldn't find any other evidence concerning the purported low quality of private schools for the poor. While I found many studies that looked at the relative efficiency and cost-effectiveness of public and private schools—most of which concluded that the private schools were better in both respects, although a couple reached the contrary conclusion, one of which was referred to by Rose—they had focused on the usual type of private school, those serving the better-off, or at most possibly included some of the poorer schools as part of their sample.[9] I could find no studies that looked specifically at the relative merits of private and public schools serving the poor.

Reassuringly, I found agreement for my conclusion, at least about the lack of firm evidence. *The Oxfam Education Report* concluded, "Surprisingly, in view of the confident assertions made in some quarters, there is *little hard evidence* to substantiate the view that private schools systematically outperform public schools with comparable levels of resourcing."[10] Oddly, although agreeing with me that there was "little hard evidence," the report was still able to summarize the position, on the same page, that, while "there is no doubting the *appalling standard* of provision in public education systems," private schools for the poor are of "inferior quality," offering "a low quality service" that will "restrict children's future opportunities." How did the author know this, if there was "little hard evidence"? Never mind, the United Nations Development Programme made the same admission of little evidence alongside an even stronger claim about the relative performance of private and public schools: "Many proponents of private education claim that private schools outperform public ones. . . . But *little evidence* substantiates these claims. *Private schools do not systematically outperform public schools with comparable resources.*"

Reading the development experts, it seemed that their sweeping deprecations of private schools serving the poor were not well founded. They could of course be right, but I'd found no proper evidence that they were. Poor parents were making difficult choices. Could they really be as foolish as these development experts were implying? I had to find out. Reading this kind of material, I knew my research had to look in detail at the relative quality of the education provided in public and private schools for the poor.

But first I needed to address one other mystery in the development experts' writings. Because the low-cost private schools are of such supposedly low quality, and because their proprietors are driven by the profit motive, the development experts were adamant about something else: the urgent need for regulators to save the poor from unscrupulous providers. As I traveled, I read what these experts said about the apparent need for increased regulation, and it too puzzled me, albeit in a different way.

8. An Inspector Calls

Flashing Policemen

The winding dirt road from Bortianor, the fishing village home of Supreme Academy in Ga, Ghana, meets the main Accra–Cape Coast highway at what locals call the "roadblock." It's where the police used to stop all the traffic plying this route, where massive jams built up throughout each day. It's no longer used; the barrier lies vandalized by the roadside. Now there are mobile police roadblocks, randomly set up anywhere along the route. Traveling back from Bortianor to Accra one day in a beaten-up old taxi, with huge cracks in its windshield, no seat belts, no functioning speedometer, and various other transgressions of the road-safety laws, we encountered one of these mobile roadblocks. As we neared the policeman who was waving us to a halt, my driver took out his license and documents and slipped a 10,000-cedi note (about $1.10) into the back pages. As we stopped, he handed his documents to the policeman, who perfunctorily pocketed the gift, and we were soon on our way. It's called "flashing." "Why don't you flash me some small money?" is a common refrain from officials everywhere in Ghana.

It's the same in Nigeria, traveling on the Lagos to Ibadan highway, where hulks of burnt-out trucks and cars lie by the road or are strewn across the median strip at disturbingly frequent intervals. The police wave you down—policemen who seem much more menacing than those in Ghana. Perhaps it has something to do with the Russian submachine guns they sport nonchalantly over their shoulders or the rounds of ammunition wrapped across their chests. Whenever I've been stopped in this way, the procedure was the same: they ask to see my passport, take it to their little bivouac on the other side of the road, make me walk all the way to meet their boss, and make me wait and wait, exchanging pleasantries about soccer (the captain of the Nigerian national team plays in the English Premier League, and they are always keen to explore my knowledge of this), keeping me waiting; perhaps my driver sorts out their "gratification."

And it's in India too. Rushing to take me to a dentist for emergency treatment in Hyderabad (fillings fall out in the most awkward of places), my car slipped through traffic lights while the lights were red. This happens a lot. Unfortunately this time, a motorcycle policeman was behind us and waved us down. My driver sighed and slowly got out, slipping a 500-rupee (about $12) note into his driver's license.

This kind of low-level corruption among government officials is all-pervasive in the countries where I was traveling. How could the development experts write about regulation of private schools without considering this reality? Was I missing something, or were they?

Last-Chance Schools Need Regulating

Their writings were clear enough. One of the reports from Save the Children stressed that "before private sector involvement should be contemplated as a possible policy option," strong regulations needed to be in place: "Without adequate regulatory capacity, private sector participation in service provision is a matter of concern, because the needs of the poor are [otherwise] unlikely to be met."[1] Another report, perhaps realizing that the horse had already bolted, emphasized how this was a grave concern: "The private sector has increased its role in the provision of services spontaneously rather than as a result of government planning," so has emerged "far beyond the capacity of state control."

Dr. Rose, too, was concerned with how private schools for the poor could be regulated. She explored the possibility of "lighter regulation to enable the private sector to operate unfettered," but didn't find this appealing. Instead, "tighter regulation" to "avoid the continued explosion of low quality private education" was required. For liberalizing regulation "runs the risk of allowing last-chance schools," her term for private schools for the poor, "to proliferate." And that was undesirable.

I read a report from the United Nations Children's Fund (UNICEF) that took the same, hard line against private schools for the poor: Regulation of "low quality" private education is urgently required, to "protect . . . citizens from exploitation in their quest for access to education." Without such regulation, the poor will continue to "pay very high costs for poor quality education." A proper "regulatory framework is fundamental to ensure that children receive . . . a quality education." The onus must be on the "central State" to "provide and implement a strong regulatory environment."

These pronouncements baffled me, not because I was against regulation per se: of course not, if regulations could be introduced that really protected the poor, who could be against that? No, they puzzled me because they didn't gel with my growing experience of how regulations—of anything, not just schools—worked in the countries I was studying. This time, the mystery was why the development experts appeared to be writing in a vacuum, far removed from the reality that always impinges on you wherever you travel and work in countries in sub-Saharan Africa and Asia.

Regulations, Regulations, Regulations

For there are already strong regulations that govern private education for the poor in all the countries I visited on my journey. And in practice, they work in exactly the same way as with the flashing policeman.

Andhra Pradesh—as do all other Indian states—already has regulations specifying every aspect of what private schools can and cannot do. In a legal bookshop in Koti, Hyderabad, I bought a three-volume tome, V. J. Rao's *Law of Education in Andhra Pradesh*, which meticulously detailed them all—and more government orders come out monthly, so it's really difficult to keep abreast of them all. It took me weeks of poring over these volumes to fathom exactly what a private school could and could not do—there are regulations on everything, including teacher qualifications, how dismissed teachers can appeal and to whom, the number of hours a principal must teach, how to advertise teacher vacancies, the necessity of "avoiding unhealthy competition among schools in the locality," what records should be kept and how, the precise details of how school income should be spent (and that no profits can be made), precise physical requirements for classrooms and playgrounds, teacher–pupil ratios, and the curriculum and syllabuses to be followed.

No private school teacher, the regulations spell out, is allowed to "read any cheap literature relating to sex in the presence of pupils or encourage students to study such cheap literature," and women teachers "shall wear traditional clothes of non-transparent material consistent with modesty." No teacher may receive a dowry, nor smoke in the presence of students. Everything is laid out meticulously, right down to the tiniest details of the "Duties of Sweepers," which reads in full, "They shall maintain the upkeep of the institutions and its premises, namely, laboratory, library, staff rooms, toilets and play ground, etc."

So many regulations, it's hard to see how any normal school manager, with more pressing demands on his or her time, could keep up. But severe punishments are laid down for any breach of these rules, punishable with imprisonment for up to three years, plus a fine. But in practice? In practice, all these incredibly detailed regulations are simply ignored. Didn't the development experts realize this?

Early on in my research, I was in Hyderabad with Pauline Dixon. Her PhD research focused on the regulatory environment, and so we had an appointment with the district education officer with authority over schools in Hyderabad, in his new government offices still under construction. He told us that he had only three inspectors working under him (and he himself didn't do inspections) for the 500 or so recognized private schools, plus the similar number of government schools. So how on earth could he get around to all these schools and ensure that they comply with every detail? So in practice, he allowed his team to simply ignore the vast body of legislation, and instead adopt the "rule of thumb" that private schools should comply with only four regulations in order to gain recognition and remain recognized. They needed to have, he told us, a playground of the correct size, a 50,000 rupees (around $1,100) fund in a joint school-government bank account, all teachers properly qualified with government teacher-training certificates as a minimum, and a library.

This type of "regulation-lite" might seem more realistic. Possibly it would even be the kind of regulatory regime that the development experts have in mind, rather than the arcane detail of the actual legislation, when they argue for the need of proper regulation?

But here's the rub: once we'd heard about his pared-down approach, Pauline quickly investigated about a dozen private unaided schools in Hyderabad whose managers I knew fairly well. None of them complied with more than two of the regulations even on this new slimmed-down list. All had the endowment fund, but only two had a proper library. None had a playground of the correct size, although most had a playground of some description. Not one had all teachers correctly qualified, although most had some of their teachers up to this level. Yet every one of these schools was recognized! And I found exactly the same story in Nigeria. A casual visit to 10 recognized private schools in the local government district of Kosofe in Lagos State, where my teams were doing the study, revealed that, according to the government regulations, only three of them should have been recognized. The remainder met few, if any, of the specified regulations.

So what's going on? How can schools be recognized when they clearly don't meet even a subset of regulations, let alone the full monty? Just as my taxi driver at the beginning of this chapter could pass through the police roadblock, which had been specifically set up to look for offenders of the road safety code, when his vehicle was in flamboyant violation, recognition is not acquired by meeting regulations. There are tried and trusted mechanisms in these countries that easily circumvent the need to meet regulations. Becoming recognized simply means bribing the inspectors with money. If you pay, you get recognized, and can stay recognized. If you don't, you won't. It's simple.

Instant Gratification

It's all quite remarkably open. On my journey, I was amazed at how candid government officials were about this aspect of their work. At the meeting with the district education officer in Hyderabad, after we'd been told about the problem of few inspectors, many schools, and almost unlimited regulations, I thought I'd try my luck with a question I assumed would get no answer at all. Prompted by what some private school managers had told me, I asked him, "Do the schools try to bribe the inspectors?" He turned to my assistant and asked for a translation of what I'd said. They spoke in Telugu, he perhaps buying time to think of the answer. But then he offered, quite openly: "Everyone gets bribes. Sometimes the inspectors give me bribes, sometimes the schools. And I know that if I don't give them what they want, then they will go above my head and bribe someone else—a politician, my boss, whoever—so I might as well take the bribe and give them what they want."

Bribery is endemic. It's the way the system functions smoothly. Pauline explored this further with some of the school managers in Hyderabad. Again, they were entirely up-front about the situation. One told her: "Everything is possible if you offer the right amount of bribe. . . . In fact, if we follow the proper channels, every path will be closed." Another said that all government officials can be bribed and that "an official will not be able to sleep at night if he doesn't ask for bribes." She asked them what happened when the school inspectors called. Only one said that the inspector came to "visit the classrooms and give suggestions." But even she added, "And at last takes the bribe." Most commonly, they said that the inspector was only interested in bribes. One offered: the inspector comes "to collect the bribe and sign the register to show the government that he has visited the school for inspection." Another said that the inspector comes and does "nothing in particular; he inspects only the records and goes with filled pockets."

Indeed, the system has become more or less formalized, with roughly set amounts required to pass through certain stages of the recognition process. If an inspector asks for too much, these set amounts can be referred to and offered instead. So in Nigeria, for instance, the school proprietors told me that the registration process first requires a name search, to ensure the chosen name is not already in use. The official fee costs 5,000 naira (around $40)—about the annual cost to parents of school fees in unregistered schools, or just over the monthly salary of a teacher in these schools. But in addition, the proprietor must pay "gratifications" of about 1,000 naira (about $8) to the officials. Then there are the requisite inspections before the registration process is completed. At least two are required, costing, officially, 5,000 naira, paid to the Ministry of Education at the payment office of the Lagos State government. But again, the proprietor must also bribe the inspectors "as gratification to the inspectors if he wants a favorable report." These extralegal fees range from 5,000 naira to 15,000 naira ($40 to $120) depending on the number of inspectors that come and the proprietor's bargaining skills. According to the proprietors, "We know that this money always reach the top," that is, the Ministry of Education officials themselves.

To be registered, the schools should have a sickbay, with a full-time nurse—an impossible expense for these schools—and a one-acre playground—inconceivable in the slums and shantytowns. The school grounds should also have a full-time gatekeeper. None of the low-cost private schools have these. To overlook these omissions, the inspector receives a bribe of 5,000 naira. The same goes for failure to employ fully trained teachers (5,000 naira to the inspectors for noncompliance).

And so it goes. At every stage of the registration process, there are official fees to be paid; and at every stage, bribes for the inspectors to overlook noncompliance.

Parents the Losers?

So I wasn't balking at the regulation of private schools because I was against regulations per se; I just couldn't actually see how they could work given the reality on the ground. And it seemed to me that the development experts hadn't thought it through at all.

Budget private schools—even the recognized ones—are, in practice, largely unregulated by, and hence unaccountable to, the state. But there is not a lack of regulations, as the development experts seem to imagine. Regulations are simply ignored as long as bribes are paid. On the face of it, the parents are the losers: for government regulation might have given them a way to sort out whether one school is better than another—if it is recognized by the authorities, it must be better. But clearly, government recognition conveys no information about school quality; it only indicates the school's ability to afford bribes. So it would seem that parents suffer as a result of this system—not only because they are deprived of one source of valuable information but, in fact, because they are positively misled by the information that is available. And since the revenue that schools use to pay the necessary bribes is derived from tuition paid by poor parents, regulations have in fact become a regressive tax on the consumption of education—working precisely counter to the goal of "education for all." Rather than being exploited by unscrupulous school proprietors, parents are, indirectly, being exploited by unscrupulous inspectors.

Of course, the development experts might counter that the whole system could be reformed. It's not this type of corrupt regulatory system they have in mind when they seek to impose "strong" regulations on budget private schools. Instead, they want something that works well, just like they might say regulations do back at home.

True, it will require slow and painstaking reform of the very fundamentals of government and society. And the poor, meanwhile? Well, they must be patient, until these reforms have been introduced. For how else can these poor "citizens" be protected against "exploitation" by for-profit providers?

Actually, as I journeyed and researched, it occurred to me that there might be another way—and it was curious to me that the development experts didn't catch on to this possibility. Indeed, it's more or less what government officials in Hyderabad told Pauline and me. In a sense, they weren't too bothered about whether the private schools met their regulations because the schools had a much stronger sense of accountability to people who could be relied on to make sure things were working well. The district education officer in Hyderabad put it succinctly: "The teachers in the private unaided schools are accountable to the parents. The parents insist on quality. The teachers in the private unaided schools are faced with the sack if they do not perform.... They can easily be removed.... The parents are rational and so the schools are accountable." Another government official in Hyderabad reiterated the same claim: "In the private schools, the manager watches the teachers all the time. In turn the teachers watch the children."

Wasn't this different kind of accountability significant? Couldn't the development experts be satisfied that it would, at least to some powerful degree, help protect parents against any unscrupulous providers?[2]

Baden Powell and the Really Important People

Near the center of the coastal city of Accra, Ghana's capital, is the shantytown of Baden Powell, called thus because you reach it by passing Baden Powell Centenary Memorial Hall. Here along the rocky shoreline ran open sewers between corrugated-iron-roofed huts, with views across the ocean that might cost millions elsewhere. There are more African-sounding shantytowns too, such as Agbogbloshie and Neema. There's also Jamestown. One hot, humid October day, I visited these shantytowns with Emma Gyamere, my team leader in Ghana. It had been a very long day; we'd been out traveling since 7:30 a.m., checking on schools taking part in the testing for the comparative survey. Our car had no air conditioning, and I was feeling exceedingly hot; my right arm was very sunburned from sticking out the window all day. Feeling weary and a little sunstroked, I hope I can be excused for what happened next.

We walked through the slum. Children pointed excitedly at the "white man" and practiced, as they did in every other African country I visited, their "how are you's"; some chanted "how are you, how are you, how are you!" delighting in their own mastery. Older men smiled and greeted us in the customary fashion. We located the school we were looking for, Sunrise Preparatory School. The proprietor was standing outside her tiny office, talking to a very thin, unkempt older man. She motioned us to sit outside and wait. The wooden chairs were small, but at least in the shade, although it was still uncomfortably humid. After a while, I looked at my watch. We'd been waiting 20 minutes while the proprietor engaged in discussion with this man. "She's very rude," I said to Emma, who agreed. Accepted was the fact that a visiting white man should be given priority, even though he had called unannounced. After another five minutes, I suggested that we leave. Emma readily agreed, and I got up to tell the owner.

"I'm sorry," she said, "but this is a parent." She said it in a way that for her demanded no more explanation. Of course, she couldn't stop her conversation with a parent, one of the really important people in her world, no matter who had come to visit her.

The proprietor of Sunrise Preparatory School understood that different kind of accountability well. Of course she was accountable—not to the government inspectors, who would be more interested in bribes than educational standards. She was accountable to parents—the really important people—and through them to the students in her school. If parents withdrew their children and thus their fees, she would go out of business. She knew that very clearly and would do all she could to prevent it.

This alternative idea of accountability didn't seem to get much consideration in the development experts' writings I reviewed. However, I read tantalizing glimpses that some were at least aware of it—but frustratingly, they didn't make anything of it at all. For instance, I'd read a report by Save the Children that had as one of its major themes the need for greater regulation of private schools for the poor. However, it had an interesting aside that raised the alternative route to accountability. Save the Children had interviewed a 12-year-old boy, Jhazeb, in a private slum school in Karachi,

Pakistan, one that they had disapprovingly noted didn't provide a playground and so fell short of its regulatory requirements. However, the boy was not concerned with this supposed failure: "Though the school is small and does not have any ground for sports, Jhazeb said they are contented playing in the fields and the streets by their houses and he would rather see the school bring in more computers and offer computer classes to their students."[3]

Young Jhazeb was aware of the opportunity cost of providing a playground, and thought that his school should have other priorities. Save the Children used this anecdote to note that private schools "are already responding to parental preferences, within the context of market forces ('If we offer computers and classes rather than playing fields and equipment we'll have higher enrolments.')."

Again, just as my experience at Sunrise Preparatory School suggested, doesn't this example from Pakistan also show, at least in some small way, private schools being accountable, perhaps more accountable than government, to the parents and children they serve? Government says that all private schools must provide a playground, which would be very expensive, given the price of land in the slums and the revenue of the schools, and may not even be possible, given the scarcity of available land. The children know better. They think they have enough play areas, thank you, and that scarce resources are better spent on other things, such as computer education, that will help them get on in life. The private schools respond to this demand and offer what children, and parents, want.

Shouldn't this be viewed as something valuable? Not for Save the Children, it appeared. For in its report, it followed this example with a discussion about accountability, suggesting that it had entirely missed the point: "Whereas proponents for an increased role of the private sector in education point to a greater accountability within such schools, this has not been reflected in the information collected." From the ensuing discussion, accountability to Save the Children meant, by definition, political accountability. It didn't find much of this, not surprisingly, in the private schools, and it was blind to any other sort. This view also seemed to be shared by everyone I else I read. A UNICEF report had exactly the same narrow conception of accountability. For UNICEF, it meant things like "parent-teacher associations" and "citizen input into state regulatory institutions," rather than the kind of accountability hinted at by

Jhazeb in Karachi, or by the proprietor of Sunrise Preparatory School in Accra.

I was puzzled by why this alternative accountability—to parents and children—didn't merit more attention from the development experts. If you are paying fees at a private school, as the parents of Jhazeb in Karachi are doing, then doesn't that lead to a relationship of accountability with the school owners that makes them interested in what you value and want for your child? How does it do this? Put simply, you can withdraw your patronage, stop paying your fees, and take your child elsewhere if you don't get what you value. Of course, there are some complications from doing so. For a start, you must find another suitable private school; your child might be quite settled in the current school so you'll have to weigh the benefits of changing schools against the costs of not changing. And school owners know that. But above all, school owners know that you can move your child, that you have the right to leave, and so will, other things being equal, strive to ensure that you don't. Otherwise, they lose income. And if enough children leave, they go out of business.

Intriguingly, some development experts did seem clear that this kind of accountability—market accountability—was effective for the poor in numerous areas of their lives. The World Bank called it the "short route" to accountability, to be contrasted unfavorably when it comes to education with the "long route," where accountability comes only through poor people's voting for politicians who then may, but usually do not, enforce accountability through the political process. But although they point to its manifest benefits in many areas for the poor, and are clear that it is a much easier form of accountability than political accountability, they are equally as clear that it cannot work for education.

I had to get to the bottom of why the development experts rejected this short route to accountability for education. Usefully, the World Bank's *World Development Report 2004* spelled out in depth the advantages of market accountability but gave detailed "good reasons" why it was not suitable for education. I carefully tried to follow its argument.

First, it favorably describes how accountability works in a typical market transaction, when, say, a person buys a sandwich: "In buying a sandwich you ask for it (delegation) and pay for it (finance). The sandwich is made for you (performance). You eat the sandwich

159

(which generates relevant information about its quality). And you then choose to buy or not buy a sandwich another day (enforceability), affecting the profits of the seller." That is, accountability is a relationship between purchaser and provider, with five constituent parts: delegation, finance, performance, information, and enforceability. All these parts are important, it says. If any are missing, "service failure" results.

Now the wonderful thing about a competitive market, the report argues, is that it "automatically" creates accountability between sellers and buyers: "The key information is customer satisfaction, and the key enforceability is the customer's choice of supplier. Competitive markets have proved a remarkably robust institutional arrangement for meeting individual interests."

On the face of it, this discussion appeared rather promising. For it would seem to show very neatly the advantages that private schools for the poor have over public schools in terms of accountability. I felt I could easily substitute parents and schools into the World Bank's formula to show the advantages of this "short route" to accountability quite clearly. In a private schooling market, it would mean this:

You choose a primary school for your child (delegation) and pay the monthly fees (finance). The schooling is delivered to your child (performance). You check on how your child is doing in school, perhaps by noting how her exercise books are marked or how well he speaks English with his friends (which generates relevant information about its quality). And you then choose either to send your child to the school next month or to change schools (enforceability), affecting the income of the school owner.

On the face of it, all the accountability stages appeared to work well. In the public school system, however, the "accountability" system wouldn't function at all well:

In sending your child to the local public school, you do not choose that school (uncertain delegation) and someone else pays for it (no finance). The schooling is delivered to your child (performance). You check on how your child is doing in school, perhaps by noting how her exercise books are marked or how well he speaks English with his friends (which generates relevant information about its quality). But then your only choice is whether to send your child to school at all or take him or her out of the public education system, neither of which affects the school principal's or teachers' pay (lack of enforceability). The only possible route to enforceability is through the political process, but that is slow, cumbersome, and, in practice, ineffective.

So the advantages of the private system of accountability seemed obvious in the schooling example. The most important difference is "enforceability" in the private case, which of course depends in part on the issue of who pays (finance). Because the parents pay fees to the private school, they can enforce quality.

However, the development experts are adamant: Although very effective for most other areas for the poor, this short route to accountability is not possible in education. The only possible route to accountability here is the "long route"—"by clients as citizens influencing policymakers, and policymakers influencing providers." The short route to market accountability, whatever its virtues, is inapplicable to education. There can be "no direct accountability of the provider to the consumer." Why not? The World Bank puts the issue thus: "For various good reasons, society has decided that the service will be provided not through a market transaction but through the government taking responsibility."

And it lists the good reasons—which are good enough for me to address later in a separate chapter. Before that, it's important to realize that the development experts are very much aware of the huge problems with political accountability. The list of problems is in fact so long that it is really hard to see how it could be surmounted. If there really were no alternative, then obviously one would need to do what one could to attempt to surmount the problems, and the poor would have to be patient. But why neglect the obvious solution of private education for the poor?

Problems, Problems, Problems

The problems with the long route to accountability—political accountability—in education seem enormous, at least for the poor in developing countries. The first problem is what the World Bank calls "voice" failure. This is the failure of the poor to have any influence over what their governments do. They have no "voice" in the political process. The state, controlled by politicians and administrators, "simply does not care about providing services" for the poor. The clear signs are "when too little budget is devoted to services for poor people, and when the budget is allocated to meet political interests."

But why don't poor people just vote bad governments out of office? Sometimes, the World Bank says, the electoral system simply doesn't work—it is itself subject to corruption. But even when it at least works at this basic level, poor people find it hard to influence politicians about the state of public education. Poor people, like everyone else, might vote along ethnic lines, not particularly concerned with evaluating how their chosen politicians have performed with public education. (A joke doing the rounds in India at the time of one election I witnessed was, "In other countries you cast your vote; in India you vote your caste.") Or they might simply take with a grain of salt politicians' promises to improve public education services because they know that politicians haven't delivered in the past. It is far easier simply to vote for candidates who offer to provide "ready cash and jobs" for one's particular ethnic group, race, or caste.

According to the World Bank, one of the severe problems with using the political process to reform education to benefit the poor is the politicization of education: schooling has become a political battleground, with different groups in society competing for scarce public resources, often with contradictory desires. The elites and middle classes may say they want universal education, but they won't vote to jeopardize more public spending on higher education, which benefits their own children. Politicians see the public education system as an easy way to provide patronage. And teachers unions, very powerful forces in many developing countries, act in their own interests, to better their wages and conditions of services by enhancing job security and extending holidays—exactly as I'd found in India, even to the extent of adding "casual leave" on top of the already-existing long school holidays—all of which can act against the interests of the poor. These contradictory pressures lead, the World Bank report said, to political inertia and corruption: "Politics generally does not favour reforms that improve services for poor people. Such reforms require upsetting entrenched interests, which have the advantage of inertia, history, organizational capability, and knowing exactly what is at stake. Policymakers and providers are generally more organized, informed, and influential than citizens, particularly poor citizens."

Using the political process has not been an effective way for the poor to improve public education. But even if solutions can be found, through reforms such as decentralization and improving information, the World Bank points out an even greater state failure, "compact failure." Here, the state fails to enforce responsibility for public services. It cannot, or will not, motivate management to organize or incentivize its "frontline workers." So even if poor people could influence politicians and policymakers, the World Bank says, the politicians and policymakers in turn cannot effectively influence the service providers. They can't or won't "impose penalties for underperformance." They won't fire teachers, for example, so absenteeism goes unpunished. Even if poor people's political voices are strengthened, at best this might make "policymakers want to improve services for the poor. But they still may not be able to." Even well-intentioned policymakers "often cannot offer the incentives and do the monitoring to ensure that providers serve the poor." Problems such as teacher absenteeism and the "rude treatment" of pupils and their parents—the social distance I often encountered whenever I visited government schools—are all symptoms of this problem, reports the World Bank.

To counter absenteeism, corruption, and underperformance in practical terms, the World Bank suggests that the authorities strictly monitor teachers and principals. But again, this only brings further problems, and it is difficult to see how they can be solved—even in theory, let alone in practice. The authorities could try to compensate teachers by results—rewarding those whose children achieve higher grades and punishing those whose children don't. But teachers unions resist anything so simple, for reasons that the World Bank also seems to find persuasive: "Good teaching is a complex endeavour," it agrees. Teaching quality can't be assessed only "on the basis of student scores on a standardized examination," it reports, because schooling "has many other objectives." Whether it's because of this complexity or simply because of teachers union intransigence, it doesn't matter as far as outcomes are concerned: the result, the World Bank reports, is that "simple proposals of 'pay for performance' for individual teachers and principals have rarely proved workable."

Perhaps governments could move away from such objective measures of student outcomes, and instead move toward subjective measures to judge teachers? Again, the World Bank says, this would only bring additional problems to systems prone to corruption and bad management: "Perhaps good teaching can be assessed subjectively by another trained educator—a head teacher or school principal. But this creates the temptation to play favourites or, worse, to extract payments from teachers for good assessments." So one must limit the autonomy of school principals and again make them accountable to the authority. One must bring in some "assessment standard" for school principals too: "But all the problems of assessing good teaching also apply to good school heads. Indeed, that is how dysfunctional bureaucracies cascade into a morass of corruption, as upward payments from those at lower levels buy good assignments or ratings from superiors."

It all seems too difficult to reward good performance. But if one can't do this, then one must reward everyone the same, so "excellent teachers working in adverse circumstances and those who never show up" all get paid the same salary. Not surprisingly, this only serves to undermine the morale of good teachers, driving them away from teaching altogether. The same is true if one simply rewards all teachers with higher wages—those who are conscientious get the same rewards as those who don't show up. As I read this report, it all seemed impossibly difficult to overcome. But aren't all these impossibly difficult problems in public education pretty easy to overcome in private schools?

Benign Big Brother

One private school proprietor whom I got to know really well was Mohammed Anwar of M. A. Ideal High School in Hyderabad, India. He was one of the first proprietors I met on that, for me, momentous trip to Hyderabad's slums in January 2000. On a later visit, I discovered that he had installed, at not inconsiderable expense, an admittedly rather primitive closed-circuit television (CCTV) system throughout his school. On his desk was a monitor, and in many classrooms a small video camera. While he worked in his office, he could switch the view to any classroom to see what was happening.

When I saw this, I politely said how nice it was. I really wondered why on earth he had used his scarce resources to do such an idiotic thing. Surely, in a school that charged fees of $2 per month, his scarce surplus could have been put to better use—why not provide computers for the children, or more books? Why waste your money on a gimmick like that! Anwar later became the head of the new Dynamic Federation of Private Schools. I noticed a couple of other proprietors had copied him and installed similar CCTV systems in their schools. And I also saw one later in a rather posh private school elsewhere in the city.

I didn't think about Anwar's CCTV again until I was reading the World Bank's detailed discussion of the problems of state accountability that I've outlined above. Suddenly it dawned on me that Anwar had done something that was incredibly rational in his context. His major problem was teacher accountability—and the major difference between his school and the government schools was that the parents expected him to effectively solve this problem. Having an efficient way of keeping an eye his teachers' activities was his solution. He knew, in his own words, "the Indian teacher mentality." He knew that teachers' accountability to him was the key to his accountability to parents. He didn't learn what to do from any management consultant or course; he worked out for himself the best way forward. And of course it was an appropriate use of his surplus, if he could keep teachers accountable. I've never ever heard of a similar thing happening in a public school.

Private school owners, of course, seemed to easily monitor their teachers' performance on a day-by-day basis. Even without CCTV (and Anwar did this too), they walk around their schools constantly, checking on teachers' attendance or whether they were teaching. They check on how often children mark their exercise books. They follow up on parents' complaints, such as a teacher's absence or a child's difficulty in grasping a lesson. They can easily reward teachers who perform well, whose children get good grades in public exams for instance. But they can be fair about this, too. In another school in Hyderabad, the school owner uses a simple computer program to monitor the children's improvement in class. He can see if very low-performing children's standards are initially raised and can reward this, even if those children still aren't performing as well as others. But again, the school owner, being closely involved, will know whether a teacher is working with a particularly challenging group of children, and can reward teachers appropriately.

And what incentive do school owners have to reward teachers in this way? They know that good teachers will be snapped up by other private schools, if they think they can get higher salaries elsewhere or believe they are not being appropriately rewarded. And of course, school owners can always be discretionary, in ways that are impossible in the state system. They don't have to be oppressive "big brothers"—indeed, such oppressors would soon lose teachers to more sensitive, more discretionary proprietors. For example, a private school owner, a benign big brother, might ask a teacher who was absent or not teaching well on a particular day whether there was a problem. If the poor performance was unusual and was due to a bad or sad experience, the school owner wouldn't fire the teacher; he or she would be satisfied that the teacher's behavior was not habitual. There are clear incentives for school managers to keep teachers who are generally good and assist them through particularly hard times.

Of course, a good government principal could also do all these things, and good government inspectors could assist them in doing so. The problem, as the World Bank so clearly notes, is how to ensure that principals and inspectors do these things—for it is just an extension of the problem of ensuring that the teachers are accountable in the first place. It simply raises the problem of accountability to a higher level. The chief problem in the government schools is that the principals and inspectors have no incentives to do any of these things. Principals will draw the same salary and same benefits if they sit in their offices reading the newspaper all day—or even if they don't show up at all—as they would if they meticulously walked the corridors checking on their teachers. Likewise, inspectors get paid the same whether they check up on schools or stay in the relative comfort of their offices.

All I read pinpointed the problem clearly: the incentive structures are all wrong in the public-sector schools. In the private schools, on the other hand, the incentive structures work in the opposite, positive, direction for each school owner. All school owners depend on parents' using their schools; if parents don't, the school owners are out of a job. So this invisible hand of the competitive market keeps all school owners on their toes, constantly monitoring the performance of their teachers, without whose high performance school owners will suffer. It's this invisible hand that is working in the educational market in exactly the same way that it does, as the World Bank points out, in the market for sandwiches.

So what's the problem with simply accepting that the short route to accountability—the accountability of the competitive market—is also good enough for education? The alternative will always be an uphill struggle at best. At worst, the long route to accountability will never serve the interests of the poor.

Actually, the development experts' objection to this conclusion was staring me in the face once I'd got this far. My emerging view was that state regulations didn't matter too much because private schools seemed to be accountable to others—parents—who appeared capable of keeping a watchful eye on what was going on within them. But of course, this brought me squarely back to the development experts' criticisms about the low quality of the private schools serving the poor. The development experts didn't appear to trust poor parents' judgment, so accountability to parents couldn't possibly be the answer. For what the development experts continually saw was poor parents being hoodwinked into accepting low-quality provision—lower even than the government alternative. Even if they didn't explicitly call them "ignoramuses," it was clear that development experts took a pretty dim view of the choices poor parents made for private education.

Were they right? I had to find out.

9. Old Monk, and Young Nuns on Motorbikes

January 26, 2004, Republic Day, India: Exactly four years to the day since I first came to Hyderabad, took an autorickshaw to the Charminar, and discovered for myself private schools for the poor, I was back in Hyderabad, with Pauline Dixon. We were there to train the extended research team that would collect the data to explore the relative quality of the public and private schools in the poor areas of the Old City.

We'd arrived two nights before. There was a power outage in the city, and we sat by candlelight to catch up with the team. The week before, Gomathi, the spirited young woman who had trained as a social worker and had been my team leader in Hyderabad since I first started doing research there, had taken her five colleagues on a team-building trip to Sri Salam, 170 kilometers away by road, where the river Krishna is dammed to harness hydroelectric power. To get there, you travel through the endless miles of dark forest that is the Rajiv Gandhi tiger reserve. Gomathi's eyes lit up as she told us of how they had sat around a campfire all night, dancing to the car radio, singing songs, playing dumb charades, and telling stories. In the morning, they swam in the lake and visited the temple. "We're ready now," Gomathi said.

And by candlelight we had worked, getting ready to train the larger team that would conduct the first round of research that would reveal whether the private schools were really of such low quality as every development expert claimed. Once we'd conducted the tests in Hyderabad, we would move on to other countries to do the same.

For the previous few weeks, Gomathi and her team had criss-crossed the poor areas of Hyderabad, visiting 150 schools that had been randomly selected from the list of nearly 1,000 schools we found in the school census and getting the school managers' permission to conduct tests. (They carried letters from the secretary of education,

Dr. I. V. Subba Rao, to persuade any reluctant government principals and a letter from me for the private schools.) In each school, the team obtained the names of fourth-grade children, from which we selected up to 30 children in each school, who would become our sample for testing. Gomathi and her team then had around 4,000 English, mathematics, Urdu, and IQ tests printed, and 4,000 copies of the pupil and parent questionnaires and around 200 school and teacher questionnaires photocopied and stapled. She visited cookie and cake wholesalers and managed to persuade several to donate entire boxes so that we could give them out to the children participating. And she purchased 4,000 pencils, rulers, erasers, and plastic bags. All were stacked in the offices. Days were spent distributing them in individual bags for the children, the right number for each school and, once a roster of researchers had been worked out, into the right boxes for each researcher to take into the field.

Research is a peculiar business. My erstwhile colleague at Newcastle University Professor Bruce Carrington used to complain that the true "messiness" of research is never apparent when one reads the abridged, polished, and sterilized accounts in academic research journals. He wished researchers would tell it like it really is, so that new recruits would know what they were in for. Bruce, this research was really messy! So many times I nearly lost my cool, aided by sleep deprivation from jet lag, and the heat and humidity, working in offices without air conditioning where the fans worked only intermittently due to power outages. Equally at times, as things went well, I was euphoric, writing in my journal that this experience was the happiest one of my life.

Gomathi, to her credit, was calm throughout. To be fair to me, she was used to the kinds of things that nearly drove me mad with frustration: researchers' turning up in dribs and drabs for training, some arriving an hour or more late; piles of photocopying that arrived stapled in the wrong order, which then had to be painstakingly unstapled and reassembled; or IQ tests printed on wafer-thin paper of such poor quality (the printer presumably skimping to cut costs) that you could see through to the question on the next page, which meant you couldn't really make any sense of the questions, and the whole lot had to be scrapped and new tests ordered from a more reliable printer. Some things happened the way they did because of the marvelous manner in which things just fall together in India: I was out of line in complaining to Gomathi when I realized that she hadn't yet ordered chairs for the training session that was to begin in half an hour. But who would think of ordering chairs more than 30 minutes before they were needed? By the time the session began, young men had arrived with chairs stacked on the open-backed freight autorickshaws and had neatly arranged them in rows in our training room. And some frustrations arose from peculiarities that one perhaps couldn't have predicted—like the disappointment I felt when the first batch of trial parent questionnaires were returned unanswered after the third question. Did this mean we couldn't get any information from the parents; was the whole project doomed? Fortunately, one of my researchers realized that question 4 asked for the ages of the parents' daughters (as well as those of their sons). The offending question was omitted, and in the new trials parents answered all the questions.

On Republic Day and the day after, 45 researchers were trained. Many were graduate students at local universities; the remainder were young nuns who were active in different types of social work in the Old City and also engaged in postgraduate study. Working through that night, Pauline and I consumed a bottle of Old Monk rum, the local brew that is my official tipple whenever I'm in Hyderabad. With the team, everything was readied into boxed sets for the next three days of intensive testing in schools. The first day, 45 researchers assembled at the Charminar bus station at 7:30 a.m., while my team of supervisors distributed their boxes and smoothly sent them off in the buses and autorickshaws to their appointed schools.

Well, that was how it was supposed to be. I couldn't really work out why, but it took well over an hour of people madly running around, boxes going this way and that, papers being taken out of one and put in another, team members shouting at one another, before each person had the correct box and knew where to go. And not everyone was on time, to say the least. And not all the autorickshaws that we'd painstakingly lined up the day before had turned up; so some of the researchers were ferried away on the back of my team's motorcycles. I have this image with me still: my researcher driving a Hero Honda 250 cc motorbike with two young nuns seated sidesaddle behind in their light-brown habits, smiling, with the boxes of tests precariously placed on their laps. Waiting for over an hour in the terrible noise and commotion and heat of the bus station had my nerves jangling. Beggars swarmed around me; a young woman carrying a baby stroked my tummy, asking for money, pointing to her mouth and the mouth of her baby. For an hour.

But eventually, everyone had gone, and Pauline and I and the six team leaders separately toured all the schools among us to check that everything was working well, carrying spare papers with us for those that would inevitably be missing, and standing in for any researcher who had not yet turned up.

Meeting at the end of the day, watching the autorickshaws pull up and researchers and their boxes of papers pile out, I felt incredibly relieved and satisfied that all had gone, more or less, as planned. And that we were beginning to accumulate data that would help us answer the questions everyone had about the quality of private schools. For three days we carried on like this. And then for months afterward, the tests were sorted and sent away for marking, the questionnaires coded and entered into spreadsheets, and the data analyzed.

Altogether, my teams tested 24,000 children. We started in India and moved on to Nigeria, then Ghana, then back to India, then on to rural China (I'll discuss the Chinese case separately). What did we find?

Not Ignoramuses After All

It turns out that poor parents are not "ignoramuses." The major research effort described above had been required to gain data on pupils' achievement—something that is considered essential before comparative judgments can be made between public and private schools. But in fact, the evidence already accumulated during the first part of the study suggested pretty strongly that parents knew they were onto something when they chose private over government schools. For when my teams were conducting the surveys that provided the evidence of the nature and extent of private education (discussed in Chapter 3), they asked to visit one specified primary school classroom (fourth or fifth grade, depending on the country). They called on the classroom only when teachers should have been teaching (that is, waiting until any breaks, sports periods, or assemblies were over before their visit). They noted what the teacher was doing, or if he or she was absent. They also noted what facilities were available in the classroom and around the school. And the data collected also told us something about the pupil–teacher ratio.

To this evidence, I was now in a position to add data on the relative achievement of pupils in public and private schools.

On all the indicators explored, government schools, in general, performed worse than both recognized and unrecognized private schools—and remember, unrecognized schools where the ones particularly criticized by development experts:

- Class sizes were smaller in both types of private schools than in public schools.
- Both types of private schools had higher teacher commitment—in the percentage of teachers teaching when our researchers called unannounced.
- Only on one quality input—the provision of playgrounds—were government schools superior to both types of private schools across all studies.
- Children in both types of private schools in general scored higher on standardized tests in key curriculum subjects than did children in government schools. This remained true even when we controlled for an array of background variables, to account for differences between children in public and private schools.
- The higher standards in private schools were usually maintained for a small fraction of the per-pupil teacher cost in government schools.

That is, the research showed that private schools were not only more effective but also more cost efficient than the public schools.

As the results came in and were analyzed, and I realized what they were showing, I began to sense that I was onto something extremely important. Early in my journey, I'd been met with denial from those in government and many development experts that private schools for the poor even existed. The evidence my teams had accumulated—and evidence from others now working in this area—showed beyond doubt that they were there, and in fact were serving a majority of schoolchildren in poor areas. Now no one could deny their existence. But development experts were still unimpressed: They were adamant that these private schools, especially the unrecognized schools, were fly-by-nights, run by unscrupulous businesspeople intent on ripping off the poor. And the poor, well they were ignoramuses (but don't let's use that word) for letting themselves be so hoodwinked. The quality of educational provision in these private schools was suspect, to say the least. You could see for yourself how bad it all was in the low-cost private schools, just by seeing the poor-quality infrastructure and by knowing that teachers were untrained and underpaid.

Well, that was not at all what the results showed. The results seemed to indicate pretty categorically that the development experts didn't have a leg to stand on. It became clearer and clearer that poor parents were keen education consumers when they chose private over public schools.

Small Is Beautiful

There's a big debate in the West about whether class size matters.[1] Whatever may be true in the United States or United Kingdom, where class sizes are already relatively small, any government intervention—hugely expensive interventions at that—would lead only to small reductions in these already small classrooms. But in developing countries, it may be different. Certainly, poor parents appear to see things differently. One of the major reasons, parents have told me, they send their children to private schools is that classes in public schools are simply too big. Parents simply believe that teachers won't be able to teach *their* children; they worry their children will get lost in such large classes. Other things being equal, for poor parents class size appears to be a key factor in their choice of private schools.

And my researchers found in every case, average class sizes were smaller in private schools than in public schools (see Figure 1). In Delhi, the pupil–teacher ratio was *three times higher* in government than private unrecognized classes. In Hyderabad and Mahbubnagar, government class sizes were nearly *twice as large* as those in private unrecognized schools. In Ga, Ghana, government class sizes were over twice as large as those in private unrecognized schools. In Lagos State, Nigeria, they were one and a half times larger.

More Committed Teachers

Calling unannounced on primary school classes, my researchers found in all cases that teaching commitment was highest in the recognized private schools, followed closely by unrecognized private schools. In all cases, it was lowest in the government schools:

- In Delhi, teachers were teaching in only 38 percent of government classrooms during our investigators' visits, compared with around 70 percent in both types of private unaided schools.

Figure 1.
AVERAGE NUMBER OF FOURTH-GRADE PUPILS IN CLASS

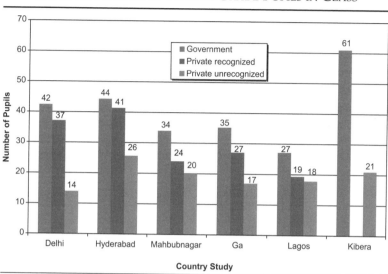

SOURCE: Author's own data.

- In Hyderabad, 75 percent of government teachers were teaching, compared with 98 percent in recognized and 91 percent in unrecognized private unaided schools.
- In Mahbubnagar, 64 percent of government teachers were teaching, compared with 80 percent in unrecognized and 83 percent in recognized private unaided schools.
- In Lagos State, 67 percent of government teachers were teaching, compared with 88 percent and 87 percent of the recognized and unrecognized private teachers, respectively.
- In Ga, only 57 percent of teachers in government schools were teaching at the time researchers arrived unannounced, compared with 75 percent and 66 percent of teachers in recognized and unrecognized private schools, respectively.

Providing What Parents Want

Language is a major issue in Indian education. Mother-tongue teaching is the prescription in government primary schools, usually up to fifth grade. While English was made an official language in India in 1967, alongside Hindi, each state also has its own official language—in Andhra Pradesh, it is Telugu—and each state has "clamoured to prioritize and preserve its own language in state schools."[2] But then in the poor areas of Hyderabad that we researched, the majority of families are Muslim, hence Urdu-speaking. Each of these languages has a different script. This means that in public schools in Andhra Pradesh, young children are taught in either Telugu or Urdu and must learn both languages, as well as Hindi. English was not usually introduced until about fifth grade, although government schools in Andhra Pradesh have recently started teaching it in first grade. But poor parents told me that they wanted their children to be proficient in English, which they perceived to be the international language, the language that would help their children get ahead in business and commerce and lift their families out of poverty. And they felt that English-medium schools (those that teach all subjects in English) were the way to do this. An important reason, they told me, for choosing private schools was that they were English medium. Private schools, they said, provided what they wanted rather than what the government said they should have.

In our research, we found that private schools were much more likely to be English medium than government schools. In Andhra Pradesh, India, they were in the majority, even in rural areas: In Hyderabad, 88 percent of recognized and 80 percent of unrecognized private unaided schools reported they were English medium, compared with fewer than 1 percent of government schools. The majority of government schools (73 percent) were Urdu medium. In Delhi, nearly half (47 percent) the recognized private unaided schools were English medium, whereas 21 percent of unrecognized private unaided schools were English medium. Many of the private unrecognized schools, however, provided both Hindi- and English-medium streams (34 percent). Only 3 percent of government schools were English medium, the majority being Hindi medium (80 percent). Even in rural Mahbubnagar, well over half the recognized (51 percent) and unrecognized (57 percent) private unaided schools reported they were English medium or had two streams, one of which was English, compared with fewer than 1 percent of government schools.

Whose "Hidden Curriculum"?

So private school teachers are more committed than their government counterparts; class sizes are smaller; and private schools provide poor parents with what they view as a preferred route out of poverty. But what of the buildings and facilities within the schools? What of trained teachers? Clearly, they are what most trouble the development experts and government officials who castigate the private schools for their low quality. One such troubled expert is Professor Keith Lewin of the University of Sussex, whom the BBC interviewed for the film we made in Nigeria. Sitting comfortably in his London flat, Indian icons on the mantelpiece behind him, he was adamant that private schools for the poor were of low quality and not part of any educational solution: "There is a *hidden curriculum* in all these places," he said. "If there are no latrines, if there is no clean running water in the school, it tells you something about the attitude of the management of that school and the motivation of the people that run it."

I put this to a father who sent his child to Ken Ade Private School in the shantytown of Makoko. He was angry. The gist of what he said went like this: "Our homes don't have water, we don't have toilets either! The school buildings are much better than our homes. Why is he insulting us like this?" The conditions of the school simply reflect—no, are an improvement on—normal life in Makoko. So why do people like Professor Lewin suggest that only schools that are up to his Western standards are acceptable? That's not what parents believe.

In any case, comparing provision in the budgets of private schools with that in government schools, the reality is *the exact opposite* of Professor Lewin's insinuations. My researchers collected data on a range of 14 quality inputs to schools. On only *one input*—the provision of playgrounds—were government schools superior across the different studies. What might this say, I wonder, about the "attitude" and "motivation" of the government authorities and their development partners? It's true also that in Ghana, Nigeria, and Andhra Pradesh, India, aid agencies, including DfID, the U.S. Agency for International Development, and the European Union, had recently been on a spending spree in the government schools, refurbishing them, sometimes providing entirely new schools, and equipping them with luxury goods like televisions. So private schools were not operating on a level playing field. No wealthy outside agencies were assisting them. Even so, often they do better.

My research teams looked at a range of inputs that could reasonably be viewed as proxies for quality. First, there were those related to the health and hygiene of students: drinking water, toilets for children, and separate toilets for boys and girls. Second were those concerning the comfort and safety of children: that is, *pucca*, proper, not temporary, buildings; desks; chairs; electricity; fans; and a playground. Third, there were those that showed some investment by the school authorities in learning facilities: blackboards, libraries, tape recorders, computers, and televisions.

In *the vast majority of cases in all areas*, both types of private schools, unrecognized and recognized, were either superior to government schools in providing these inputs, or there was no significant difference between school types. In Hyderabad, for instance, this was true of *all* indicators. In Delhi, it was true of 10 out of 13; in Mahbubnagar and Lagos State, 11 out of 13; and in Ga, 10 out of 14.

For a small number of inputs, government provision was superior to that in private unrecognized schools, but not to that in private recognized schools. In Delhi, this was only true for tape recorders; in Hyderabad, it wasn't true for any inputs; whereas in Mahbubnagar, it was true for playgrounds and televisions. (Interestingly, a large aid project in rural Andhra Pradesh has provided televisions ostensibly for learning purposes, which might explain their more common presence in government schools. However, the research disappointingly showed that they weren't actually used for learning but remained in the principal's office.) In Ga, it was true for proper buildings, desks (the private unrecognized schools usually made do with a combined bench and worktop rather than a desk), playground, and blackboards, whereas in Lagos it was true only for *pucca* buildings.

Finally, in only a tiny proportion of cases (a total of three indicators for the entire sample) were amenities in government schools superior to both types of private schools: in Delhi, separate toilets for boys and girls and playgrounds, and in Lagos, playgrounds. That's all.

If there is a "hidden curriculum" in schools for the poor, my findings clearly indicate that private schools are not the rogues.

Children in Private Schools Outperform Those in Public School

What about teacher training? Government schools are very likely to have more extensively trained and educated teachers than private schools. In Hyderabad, for instance, only around 7 percent of government school teachers lacked a college degree. In the private recognized schools, the figure was nearly 30 percent, whereas in unrecognized schools it was over 40 percent. In Ga, Ghana, around 75 percent of all teachers in private schools (both registered and unregistered) had attended school only until senior secondary (equivalent to 12th grade), compared with only 40 percent of government school teachers. In Lagos State, Nigeria, over 25 percent of teachers in unrecognized private schools were educated to senior secondary, whereas there were no teachers whose education had stopped at this level in the government schools. But when critics dismiss private schools for not having extensively trained teachers, the key reason they do is because they assume the teachers will be less effective. We've already seen that these untrained teachers are far more likely to show up and teach than their more heavily trained counterparts in government schools. Does their lack of training make any difference to student achievement—a key indicator of their effectiveness? It turns out that it does not. Private schools again turn out to be superior to government schools.

In all the studies, the same pattern was found for the "raw" mean scores, with private recognized schools achieving the highest, followed by private unrecognized and government schools achieving the lowest scores—except for the sole case of Urdu-language achievement in Hyderabad (see Figures 2 and 3).

The results from Delhi were typical. In mathematics, mean scores of children in government schools were 24.5 percent, whereas they were 42.1 percent in private unrecognized schools and 43.9 percent in private recognized. That is, children in unrecognized private schools scored nearly 18 percentage points more in math than children in government schools (a 72 percent advantage!), while children in recognized private schools scored over 19 percentage points more than children in government schools (a 79 percent advantage). In English, the performance difference was much greater (children in unrecognized schools enjoyed a 35 percentage point advantage over their public school counterparts, whereas children in recognized schools scored 41 percentage points more). However, these differences might be expected, given that government schools are not providing what parents want, English medium. (On the other hand, they might *not* be expected, given an oft-repeated criticism that private schools are English medium in name only—that this is just another way they pull the wool over ignorant poor parents' eyes.

Figure 2.
INDIA: RAW SCORES

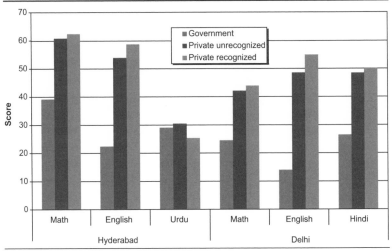

SOURCE: Author's own data.

What we found showed that the private schools were in fact educating their children to a much higher English standard than what children might pick up naturally in the local community, through radio, television, and advertisements, for instance—which is perhaps what the tests were measuring in children in government schools.)

But in any case, if more private schools are English medium, we might expect government schools to be superior in achievement in Hindi; the opposite was true. Children in private unrecognized schools achieved on average 22 percentage points more than children in government schools (an 83 percent advantage). In recognized private schools, children scored on average 24 percentage points more (an 89 percent advantage).

In Hyderabad, similar results were found for mathematics and English. However, in Urdu, the results for government and private schools were roughly similar—although private unrecognized schools had the highest average score (30.5 percent), followed by government (29.1 percent); private recognized had the lowest (25.4 percent).

These raw scores are indicative, but not the end of the story—for it may be that there are simply brighter children from slightly

Figure 3.
AFRICA: RAW SCORES

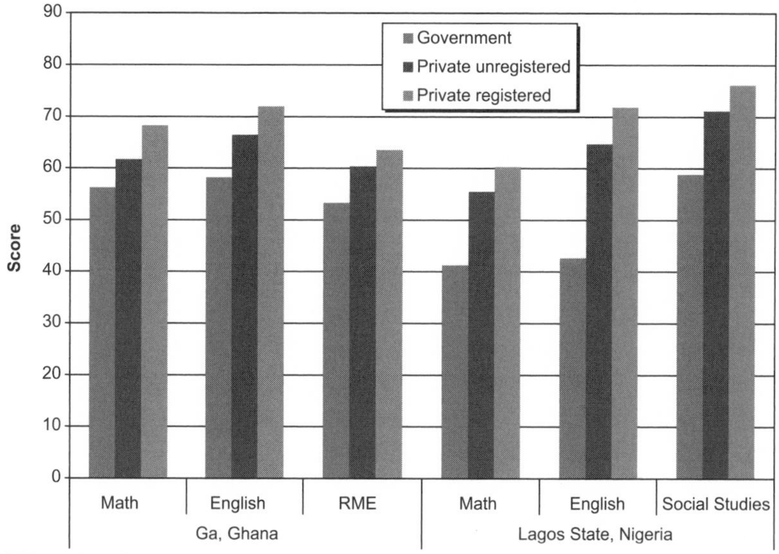

SOURCE: Author's own data.
NOTE: RME = religious and moral education.

wealthier backgrounds (although all parents were of course quite poor) going to private schools, and hence the private schools have an unfair advantage over government schools. In any case, we've seen that the private schools have better inputs in general than government schools—so perhaps these also make a difference to attainment? What we need is some way to statistically adjust the data to see what would happen if children with the same characteristics were in government and private schools—and for these schools also to have the same characteristics. Things get rather technical at this point—interested readers can consult the academic papers on my website to explore the range of statistical methods used and the results obtained (www.ncl.ac.uk/egwest). But the simple message from all the detailed statistical analyses is that they made no important differences to the "raw" scores above. Controlling for the range of background variables, including education and wealth of parents, students' IQs, and peer-group effects, the differences were usually slightly reduced but generally still large and still favored both types of private schools in each study. For instance, in Hyderabad, a child attending a private unrecognized school would be predicted to gain 16.1 percentage points more in mathematics than the same child attending a government school. In a private recognized school, the difference in scores would be 17.3 percentage points. In English, the advantages would be even greater—16.9 percentage points more in an unrecognized school and 18.9 percentage points in a recognized school. Interestingly, in Urdu, after controlling for the background variables, there was no statistically significant difference between government and either type of private school.

More Effective *and* More Efficient

Do the private schools achieve better results because they are better financed? This is what the development experts claim, on those occasions when they acknowledge superior private-sector performance. *The Oxfam Education Report* states it thus: "There is little hard evidence to substantiate the view that private schools systematically outperform public schools *with comparable levels of resourcing.*"[3] And the United Nations Development Programme makes the even stronger claim that "private schools do not systematically outperform public schools with comparable resources."[4]

Is either true? In my research, I wasn't able to obtain detailed information on actual income and expenditure within any type of school—private school managers in general were understandably wary of divulging sensitive financial information to researchers (although I did get figures for case study schools, which I'll come to later), while government principals said that this information should be obtained from the Ministry of Education, which was not generally forthcoming. However, it was possible to elicit data from the primary school teachers in the random sample on what is, in any case, the most significant element of school budgets—teacher salaries—estimated to make up the vast majority (80 to 96 percent) of all recurring expenditures in government primary schools in developing countries.[5]

In every case, the same picture began to emerge: government school teachers were paid considerably more than private school teachers—up to seven times more. But government teachers' higher pay does not in the slightest seem to translate into higher perfor-mance (see section on teaching commitment above), nor into higher achievement of children (see previous section on academic perfor-mance). But then the development experts might come back and say, OK, it might not lead to better performance, but, clearly, the private school proprietors must be exploiting their staff because they are paid much less than public school teachers. This doesn't seem to be borne out by discussions with school managers. On the contrary, it seemed that there was a large enough pool of unemployed people to satisfy the demand for jobs. Instead of condemning private schools, perhaps they might be viewed as providing a useful public service by mopping up thousands of college and high school graduates in countries where unemployment is a huge problem among those groups.[6] In fact, the much lower wages in private schools are more likely indicative of the public schools' over*paying* their teachers—that the rates negotiated through union activity within the govern-ment-run monopoly school system were in fact much higher than the market rate for teaching.

In every case, private school teachers were paid considerably less than government teachers. The differences for Delhi are shown in Figure 4. Here, the average monthly salary for full-time fourth-grade teachers is *seven* times higher in the government schools than in unrecognized private schools. In Delhi, government teachers were paid on average 10,072 rupees (around $224), compared with 1,360 rupees (around $30) in unrecognized private. Government teachers were paid around three times more than teachers in recog-nized private schools (who received on average 3,627 rupees [or about $81]).

However, class sizes were smallest in unrecognized private and largest in government schools, so computing the unit cost per pupil might give a more valid comparison. In no case did I find, even on this measure (which might, in any case, seem to be excusing the government schools for large class sizes), that the private schools had more resources per pupil than the government schools. In all cases, the unrecognized schools had considerably lower per-pupil expenditures. Public schools in Delhi were spending nearly two and a half times as much per pupil as unrecognized private schools. In all cases apart from Ga, Ghana, the recognized schools also had considerably lower per-pupil teacher costs than the government schools.

Figure 4.
AVERAGE MONTHLY TEACHER SALARY AND AVERAGE PER-PUPIL
TEACHER COST

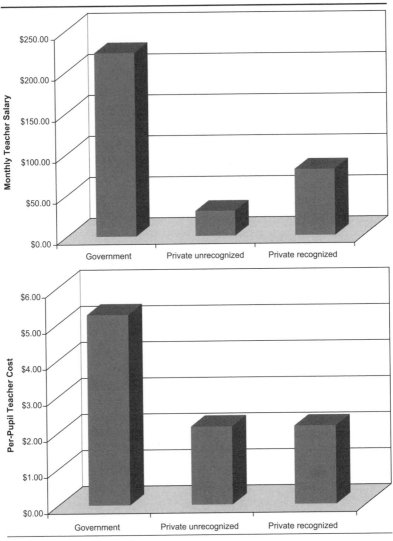

Private schools are outperforming public schools, usually for a fraction of the cost. And of course, this takes into account only the costs *within the school itself*: public schools are also supported by a mammoth and expensive bureaucracy. Private schools have no such financing behind them.

The Special Case of China

What I found in China was significantly different from the other studies. My first visit had told me that the main reason proprietors established private schools was not because public schools were, in general, perceived to be of low quality, as in all the other studies, but simply that the public schools were geographically much too inaccessible to the poor villagers. This was also the parents' main reason they sent their children to private schools. Children would have to walk for at least an hour, oftentimes more, across mountains to reach the public schools. This was too far, especially for the girls, parents said. And during much of the year, the journey was simply impossible, with the heavy rains and snow.

Given this, what I found may not be surprising. The private schools were not, in general, better equipped than the public schools, and class sizes and teacher commitment were roughly equal in both:

- **Pupil–teacher ratios** were more or less identical in public and private schools: 25:0 in private, compared with 25:1 in public schools.
- **Teacher commitment** (defined as the proportion of teachers teaching when the researchers called unannounced) was also more or less the same in public and private schools. We found 92.2 percent of teachers in private schools teaching, compared with 89.3 percent of government teachers—a difference that turned out not to be statistically significant.
- **School inputs, health and hygiene**, were better in public schools than in private. Drinking water was provided for children in 15.7 percent of private schools, compared with 28.2 percent of public schools. Toilets for children were provided in 79.3 percent of private schools, compared with 93.5 percent of public schools.
- **School inputs, comfort and safety**, were, in general, better in public schools, although there were sometimes only small differences. In 87.5 percent of private schools, desks were available

in classrooms, compared with 97.4 percent of public schools. In 65.4 percent of private schools, children were provided chairs or benches, compared with 75.6 percent of public schools. In 60.3 percent of private schools, electric lighting was provided in classrooms, compared with 84.4 percent of public schools. Playgrounds were provided in 63.9 percent of private but 86.4 percent of public schools.

- **School inputs, learning facilities.** The vast majority of both school types provided blackboards. Only a minority of private schools (4.1 percent) had a library for the children, compared with 27.4 percent of government schools. Similarly, only 3.9 percent of private schools had one or more computers for their students, compared with 27.3 percent of public schools.

Given this lack of advantages, it is worth repeating that private schools, however, obviously provided what poor parents wanted, namely, a school that was accessible to their children, whereas public schools did not, instead being rather remote and inaccessible. It is also important to stress that school fees in both public and private schools were approximately equal. But private schools had to provide *all* the facilities above, plus teacher salaries from these school fees, whereas government schools did not have to cover any of their costs. Public schools, in other words, were spending far more per pupil.

However, in terms of pupil achievement, something very interesting emerges. For this part of the research, we tested children in the Ding Xi region, which included Zhang County where I'd found my first private schools for the poor in the remote villages. We chose Ding Xi because it was one of the poorest and least-developed regions in Gansu province.[7] It was poorer than Ling Xia, where DfID was conducting its work on school development plans. My team tested 2,616 children in 218 schools, using standardized tests in mathematics and Chinese. We were able to divide the schools into three types: private schools run by proprietors (for-profit private), private schools run by villagers (nonprofit private), and public schools.

On both tests, *students in the for-profit private schools achieved higher scores than those in both the nonprofit private and public schools.* The mean score in for-profit private schools was 62.38 percent (math) and 68.83 percent (Chinese), compared with 57.72 percent (math) and 66.72 percent (Chinese) in public schools. Nonprofit private schools came out lowest, at 53.48 percent (math) and 60.71 percent (Chinese). These differences, although small, were statistically significant. However, it must be reemphasized that public schools spent far more per pupil than either type of private school.

That is, of all schools in our Chinese study, the for-profit private schools performed the best—so much for the criticisms of the development experts against the profit motive in education. And once we statistically controlled for background variables, the differences in achievement between public and nonprofit private schools became insignificant, but the differences between for-profit and the other two types actually widened.

This was because, importantly, the children in both types of private schools were much less privileged than those in the public schools—as might be expected, given that they came from the poorest villages, whereas children in the public schools were from the larger, wealthier villages. The students in public schools *had the highest IQs*—which is normally associated with higher achievement. Moreover, children in the private schools were significantly poorer than those in public schools: 93 percent of the students' fathers in the nonprofit and 84 percent in the for-profit schools were peasant farmers—the lowest-income occupation possible in the mountains, compared with 81 percent in the public schools. Fathers of children in the for-profit private schools were also the least educated—they averaged 5.1 years of education, compared with 5.4 years in nonprofit and 6.4 years in public schools. The same was true for mothers (for-profit private schools, 2.3 years of education, compared with 2.7 years and 3.7 years in nonprofit and public schools, respectively). All this was reflected in the average family income, which was lowest for students in the for-profit private schools—2,692 rembini ($332) per year, compared with 2,716 rembini ($335) in the nonprofit and 3,355 rembini ($414) in the public schools.

Again, it is important to note that these superior (or equal) achievement levels in the private schools were *not* obtained from higher spending inputs, at least in terms of teacher salaries. For teacher salaries were *much lower* in private than public schools. The mean average teacher salary was nearly twice as high in the public as the private schools.

Private schools in rural Gansu province, China, are providing parents with what they want, a nearby school, rather than a remote and inaccessible one. Although definitely poorer in terms of school facilities, the private schools are not inferior in terms of achievement to the public schools. They achieve similar or higher results with teacher salaries only a fraction of those in public schools.

China is a special case; but it still shows remarkable advantages for the private schools for the poor, probably the most remote private schools anywhere on this planet.

Good Choices

On my journey, I had read the development experts' thoughts on low-cost private education. They universally appeared to condemn it. Curiously, they appeared to condemn it without any real evidence. My research showed that they appeared wrong on all counts. Perhaps the private schools are in pretty meager buildings, perhaps they do have less-trained teachers, paid much below union rates. But these perceived disadvantages seem to be irrelevant: Well-trained and well-paid teachers don't lead to higher teacher commitment—in fact, the opposite seems to be true. What I found was that poor parents send their children to private schools *because they are better*. They are better than public schools with regard to higher teacher commitment and smaller class sizes. They are better on the vast majority of school inputs. They are better in academic achievement, even after controlling for background variables. And not only are they better in all these respects, they are cheaper to run, at least in terms of teachers' salaries. Parents are not ignoramuses. They know what they are doing.

By this point in my journey, I was ready to burst. I knew I had to share my findings with the development experts. But would they be pleased to hear that the poor have found a way of sidestepping the massive problems in public education? It was time to find out.

10. Making Enemies with Joy Beside Me

Return to Zimbabwe

He tosses my moleskin notebook down onto the low table in front of him. Thank God that my writing is so terrible; surely he cannot have deciphered much? He had been unsmiling throughout while he flicked through the pages. He is unsmiling still. He avoids looking at me, me sporting my open, receptive expression that usually works in winning over even hostile audiences. Instead, he glowers into the middle distance. He is one of the most unpleasant and angry men I have ever met. I allow myself the luxury of thinking that he is also one of the ugliest men I have ever met too; and incongruous, given all that he is saying. His "Forward with Zanu-PF, Down with Colonialism" African-style open-necked shirt sits uncomfortably with his baseball gap, advertising some American brand, and his Nike sneakers. But sitting in front of him, he in his comfortable leather swivel chair and I on a bare wooden bench, I don't know how this is all going to end.

I've started to have that terrible fear in my lower back—I've only had it once or twice in my life, way back, confronted with ugly, huge, glowering bullies in distant school bathrooms, but recognize it immediately. It's a horrible, hollow tingling somewhere at the base of your spine, or is it in your bowels? Perhaps it's your body getting ready to evacuate and flee from danger. I cannot flee.

I'm back in Zimbabwe, in the ruling party Zanu-PF regional offices in Marondera, some 100 kilometers from Harare, the capital. Worse, I'm in the dingy underground windowless security offices, sitting in front of the regional head of security. Blocking the only exit is his assistant, who stands with a completely blank expression by the closed door. It is two days before the elections in April 2005, which will return Robert Mugabe to power under widespread accusations of vote rigging. Two Western journalists working undercover for the British *Sunday Times* have just been arrested outside Harare and thrown into the notorious Chikurubi prison, from where they'll be lucky to escape unharmed.

He ignores me. I have tried to speak to him in my limited and half-remembered Shona, the language of the majority tribe in Zimbabwe, a language I learned 22 years ago when I was a mathematics teacher in Zimbabwe, helping to build the new Mugabe regime. This normally ignites warm laughter and friendship whenever I attempt it in this country. He flinches when he hears me; I'm an unwelcome object in his world whose future hangs in the balance. There is no room for warmth or camaraderie here. He turns to my new friends, sitting on either side of me. They talk fast in Shona; I understand none of it. But I get the gist. I'm not welcome.

On one side is Mrs. Joy Farirai, the proprietor of Bright Dawn School, which is operating on the outskirts of Marondera. On the other side is her 21-year-old son Tichaona, who is the school's finance manager. I had met them both just 45 minutes ago. At 9:00 a.m. precisely, I'd arrived in a battered old taxi outside their school.

Mrs. Farirai had seemed very nervous and uncomfortable when I'd introduced myself and Leonard, a young Zimbabwean who had been acting as my guide for the last three days, although her son was warmer and more welcoming. There had been a phone call, it transpired. Tichaona explained that his mother had told the chairman of their parent-teacher association (PTA) that I was visiting after I'd spoken to her last night, just to keep things regular. Now he wanted to meet me. That seemed fair enough. "We should meet him before you tour the school," Tichaona explained, in his beautifully deep, rich English accent. Fair enough, too, I thought. I'm always keen to meet any officials and keep things regular.

Mrs. Farirai had tried many times to call him on the landline. Eventually she got through. "Okay," she said, "he's at his office. We will just go to visit my chairman now, and then we can talk properly." We piled into my taxi and drove the short distance across town. As we passed our hotel, suddenly Leonard said that he had left his "small watch" in his hotel room and needed to get out and pick it up: won't I come and look for it with him? Only later did that strike me as odd—his watch must have been *so* small that he had been asking me for the time ever since I had met him. "Don't be silly," I'd said, "I've got to meet the chairman." I become annoyed at his insistence, thinking that now he was showing his true colors.

Only over breakfast I had been thinking how sweetly respectful he had been toward me and my work over the three days I'd known him; now he's become insolent and hotheaded. He changed tack: "You need to get your bag," he insisted. Equally I insisted that I could get it later. So we dropped him off at the hotel and drove around the corner . . . through the imposing steel gates of the Zanu-PF regional headquarters. At the time, this only merited an internal chuckle from me, so the chairman of the PTA is also the chairman of the regional branch of Zanu-PF!

Although the chairman had been there five minutes before when we had phoned, he had now mysteriously disappeared. We were led into the downstairs security room, where one Zanu-PF official brusquely questioned us. What was I doing here? Why did I want to visit private schools? He abruptly left, to return 15 minutes later with the regional head of security.

He speaks to Joy and Tichaona for some time; they argue with him; he is having none of it. Then he turns to me:

> "Why are you here doing research on our private schools? What did you announce when you came through immigration?" he asks, unsmiling still.
>
> "I said I was coming to visit friends and to do business," I say truthfully. I had ticked both boxes on the immigration form when I'd arrived.
>
> "Then you shouldn't be here doing research. You're here illegally."
>
> "No, no, I'm not, business means research too."

He laughs for the first time, but it's not a happy laugh: "Business is business, research is research. You need a completely different permit to do research. You're here illegally."

"Oh," I respond. I'm starting to feel uncomfortable. I don't feel proud later of how I implicated my new associates in my visit, who might prefer not to be so implicated: "I'm visiting friends. I came to visit my friends here, who happen to run a school, to see if I could *come back* to do research. I would have got permission; of course, I wouldn't do anything illegal."

He shakes his head contemptuously. "No, you are here illegally. All countries are the same, this is all a matter of immigration; we wouldn't be allowed to visit your country and go to a school without permission; we would be thrown out straightaway." This thought seems to remind him of other, more painful thoughts. He continues: "There are many Zimbabweans who are being thrown out of . . . Britain," he spits out the word disdainfully, as if it is vile even to utter it. "Zimbabweans are being thrown out of Britain every day— how dare you throw out Zimbabweans, it's so embarrassing to us, can you imagine it, the shame it brings on us?"

He pulls his handkerchief from his trouser pocket and wipes the copious beads of sweat off his forehead. I feel no sweat on mine, although it is pretty warm down there. "The trouble with you British is that you are still colonizing us, you still think you are our masters. . . ."

> Oddly, I choose to interject and challenge him on this point: "But that was 25 years ago; of course, we don't think that now!"
>
> He doesn't like being challenged. He looks away from me. He motions down to my notebook: "So why are you writing this *shit*!"
>
> It's not a question that requires an answer: "Why are you writing this shit about us?"

It was true; my notebook was pretty gruesome evidence. What had I written? Just normal stuff. About how I'd been in Zimbabwe staying with an old friend from my teaching days of 20 odd years ago, Peter, a white Zimbabwean, and his Shona wife, Caroline. About how they'd said there were definitely no private schools for the poor in Zimbabwe; that perhaps it was true this time, as, *oh dear*, *"Zimbabwe is unique in having Mugabe as leader: uniquely bad, uniquely evil."* Then about my normal detective work, trying a different tack, asking Caroline, who was a lecturer in a government teacher-training college, what morale was like in the teaching profession, in government schools? And recording what she had told me: "Morale is at rock bottom. Teachers are not paid enough. Most of my students are just there to get the diploma so that they can get their secure government job that they've been promised. 'If you pay peanuts, you get monkeys,' as the old saying goes, and monkeys are lazy." Then recording my observation that, if government teachers are really so bad, this means that there are likely to be low-cost private schools, if Zimbabwe is anything like any other country I've visited.

Then there were details of my further detective work, following many dead ends, nearly believing Peter and Caroline and everyone else I spoke to in Harare, but eventually finding what I was looking for in Dzivaresekwa. This was one of the "black townships" built by the Rhodesian government some miles outside of Harare on the main Bulawayo road to house the African workers, seemingly as far from the white suburbs as was possible. It was still one of the poorest settlements, home to many more people than it was built for. We'd gone there after we'd happened to give a lift to Leonard, a worker at a small game reserve just outside Harare near the airport, who was to become my guide as I traveled to Marondera. We'd seen wonderful birds: iridescent kingfishers, African pied wagtails, jacandas, and fork-tailed swallows, I recorded. But most exciting to me, I obsessively wrote in my notebook, was hearing Leonard say that he had a friend who was teaching in a low-cost private school in the township.

About Dzivaresekwa my notes were more positive, had my interrogator read them. I'd favorably compared Dzivaresekwa with places like Kibera and Makoko, saying it all seemed positively rich by comparison—neatly planned, charming if tiny, brick bungalows with small gardens, not poor in the way that the slums of Kenya and Nigeria were poor. It was true that many people were also living in sheds in these small gardens, but these tin shacks were no different from where *everyone* lived in the slums of other African countries. I'd been positively surprised by what I'd seen of living conditions in Zimbabwe. But I wished I hadn't recorded some of the graffiti I'd seen on the walls, though, proclaiming, "Mugabe must go."

From Dzivaresekwa there were copious notes about the low-cost private schools I'd found—but my writing was so bad, he couldn't have understood any of it, could he? Like Fount of Joy School, renting the eponymous church property, but having nothing else to do with the church. I recorded the low fees and why the owner Edwin, a very friendly, articulate, erudite, and soft-spoken man in his late 30s, told me he had opened the school—which wouldn't make very favorable reading to a government official, let alone my interrogator. I'd recorded that many migrants from the rural areas were not allowed in the government schools, as zoning had been introduced. If you weren't an official resident of the township, you couldn't go to the government school. "We take students from wherever they come, we don't discriminate," I'd recorded Edwin saying.

"Unlike in the government schools," I'd observed. And Edwin reporting that his school "upholds good Christian values, good orientation as far as morality and religion is concerned. In the government schools, they have . . . divergent values, and parents prefer what we offer." I'd also recorded Edwin's views on a private primary school he knew of nearby, where children sat under trees rather than in classrooms, that was threatened with immediate closure: "It all comes out of a quest for education. Sitting under a tree is not a criminal activity."

Another low-cost private school I'd taken notes on was Daybreak College, a secondary school that had just opened nearby. The owner, 25-year-old Watson, had been a teacher at another low-cost private school but had decided to go it alone. His father had recently died, and with the "small money" left to the family, Watson had extended his home to create a brick building for six classrooms. The family lived in the original two rooms as you entered the school. I recorded why he too had opened the school—because there was an acute shortage of secondary schools in and around the township, so he wanted to cater to this demand. Because the government schools took only those who scored highest in the state exams, those less clever had nowhere to go. Watson himself had originally wanted to go to university but couldn't afford to; with his father's passing away, "Automatically I became the breadwinner." I recorded that his fees were lower than the government schools' and that he now had 72 students but could—and would soon—accommodate 300 in two shifts. I recorded that Watson seemed to have thought a lot about marketing, even down to wearing a T-shirt emblazoned with the school name. And I recorded, word for word, how Watson had told me: "Our own market research shows that the reasons why parents prefer our college is the teacher–pupil ratio; in government schools, it is 60 to 1, in ours it is 20 to 1, so in a government school pupils have much more divided attention. Sometimes classes in government schools reach 200, so teachers are discouraged that they can make a difference. Teachers too rarely turn up, they absent themselves from work all the time. But in my school, once you absent yourself from work, you have to explain yourself, and if your explanation is not satisfactory, then you'll be out." In the notebook too, I had a copy of Watson's carefully devised code of conduct for his staff, copies of which were handed out to all new staff members, and which hung on the office wall. And I had recorded Watson telling me that government schools had a real problem with staff behavior. (I'd recalled similar stories when I'd been a teacher in Zimbabwe: reports of teachers having sexual affairs with students. And when the girls had become pregnant, as they often did, they were expelled while the teacher remained in post.) This is item number one on Watson's code of conduct: "1. No member(s) of staff is allowed to fall in love/have an indecent affair with a student both in and out of the school. Any member of staff caught in a love nest with a student will be automatically dismissed and handed over to the police." It is followed by strict instructions about punctuality ("Every member of staff must report for work by 7:00 a.m."), absenteeism ("No member of staff shall absent him/herself without a genuine reason. In case of absenteeism due to illness, a medical proof must be produced. Failure to produce medical proof/give notice is an offence which carries a fine."), and other important matters. I had written in my notebook how Watson seemed to be dealing very positively with "the very real problems that are present in government schools." I'd also recorded that, because my visit coincided with the penultimate day of term, the school was having a drama festival, with plays created by the students themselves. I'd written how "the students are great actors, full of life, exuberant, joyful." This was no cram school.

And many other details too, of the many other low-cost private schools I'd found. And how one parent had told us about Bright Dawn School in Marondera, where her family lived, and my journey with Leonard to visit its proprietor Joy—who sits beside me now, shooting me a glance that seems to say it will be all right, while the Zanu-PF regional head of security continues his tirade.

"What shit are you writing here? You British, you are still colonial racists."

I've told him already that I came to Zimbabwe as a young man, laid it on a bit that I'd given up years of life to work for his people. I had told him, truthfully, that I loved Zimbabwe more than any other country I visited, because it had been my "first love," the place where I'd spent my formative years. I didn't know what more to tell him. But I say it all again, my voice uncomfortably pleading now. He growls back: "Look, how do I know that you are a friend of Zimbabwe? So you came here 20 years ago as a teacher, but then so many of your compatriots, they come here and pretend they care for us, and will do this, and do that, do all for us, but then you leave, go back to your own country and write so much evil about us; you're all like this, we don't want your interest. You British imperialists, you all think you still run Zimbabwe, well you don't, we are sovereign and independent now, and you're here doing illegal things."

Then he turns to Joy and Tichaona, again they go back and forth, his glowering at me then ignoring me, as they all converse in Shona. How is it all going to end?

But then it does end. He gets a phone call. He listens. And he then says, "Go."

The three of us stand up. He refuses my handshake and Shona farewells. But I leave with the others! We pile into my waiting taxi, drive out of the compound to find Leonard anxiously waiting for us. "I was really worried for you," he says. And the funny thing is, before that interview, I would not have written anything bad about Zimbabwe—as my friend Peter had remarked, I was feeling only good things about the country that I loved so much, convinced that journalists had exaggerated the problems for their own self-aggrandizement, to make their own adventures sound more glorious. Poverty and corruption in Zimbabwe, it seemed to me, were nothing compared with the other African countries I visited. And I had been traveling unharmed and untouched, at ease, into the townships and rural areas, talking with whomever I liked, seeing whatever I wanted to see. The Zanu-PF regional chief of security had put a bit of a damper on all that.

We drive off, now laughing together, my relief palpable. Now I'm sweating! I tell them that of course they don't have to speak to me now, that I don't want to put them in any more danger. No, no, they insist. Equally I insist too, I'll drop them off and leave them in peace. But their insistence is greater. "My dear," Joy says, "we all need a good cup of tea." Yes, I feel very much in need of a cup of tea. So we drive off, significantly though not to her school but to her sister's place some miles out of town.

We laugh together now; the shared experience of being cooped up in the interrogation cellar has, of course, brought us closer. I tell them what I've been seeing around the world on my journey. And as they tell me of what they've achieved, and what they plan, I realize that I'm meeting two wonderfully dynamic entrepreneurs, who were creating something of immense value here in Zimbabwe. Joy's school had grown from 15 students in 1998 to around 300 now; it is the only indigenous preschool to high school in the whole country, she told me. Joy had also started a second school deep in the rural areas, in Weya, near Headlands. Here, in addition to academic subjects, children took other courses, such as poultry raising, welding, pig farming, and dressmaking, and they also ran a shop—technical subjects that were also used to raise funds for the school and to train entrepreneurs. She had also been asked to open a third school in Macheke and to extend her chain to Mutare, Odzi, and Nyazura—all in the Eastern Highlands where I'd lived so many years before—where the local communities have promised her land, inspired by what they have seen her achieve in Marondera. And she wanted to extend her Marondera operations to a university. "My dear," she said, 'I want to have a 'one-stop shop for education.'" And Tichaona, her son, taking seriously the running of the financial side of the business, was currently enrolled in an MBA program with the Zimbabwe Open University, from where he already had a diploma in financial management. We share stories, and I feel inspired by all they have achieved and want to be involved in their future.

As we part, I ask them the obvious question that somehow I'd forgotten to ask in the euphoria of being released, "Why did the security chief let me go?" Joy says perhaps they believed that I was a friend of Zimbabwe; and the regional Zanu-PF chairman has his daughter in her school. Of course, he was the chairman of her parent-teacher association, I recalled, he would have had a child in her school. "So he doesn't send his daughter to a government school?" I ask. Joy laughs: "Our school is better. They all know that." And then adds: "They weren't going to harm you, not with me there. They were just trying to frighten you." With Joy beside me, I could be safe.

We part, and Leonard and I hitch a ride back into Harare; six of us crammed into a small, very slow private car. Just outside of Marondera, our car is stopped at the police roadblock, only ours, all the others in the traffic queue are allowed through. My heart sinks; has Zanu-PF radioed ahead to have me arrested? Without Joy next to me, am I no longer safe? But nothing untoward happens;

the driver shows his papers, pays his dues, and we are off, back to Harare.

That was the only time I ever really felt threatened while doing my research. But it wasn't the only time I ruffled feathers. When I presented the results of my endeavors to academics and development experts, I felt that if they could have detained me in some dank cellar, they would have been happy to do so. Some accused me of imperialism, racism, and colonialism, just as the Zanu-PF interrogator had done. And although I never again felt that horrible tingling fear at the base of my spine, there were some uncomfortable times ahead.

My colleague at Newcastle Professor Sugata Mitra—whose work in India has shown how poor children can learn through the Internet without the assistance of teachers—once told me that if ever he felt apprehensive before giving an important lecture, he would look at a photograph of children his work was helping, and that would inspire him to get on with his talk and ignore his nerves and any potentially hostile audience. I have a photograph of me with Joy, and with Reshma too, a Muslim woman whose private school serves poor children in Hyderabad, which I use to the same effect. If Joy and Reshma can endure all that they must go through, overcome all the odds to help the poor benefit from a decent education, then I can get on with telling people what I've found.

Not long after I flew home from Zimbabwe, I presented some of my findings at an important education and development conference in Oxford. I presented the results to many academic conferences; this one was typical. I outlined my findings about private schools serving the majority of schoolchildren in poor areas of Africa and India. China too had interesting lessons to tell. I described how, after testing many thousands of children, and observing a few thousand schools, these private schools seemed superior to government schools with regard to inputs and pupil achievement. And they were doing it all for a fraction of the cost. And that free primary education might not be as beneficial as many believed, because it seemed to have the effect of crowding out existing private schools that were better serving the poor. At least in Kenya. . . .

As I finished my PowerPoint presentation and the chair invited questions, one professor, metaphorically flinging down my notebook onto the table in front of me, dismissed what I'd said, "Tooley is plowing a lonely furrow, long may it remain that way." Another stood up to condemn my approach: "Tooley's work is dangerous, in the wrong hands it could lead to the demise of state education." "You've painted a glowing picture of markets in education," said another, "but have you never heard of market failure?" Sighing deeply, another said: "It doesn't matter what your evidence shows. Statistics, statistics, statistics, who cares about your statistics? Private education can never be pro-poor." Development experts are all pro-poor. I, by celebrating poor families' decision to use private education, was not: "The poor must have state education because they mustn't pay fees." A young woman near the front was equally as dismissive: "You obviously know nothing about human rights. Free and compulsory education is enshrined in the Universal Declaration!" An elderly Indian professor, more kindly than the others, nevertheless had disagreed with all I'd said: "You're trying to pull the ladder up behind you," he smiled, "the only way your country developed was through free government schools. Why are you trying to deny it to the rest of us?"

They were all united in dismissing my findings. Why was I ignoring the many good reasons that we all know why private education cannot be part of any solution to "education for all"? Why was I ignoring the many good reasons why markets are inappropriate for education—that the short route to accountability I explored in the last chapter had to be abandoned in favor of the political long road? Why was I being so perverse as to ignore the years of accumulated wisdom to this effect?

After I'd given my paper, the conference chair, a professor at one of England's top education departments, took me aside. He was trying to be helpful: "You're silly, very silly, saying all of that. You'll never get another job. Be sensible, old chap."

Five Good Reasons?

What are these good reasons? Each of the objections given above summarizes one of the major reasons the development experts have for rejecting private education for the poor as part of any solution—apart from the issue of low quality, which we've already looked at. I read of these reasons as I studied on my journey, talked them through with whomever I could, and weighed them against what

I was seeing for myself. The more I saw, the less convincing I'd found them.

The first reason seemed easiest to dismiss. It was what one attendee was getting at when he said my ideas were "dangerous"—that, if taken up by the wrong people, they could lead to "the demise of state education." I'd read it in several places. The PROBE Report said that if poor parents support private education, this "carries a real danger of undermining the government schooling system."[1] Kevin Watkins, the author of *The Oxfam Education Report* and now director of the United Nations Development Programme, wrote that parents should not "withdraw their children from the public education system and put them in private schools," for this "reduces parental pressure to improve government schools." It was what I had heard way back when Sajitha Bashir challenged me after my first visit to the slums of Hyderabad. If poor parents continue to flee public education en masse, the experts fear, the very existence of public education itself is threatened.

But to me this seemed to be what the Americans call a no-brainer. If the education of the poor is what we desire, why should we care whether they get it in public or private systems? If private schools could be made available to all, including the poorest and most excluded, and to girls—and there could be ways of ensuring this (see below)—and if their quality, already higher than the government alternative, can be improved through judicious support (again, see below), then from the poor's perspective, why would it be relevant whether this would undermine the state system, providing that education for all was achieved? As the Chinese leader Deng Xiaoping once observed: "Who cares if the cat is black or white? It's a good cat if it catches the mouse!" Why should the poor mind what color their cat is?

The second major reason why private education wasn't the way forward for the poor had to do with "market failure." Development experts tend to use this term synonymously with education being a "public good," and there being "externalities" of education that need to be taken into account. At issue here, perhaps surprisingly given the complex way it is often described, seems something rather simple. The UNDP puts it like this: Governments should "finance and provide" primary education because "market prices alone" would not capture its "intrinsic value and social benefits." Why not? Because basic education "benefits not only the individual who gains knowledge, it also benefits all members of society by improving health and hygiene behaviour and raising worker productivity."

The basic idea, then, is that there are social benefits to be had from people being educated. If a parent educates his child, this child, so the theory goes, will contribute to society by being healthier, by being more productive at work, by being literate, and so on. But these *public* benefits, it is claimed, are not reflected in the market price of education, so there will be "market failure." That is, in the absence of the state's providing and financing education, not enough people will buy enough education, of the right sort, to provide these social benefits. That's what the conference critic was claiming about my position.

I've wrestled with this, and it seems to me that it's not as powerful an objection as the development experts imagine it to be. Suppose we're in a system where there is no public provision and financing of education. A poor parent is deciding whether to educate her child. Private schooling costs a certain amount, and her resources are very limited. She certainly values the benefits that education brings to society generally. She values low incidence of disease, the benefits of democracy, and social cohesion—in very practical terms. Disease hits her hard, for instance, and may have already killed some of her children. A lack of democracy leads to corrupt bureaucrats who pester her and her family for bribes. A lack of social cohesion leads to communal riots, which adversely affect her family and livelihood. Clearly, she would benefit from every child, including her own, being educated.

But, weighing it all, she decides not to educate her child because she chooses to allocate her resources to different ends. She can "free ride" on others getting educated, so some social benefits may come her way. But every other person will be in the same boat and will make the same calculations, so in fact society won't get educated at all, and so no one will benefit. That's the perceived problem of collective action that so troubles most development experts.

But is it really that problematic? Surely not: because the poor parent also knows that there are *private* benefits from being educated—especially for a poor person, as precisely the development experts also argue, it's one of the best routes out of poverty. And the child will not only be able to get a middle-class job with education but will also likely assist her parent as she gets older. So instead of the pessimistic conclusions reached by the development experts, a much more favorable outcome emerges: Because these *private* benefits are so great, she'll pay fees to educate her child, even if it means sacrificing other goods. But so will many other parents, and so all will enjoy the social benefits this brings, even though they weren't a significant part of their initial decision to educate their children.

The key points seemed to be the cost of schooling and the value of the private benefits. It is a mistake to blithely assume that the cost of schooling will be so high, and the private benefits so low, that parents will decide not to educate their children. The only way to address the issue is not in the abstract, as the UNDP and my conference critic had, but by looking at the evidence and seeing whether poor parents are actually willing to spend on education, and so produce the desired social benefits.

The evidence adduced in my research demonstrates quite categorically that poor parents *are* prepared to pay for schooling, for this is in fact what they are already doing. In slum areas, the vast majority of parents *are* prepared to pay, and are paying. It seemed to me then—and still seems now—that this evidence is enough to refute the "market failure" argument. Poor parents have shown that there is no problem of collective action and no grounds for assuming that the externalities of education will lead to market failure. The perceived private benefits are enough to make them pay for education and, hence, obtain the social benefits that arise from that decision. Furthermore, I'd found that the price paid for schooling also includes an element to cover scholarships for the poorest in society— that's another way of looking at the fact that school owners admit up to 20 percent of their children free of charge or at a concessionary rate. So not only are parents willing to pay for private education, they are also apparently willing to subsidize the cost to others who are not as fortunate as they. Furthermore, since the quality of education in parent-funded private schools exceeds that provided by the government sector, the corollary social benefits of education would be commensurately greater as well. And because private schools are locally owned and funded—not dependent on foreign aid as are most public schools in the countries I studied—they generate self-sustaining domestic economic activity that public schools do not. Since indigenous, self-sustaining economies are the ultimate goal of developing countries, private schooling intrinsically represents a larger step forward on the path of development. Private schools, in other words, appear to be *superior* to government schools in the creation of public goods. All this, I believe, indicates that the second "good reason" not only fails to pass muster but in fact puts things precisely backward.

The third reason comes out of the "pro-poor" idea. Of course it arises from a well-meaning desire to ensure that no child is left behind. So state financing is the only way to provide equality in education, for if poor people must find fees for schooling, some may be unable to "use them—making it difficult to escape poverty." Again, that all seems plausible in theory. But the same development experts who argue this seem to have no difficulty admitting that current *government provision* is itself inequitable, in general benefiting the wealthier in developing countries rather than the poor. Government education provision is unfair too. The key question is, could private provision be made fairer and actually turn out to be fairer than government provision?

The main reason given by the development experts as to why it can't be made more equitable is simply that private education requires tuition fees to be paid. *The Oxfam Education Report* was clear about this: Private education "does not offer a route to universal primary education, because poverty often excludes the poor from private markets." Even though private education is "filling part of the space left as a result of the collapse of State provision," its potential "to facilitate more rapid progress towards universal basic education has been exaggerated." Why? Because poor parents cannot afford private education. The PROBE Report made the same objection: "Private schools are out of reach of the vast majority of poor parents."

The issue of not everyone being able to afford tuition fees for private schools is an important one. But why would this be viewed, other things being equal, as an objection to a greater role for private education? If private schools have all the above-listed advantages over state schools, with regard to quality and accountability, why would we see the tuition fee problem as such a huge obstacle? We shouldn't, for there is the obvious possibility of creating *targeted* vouchers or scholarships for the poorest, or for girls, which overcomes the objection. The UNDP seems to agree that this is a possible way forward. In a section of a recent report, "Making Private Provision Work for Poor People," it notes: "Public funding of private schools can help in certain circumstances. . . . To ensure that children from poor families unable to pay school fees are able to attend private schools, governments could finance their education through vouchers." It gives the example of vouchers targeted at the poor in Colombia for secondary schools that helped "expand schooling at lower cost for the government, because the only cost the government bears is the voucher."

Similarly, the World Bank, noting the difficulties of the political "long route" to accountability, says, "Given the weaknesses in the long route of accountability, service outcomes can be improved by strengthening the short route—by increasing the client's power over providers." It too gives the example of targeted vouchers, which enable clients "to exert influence over providers through choice." This will allow parents a choice of providers so that they can "vote with their feet." "The competition created by client choice also disciplines providers. . . . Reimbursing schools based on the number of students (or female students) they enrol creates implicit competition among schools for students, increasing students' choice."

And *The Oxfam Education Report* also notes the success of two targeted voucher programs, the aforementioned in Colombia and one in Pakistan that targets the poorest and most disadvantaged, girls, enabling them to attend private schools. Surely these are positive ways forward that could embrace the choices that parents seem to want to make, and help extend them to everyone? No, for the author, they are just short-term expedients: although he agrees that "support for good-quality private providers can create equity gains," this must be viewed as only "a transitional arrangement in countries where public education systems are failing to reach the poor." But that is all they can be: "In terms of achieving the 2015 target of universal primary education, there is no alternative to comprehensive public provision of good-quality basic education. Private-public partnerships have a role to play in some countries, but only at the margin. They do not solve the problem of mass exclusion, and do not diminish State responsibility for providing education for all."

Why is this position so obvious that it is the one reached by apparently all the development experts, even those who acknowledge that private schools for the poor exist, and that targeted vouchers are a possibility? It didn't seem obvious to me in the context of the evidence I'd found around the world. Even if you are pro-poor, there didn't seem to be any reason to accept that tuition fees are an impassable obstacle to harnessing private schools for the poor as a path to universal education. There is an obvious solution to this problem—targeted vouchers.

So the third "good reason" didn't seem to me to be good enough either.

What about human rights? The fourth "good reason" is that education "is a fundamental human right." Both the World Bank and the UNDP spell this out as a major objection to private education playing a role in education for all. But what role does this imply for governments, and does it rule out private education's playing a significant role in promoting education as a human right?

Interestingly, when I looked up the academic literature on the subject, I found two versions of the rights-based commitment to education that were adopted by the international community in 2000. The second Millennium Development Goal commits governments to "ensure that, by 2015, children everywhere . . . will be able to complete a full course of primary schooling." Then there is the second goal of the Dakar Framework for Action, commonly known as the "education for all" (EFA) goal, which commits signatories (principally governments and nongovernmental organizations) to ensure "that by 2015 all children . . . have access to and complete, *free* and compulsory primary education of good quality."

Now the United Nations Educational, Scientific, and Cultural Organization, the champion of the EFA goal, is adamant that the education MDG is only "different in detail, but not in intent" from its own EFA goals. But clearly I could see there was a crucial difference. Under the MDG version, governments are only committed to ensuring that all children have *access* to primary schooling; it says nothing about whether it should be *free*. Under this goal, then, it doesn't seem to rule out that the human right of education could be met, in full or in part, by fee-paying private schools, if everyone could obtain access to them—perhaps by providing targeted vouchers to those who could not afford fees. So the MDG version would *not* be an objection to private education playing an important role in providing "education for all."

However, the Dakar Framework version is more particular. Here, the commitment *is* to *free* primary education. On the face of it—

the criticism that the young woman threw at me at the Oxford conference—the EFA goal clearly provides an impossible stumbling block to private-sector involvement. If primary education must be *free*, then of course this rules out a large role for private education. Is that enough to make all my evidence beyond the pale? I think if we look at the *motivations* behind the Dakar Framework, we can see that, in intent, if not precise wording, it is not incompatible with private fee-paying education.

For UNESCO helpfully published an expanded commentary, meant to clarify any ambiguities within the framework. Here it notes that "user charges continue to be a major deterrent to poor children attending school," and that education "must neither exclude nor discriminate." Hence, it concludes, "Every government has the responsibility to provide *free*, quality basic education, *so that no child will be denied access because of an inability to pay.*" But this clarification surely reveals the true intentions behind "free" education: that *poverty* shouldn't lead to any child being "denied access." This is entirely different, of course, from requiring *no one* to pay fees. It could be perfectly compatible with this formulation of words to have fees at primary school, with the poorest being allocated targeted vouchers, as I've already discussed, so that they are not excluded by poverty.

This is further reinforced by UNESCO's continued clarification as to why governments "must fulfil their obligation to offer free and compulsory primary education." It writes: "*For the millions of children living in poverty,* who suffer multiple disadvantages, there must be an unequivocal commitment that education be free of tuition and other fees. . . ." Again, the commitment to free schooling seems to be for those who can't afford even the low fees at budget private schools, not necessarily everyone. Again, targeted vouchers for the very poor to use for private schools could easily be permitted under this interpretation.

Moreover, it might again come as no surprise, given the discussion in the previous section on the range and quality of government provision, that the major reports from the UNDP and the World Bank say that, in reality, the fact that education is a human right doesn't make much difference as far as government behavior is concerned: the World Bank reports that "many governments are falling short on their obligations, especially to poor people." The UNDP points out, very significantly, that "public provision of social services is not always the best solution when institutions are weak and accountability for the use of public resources is low—often the case in developing countries."

So again, what education as a human right means in practice for public and private involvement in education would seem to be an open, practical matter. In practice, if governments are not living up to their promises, then it surely is an open question whether the private sector is serving the "human right" better than the states. Again, the fourth "good reason" does not seem to be too powerful an objection either.

The final "good reason" was the one put to me by the Indian delegate at the conference, who said that I was trying to pull the ladder up behind me. Nobel Laureate Amartya Sen espouses this position well. Taking to task some unnamed "market enthusiasts" who recommend to developing countries "that they should rely fully on the free market even for basic education," he says that this "rather remarkable" approach would withhold "the very process of educational expansion that was crucial in rapidly spreading literacy in Europe, North America [and] Japan . . . in the past." It was certainly not through the market, but through the state, that educational expansion was achieved in the West, he says. And if it was good enough for the West, then it must be good enough for developing countries, too.

Amartya Sen isn't alone in espousing this position. The World Bank also gave it as a "good reason" for the long route of accountability: "In practice no country has achieved significant improvement in . . . primary education without government involvement." The UNDP agrees: "Only when governments intervened [in education] did these services become universal in Canada, Western Europe and the United States."

However, I don't think things are as clear-cut as these development experts believe. For a start, I'm not convinced that this was really the way education developed in the West. There is strong, if counterintuitive, evidence that universal primary school provision was more or less achieved in 19th-century England and America before the state got significantly involved, through private means, such as the church, philanthropy, and the much maligned "dame" schools, that is, private schools run by small-scale proprietors, much like the ones we see in the slums of developing countries today. Less controversially, I suspect, there can also be doubts about whether we in the West *are* actually enjoying education for all under our existing public school systems, once truancy and dropouts are taken into account.[2]

More fundamentally, why does it *matter* what happened in the West? Can't I throw the "imperialistic" label back at these critics who say that the only way forward for poorer nations is to follow what they imagine the West has done? In the foreword to *The Rough Guide to A Better World*, sponsored by the Department for International Development, Sir Bob Geldof notes that development sometimes— and "admirably"—succeeds in countries, by people "ignoring all the advice of 'the experts' and finding their own *culturally appropriate* model." Perhaps "ol' Bleak Bob" (his own self-appellation) has hit on something crucially relevant to our concerns here? If many poor parents, in Asia and sub-Saharan Africa in particular, are choosing private schools because public education clearly is not working for them, then perhaps this says something about the *cultural appropriateness* of the private model in their developing country context, and the inappropriateness of trying to do things in the contemporary Western way? At the very least, one might be open to this possibility.

Even if the West was won, educationally speaking, through public schooling, this would not in itself mean that it is the only, or the best, way forward for people in very different circumstances—with very corrupt and unresponsive governments, for instance. Perhaps what I was finding—so many poor parents choosing private schools because public education is not working—says something about the *cultural appropriateness* of the private model in developing countries, and the *in*appropriateness of trying to do things the current Western way? On this ground alone, I would have thought, the final "good reason" should be considered pretty insubstantial.

But hearing this criticism, I wondered how *were* people being educated in developing countries *before* the Western powers colonized them? People I'd spoken to on my journey clearly carried the assumption that the colonized peoples simply weren't being educated at all until the imperialists arrived. I heard Claire Fox, director of the London-based Institute of Ideas, whose radical views I usually found inspiring and palatable, tell a conference that there wasn't much she liked about Western imperialism in India, but one of the few good things it did bring was education to the previously uneducated masses. Funnily enough, I heard the same thing from the elderly guide at the first-ever primary school in Nigeria, St. Thomas School, founded in 1845, on the edge of the coconut tree–lined lagoon in Badagry, Lagos State. He showed me around a rather ordinary-looking whitewashed brick building, with planks, hinges, doors, and corrugated roof all imported from England, still standing after 159 years. Upstairs was the room that contained the first Bible imported from England to Nigeria, a tatty book with the first chapters of Genesis and all of Revelation missing, and the first Bible translated into Yoruba. Downstairs was the room where a Mr. Philipson, the first Western teacher in Nigeria, had lived for 23 years; he had started the school across the compound with 40 children. The school had soon been inundated with children, my guide told me, so the rule had been devised—a rule in existence until as late as 1989—that required a child to reach his hand over to touch his opposite shoulder before he could be admitted to school, something, apparently, that children younger than five cannot do. It was the most extraordinary place. My guide told me, "The British brought with them three good things to Nigeria: Christianity, Agricultural Science, and Education." "And," he emphasized, "all three began here."

Was it true? I realized that I didn't have much of a clue about what education was like, or if schooling existed at all, before the imperial powers brought it to their colonies. This was to require another journey, this time back in time. And like my other journey, this one too began in Hyderabad.

11. The Men Who Uprooted the Beautiful Tree

Dalrymple's Footsteps

I didn't read only the reports of development experts as I traveled. On one of my visits to Hyderabad, I read William Dalrymple's *White Mughals*, the account of James Achilles Kirkpatrick, the British representative to the court of the Nizam of Hyderabad in the late 18th century, and his tragic love affair with the young and beautiful Mughal princess Khair un-Nissa. On a Sunday afternoon, waiting for our evening flight to Delhi, Pauline and I took my team to follow in Dalrymple's footsteps, to weave through the crowded streets of Koti, to visit the old British residency, now the crumbling home of the Osmania University College for Women. No one challenged us as we wandered around by the glow of our mobile phones in the bat-infested, dank cellars or upstairs in the magnificent old ballrooms and once-elegant parlors. We admired the rusting chandeliers and wall-length mirrors, marveling at the incongruity of these magnificent decaying features juxtaposed against tatty blackboards plastered with economics' formulas. From there we drove again, to climb to the balconies of the 16th-century Charminar, taking in the vistas across the Old City in which we had been working for the past five years.

I remembered that in Dalrymple's introduction, he had described how he had had a "moment of pure revelation" in an old bookshop in the labyrinth behind the Chowk Masjid, the teeming bazaars surrounding the Charminar. Serendipity had led him to the "dusty, ill-lit shop the size of a large broom-cupboard,"[1] where he had found important Persian manuscripts that had been a crucial help in his investigations. Why didn't we follow his footsteps there too?

The bookshop wasn't actually too difficult to find, and clearly we weren't alone in making this pilgrimage, given the blasé, if still curious, way in which other shopkeepers pointed us in the right direction. It was as tiny as Dalrymple had said, with books piled from floor to ceiling, curiously with their spines facing inward so that you couldn't see the title of any book without pulling it from the shelf. It was also as dusty as Dalrymple had said, and I began to sneeze in the enclosed space.

The old owner who appeared after a while was friendly, if hard of hearing. We told him that we had just been exploring the old British residency, you know, "Osmania University College, following in Dalrymple's footsteps. . . ." He apparently picked up only on the university bit: "So you're in education?" "Yes," we repeated, "we're following Dalrymple" and that's why, we explained, we'd come to his bookshop. He looked interested, but promptly went away, leaving us alone in the dark shop, and I thought he'd forgotten us. We browsed, finding some wonderful old maps of Hyderabad, and a fascinating slim volume debating the case for and against Hyderabad's joining India in 1949. (The Nizam of Hyderabad had prevaricated about wishing to become independent, to join Pakistan, or to remain part of the British Empire. In the end, Indian tanks decided the issue.)

But then the owner returned. And just as Dalrymple had had a stroke of fortune in this antiquarian bookshop, so did I. He returned with *The Beautiful Tree* (the same title that, in homage to Gandhi, I chose for my book). "Dharampal" he beamed triumphantly. "Oh," I said, "we've been reading William Dalrymple, an Englishman, not your Dharampal." I continued: "The Englishman visited your shop a couple of years ago and found some Persian manuscripts. Do you remember?" He reflected for awhile, then said: "Oh yes, that man. Too hard bargaining." He shook his head, "Too hard bargaining." He bade me look at his preferred Dharampal.

I opened the green book. It wasn't old—dated 1983—but was tatty and dusty. I read as I stood. Dharampal opened with an extended quote from Mahatma Gandhi, at Chatham House, London, October 20, 1931:[2]

> I say without fear of my figures being challenged success-
> fully, that today India is more illiterate than it was fifty or
> a hundred years ago, and so is Burma, because the British
> administrators, when they came to India, instead of taking
> hold of things as they were, began to root them out. They
> scratched the soil and began to look at the root, and left the
> root like that, and the *beautiful tree* perished.

Hence the title of this book. I was going to buy it anyway just as a souvenir of that day, but I wasn't then a great fan of Indian revisionism that claimed all the British brought to India was harm, so didn't think it would be a particularly enjoyable nor enlightening read. But then as I read on, the next few sentences of Gandhi's speech began to resonate with things that I'd been finding myself:

> The village schools were not good enough for the British administrator, so he came out with his programme. Every school must have so much paraphernalia, building, and so forth.

Wasn't this a bit like what the development experts and national governments were saying *now*? The private schools for the poor weren't "good enough," hence the need for aid programs for "paraphernalia, building, and so forth" in the public schools? I read on, growing more curious:

> There are statistics left by a British administrator which show that, in places where they have carried out a survey, ancient schools have gone by the board, because there was no recognition of these schools.

I'd never heard of such evidence of schools that existed before the British; moreover, this was apparently British contemporaneous evidence itself, so unlikely to fall victim to the desire to trash what the British had ever done for India. Gandhi concluded:

> And the schools established after the European pattern were too expensive for the people.... I defy anybody to fulfil a programme of compulsory primary education of these masses inside of a century. This very poor country of mine is ill able to sustain such an expensive method of education. Our state would revive the old village schoolmaster and dot every village with a school both for boys and girls.

It seemed to chime what I was thinking and finding. Certainly "compulsory primary education of these masses" had not been successfully achieved, "inside of a century," following the British state education model, as predicted by Gandhi. Indeed, all the "very poor countries" that we were researching, including India, seemed "ill able to sustain" the "expensive method[s] of education" that were being championed by the development experts, whether because of lack of funds, corruption, or a mixture of both. My thoughts rushed ahead: wouldn't it be strange if what Gandhi was proposing—to "revive the old village schoolmaster and dot every village with a school"—was actually what we were *finding* in the slums and villages of India today?

I bought the book, for what seemed a victory for my own "hard-bargaining" prowess (although my Indian team gasped in horror at how much I was prepared to pay). And I read it from cover to cover on the flight back to Delhi and to England. That Sunday afternoon, I embarked on another journey, back to 19th-century British India. It was to take me to libraries across London, following up Dharampal's sources. What I found seemed almost as remarkable, and as challenging to the accepted wisdom, as what I'd found on my physical journeys across Asia and Africa.

Munro's Minute

In the early 19th century, Sir Thomas Munro, governor of the Madras Presidency, wanted to do something about education in India. Everyone in England seemed to have an opinion about "the ignorance of the people of India and the means of disseminating knowledge among them." But no one had any *evidence*. It was idle chatter, based on prejudice, "mere conjectures of individuals unsupported by any authentic documents."[3] Munro proposed to discover the truth, by conducting a survey of what was actually happening on the ground.

Munro's Minute (memorandum) of June 25, 1822, was sent to all district collectors. The terms of reference themselves are interesting—clearly pointing to an awareness that there were schools in the villages before the British intervened. Each collector was asked to submit "a List of the schools in which reading and writing are taught in each District showing the number of scholars in each and the caste to which they belong."

The collectors' reports filtered back slowly—several taking a year or more, and one taking three years! It was a very long research process. All but one collector took the job seriously: the principal collector for Canara complained that filling in the form "would take up a considerable time," which would be wasted because everyone knew there are "no Colleges in Canara" nor "fixed schools and Masters to teach in them."[4] Fortunately, his was the only such report. All the other collectors furnished the required information.

The data are quite remarkable. Far from there being no schooling in India before the British brought their system, the figures show an abundance of preexisting schools and colleges: In the 20 districts returning data, 11,575 schools and 1,094 colleges were reported, with 157,195 and 5,431 students, respectively.[5] In addition, many collectors reported that considerably more scholars and students were educated in their own homes. Although such numbers were difficult to discern, some estimates were made—for instance, the collector of Madras who had reported 5,699 scholars in school reported that an additional 26,963 school-level scholars were then receiving tuition in their homes, that is *five times more* than were in schools. Munro suggested that such "home-schooling" would be common throughout the presidency.

Satisfied that his research had not been in vain, Munro summarized the evidence in his Minute of March 10, 1826. The existing indigenous schools were serving about 25 percent of the *male* school-age population, he wrote. But given that many more were reportedly being educated in their own homes, he estimated that at least one-third of the male population was being schooled. For girls, the numbers in school were much lower, but this could be explained by the fact that they were educated almost entirely in the home.

This level of educational enrollment, reported Munro, "is higher than it was in most European countries at no very distant period."[6] Moreover, the indigenous schooling system found by the British did not just focus on the elite but included the *most disadvantaged and poorest*. What are today classified as "backward castes" in India amounted to a substantial minority of enrollment in each district— for instance, 38 percent of the school population in Tinnevelly and 32 percent in Salem and Madras.

From Madras to Bengal, Bombay, and the Punjab

But there was more evidence than just Munro's. Thirteen years later, a more limited survey was carried out in the Bengal Presidency, which led to the celebrated Adam reports, "State of Education in Bengal 1835–38," published in 1841 by the University of Calcutta. Adam's first report featured his headline conclusion that there were about 100,000 village schools in Bengal and Bihar in the 1830s— something that Gandhi had announced at his talk in London. Adam noted that it appeared "that the system of village schools is extensively prevalent; that the desire to give education to their male children must be deeply seated in the minds of parents *even of the humblest classes*; and that these are the institutions, *closely interwoven as they were with the habits of the people and the customs of the country*."[7] Again, his work revealed an extensive system of indigenous Indian education, responding to the situations and needs of the poor.

Similarly, there was a report around 1820 on areas of the newly extended British Bombay Presidency that said, "There is hardly a village, great or small, throughout our territories, in which there is not at least one school, and in larger villages more." And from the Punjab, a report documented around 330,000 pupils in "the schools of the various denominations who were acquainted with reading, writing and some method of computation."

From Madras to Bengal, from Bombay to the Punjab, the accumulated evidence showed that any claim of no indigenous schooling worth speaking of before the British intervened was completely wrong: on the contrary, it all pointed to a vibrant indigenous system serving at least as high a proportion of boys as in European countries, including England, just a few years earlier. This was quite an extraordinary finding. In fact, in India, there were schools in almost every village before the British replaced them with the system that provided the foundations for today's public system.

The crucial question for me as I first read Dharampal's account of Munro's survey was, how was all this schooling funded? Could it be that what Munro uncovered was similar to what we were finding today, a vibrant *privately funded* education system, operating underground, with no official recognition, about to be replaced by an alien system? If so, then I could posthumously recruit Gandhi as a supporter of private schools for the poor in India, for he had written that he had wanted a return to this system. It turned out that was exactly what it was, a system funded almost entirely by student fees, plus a little philanthropy.

Private Schools for the Poor in 19th-Century India

How the system was funded was one of the questions Munro asked of his collectors. Of the 21 districts of the Madras Presidency, there is an open verdict about funding from two—one because the collector didn't take the exercise seriously, whereas the second didn't supply any notes on school funding. Of the remaining 19 collectors' reports, I could see that 16 described the system of schooling as *100 percent privately funded*, whereas the remaining 3 reported predominantly private—with only a tiny proportion (from 1 to 2 percent of schools) in each funded by government. Indeed, for one of these three, the information on funding for schools and colleges is collated, so it may well be that it was only the colleges that were funded in this way, as in most other districts, rather than schools too.

The collectors' reports show the careful and scholarly way in which the data were collected and collated. To take one example, the collector from the North Arcot district, a Mr. William Cooke, one of the three that reported a small amount of nonprivate funding, even tells us the cook's pay at one school and the daily allowance for boiled rice! You get the feeling that he took his assignment very seriously indeed. All his figures are collated in Table 3. Cooke recorded 583 private primary schools teaching in the local languages. Of these, 3 charged no fees, while the remaining 580 charged monthly fees, ranging from 15 annas to 21 rupees per year. There were also 40 Persian schools, 31 of which were private fee-paying schools, with 308 pupils, supported entirely by fees ranging from 1 rupee and 14 annas to 24 rupees per year. Seven of the Persian schools were "public schools," funded either by the villages or with a yearly government allowance, whereas the remaining two Persian schools provided free tuition. Finally, there were seven English private schools, three of which were free of charge, while four charged fees from 7.5 to 42.0 rupees per year.[8]

The other collectors gave similar levels of detail. They revealed that, in the Madras Presidency, the extensive system of schools was more or less entirely *privately* funded. The same conclusion also stands out from Adam's evidence for the Bengal Presidency:[9] Before the British took over and imposed their alien centralized public education system, India had an extensive system of private schools that catered to the masses. Or put another way, before the British came, the Indians already had a system of private schools, including schools for the poor.[10]

The collectors also told us something about the different motivations of those who set up private schools. One observed that private schools "are partly established occasionally by individuals for the education of their own children, and partly by the Teachers themselves, for their own maintenance."[11] Some parents, he continued,

Table 3.
PUBLIC AND PRIVATE SCHOOL FUNDING, NORTH ARCOT, 1823

Medium	Schools	Total students	Free (charity)	Private		Public			
				Fees, no subsidy	Free (public)	% public funding	% charity	% fee paying	% private
Indian languages	583	6,867	131	6,736	0	0	2	98	100
Persian	40	398	15	308	75	19	4	77	81
English	7	61	17	44	0	0	28	72	100
Total	630	7,326	163	7,088	75	1	2	97	99

SOURCE: Collated from C. Hyde (1823), "Principal Collector of South Arcot to Board of Revenue: 29-6-1823, Cuddalore, (TNSA:BRP: Vol. 954, Pro. 7-7-1823, pp. 5622–24, Nos. 59–60)," in *The Beautiful Tree: Indigenous Indian Education in the Eighteenth Century*, by Dharampal (Coimbatore: Keerthi Publishing House, 1995), pp. 145–46.

"who are anxious to have their children educated" cannot "sufficiently pay the Teachers out of their own money." In which case, they "procure some other children in addition to their own for being educated and get adequate allowance to them by way of subscription from these children, from one quarter, to one Rupee each monthly." This all seemed strangely reminiscent of what I had discovered in India today, where some parents who want to provide their children with what they view as a better education sometimes start a school and "procure some other children" to make it a viable undertaking.

The collectors also gave details of how the system accommodated the ability of parents to pay. For instance, one noted that the school fees were paid according "to the circumstances of the parents."[12] Another observed that "school Masters receive monthly from each Scholar from one quarter to four Rupees, according to their respective means." Again, this flexibility in payment mirrored what I found in today's private schools for the poor.

Moreover, the collectors were clear: the schooling system had always been privately funded—the British didn't come to India and supplant an effective state system of revenue collection that could have funded schooling.[13] Most of the collectors provided information on whether the funding had changed over the years. They reported— apparently from detailed investigations—that there were no records, verbal or written, of there having been any public funding in the past. A typical comment came from South Arcot, where the collector argued, "No allowance of any sort has *ever been* granted by the Native Governments to Schools, the Masters of which are entirely supported by the Parents of the Scholars."[14]

The conclusion is clear. The "deep-rooted and extensive" education system, catering to "all sections of society," uncovered by Munro's careful survey of the Madras Presidency of 1822, was a private education system. Indeed, when the Board of Revenue to the Chief Secretary to Government summarized all the evidence collected on February 21, 1825, to be given to the governor, Munro, the secretary agreed with this conclusion: "It will be observed that the schools now existing in the country are for the most part supported by the payments of the people who send their children to them for instruction. The rate of payment for each scholar varies in different districts and according to the different circumstances of the parents of the pupils."[15]

When Gandhi spoke at the Royal Institute of International Affairs in London on October 20, 1931, I could now see more clearly what was at stake. When he said that the British came to India and uprooted "the *beautiful tree*," he was referring to the beautiful tree of a private education system, serving the poor as well as the rich. Instead of embracing this indigenous private education system, the British rooted it out, and it perished. And this left India "more illiterate than it was fifty or a hundred years ago."[16]

I was truly astounded when I discovered this, from reading Dharampal and following up the original sources in the India Office Room of the British Library. Why wasn't this extraordinary fact more widely known? And why did people—well-meaning people who might have known better—persist in claiming that the British brought education to India, and it, at least, was a positive legacy of colonialism? Quite a lot of the blame could be laid at the door of Sir Philip Hartog, it would seem. My journey shifted across London's Bloomsbury district, from the British Library to the annals of the Institute of Education, where I found the Joseph Payne Lectures, delivered there by Sir Philip Hartog in 1935 and 1936, under the title "Some Aspects of Indian Education, Past and Present."

Enter Sir Philip Hartog

Not everyone was happy upon hearing Gandhi's version of events. In the audience was Sir Philip Hartog, a founder of the School of Oriental Studies, University of London, and former vice-chancellor of the University of Dacca, who was positively incensed about what he heard. He questioned Gandhi at the meeting itself, and, unsatisfied by the answers, entered into a long correspondence with him, culminating in an hourlong interview. Gandhi directed him to articles based on the findings noted above, from Bombay and Bengal (it would seem there were no parallel articles written about Munro's evidence from Madras). But Hartog wasn't convinced and repeatedly insisted that Gandhi publicly revoke his comments.

On his return to India in 1932, Gandhi was arrested and imprisoned. Meanwhile, Hartog set out to prove him wrong—still parrying Gandhi for answers, who, not surprisingly, politely wrote to inform "of his inability at that moment to satisfy him." Hartog's endeavors, however, resulted in his being invited to lecture at the Institute of Education, University of London, aiming to "remove, if possible, once and for all, the imaginary bases for assertions not infrequently made in India that the British Government systematically destroyed the indigenous system of elementary schools, and with it a literacy which the schools are presumed to have created."[17] It seems he was pretty successful at doing so.

Hartog disagreed about both the *quantity* of indigenous educational provision before the British and its *quality*. His disagreement about the quantity is relatively easy to dismiss. First, Hartog did not appear to dispute that there had been a spontaneous "mushrooming" of private schools in India before the British got involved. He concurred that "English-teaching schools, sprang up all over Bengal," prompted in part by ordinary people's desire to learn English and, hence, to enter British service. Moreover, he conceded that these schools had nothing to do with the British: the movement "received little encouragement or stimulus from Government," for at the time there was "no deep-seated desire of Great Britain to westernize Indian education." No instead, the growth of the schools *"was spontaneous and voluntary."*

But, whatever this agreement, he believed that the commentators, including Munro, exaggerated the extent of educational entrepreneurship in 19th-century India. In his lectures, Hartog was curt and dismissive about this evidence: "I have grave doubts as to the accuracy of these figures." But that's all he said to his audience about Munro's detailed survey. Those who wanted more detail were referred to a memorandum, published as an appendix to his book ("Note on the Statistics of Literacy and of Schools in India during the Last Hundred Years"). Reading this, I could see how completely off-target his criticisms of Munro were.

For Hartog cited the writings of only *one* of Munro's 21 British collectors to dismiss the findings of the entire group, that of a Mr. A. D. Campbell, collector from Bellary. Campbell, he noted, "gave figures for Bellary far below the average reported by Munro." If Munro's findings had been applicable to Bellary, he argued, then Campbell should have found twice as many scholars in schools. This is the proof that Hartog was looking for: "The contrast between the figures of Munro for Madras as a whole with those of Campbell for Bellary . . . suggests that Munro's figures may have been overestimates based on the returns of collectors less careful and interested in education than Campbell." Campbell supposedly showed that

Munro was wrong, because Campbell found only half the schools identified by other collectors and Campbell was purportedly the only conscientious collector.

But this conclusion seemed to me to be totally unsustainable, once the collectors' reports were examined in detail. To support his thesis that Campbell's report was the only one to be taken seriously, Hartog noted that the collector from Bellary was "singled out" by the Court of Directors of the East India Company as "the only one among the collectors who wrote '*concerning the quality of the instruction* given at the elementary schools.'" However, far from pointing to a strength, this actually pointed to what the Court saw as a major *weakness* with Campbell's evidence. For the collectors *weren't asked* by Munro for their subjective judgments about quality. Munro was after the facts, not opinion. It is true, Campbell thought that the quality of education could be improved, although he wasn't actually that damning; he wrote, "The chief defects in the native schools are the nature of the books, and learning taught and the want of competent master."[18] Hardly enough to support Hartog's assertion of the "miserably inefficient" indigenous schools. But as for the *quantity* of indigenous education, Campbell's evidence is the weakest of all the collectors'. Whereas other collectors gave pages and pages of detailed statistical tables broken down by districts and villages, by schools and colleges, and by sex and caste of the scholars, Campbell provided only *one* table, featuring *one line of data*. That's all.

It would seem much more appropriate to turn Hartog's comment on its head. It was *Campbell* who was careless and inattentive, not the other collectors. It's hard to concur with Hartog that Campbell's figures should be taken more seriously than, say, the collector for Trichinopoly, with his 10 pages of scrupulously prepared quantitative tables; or the collector for North Arcot, with his 14 pages of meticulous statistical detail. It is hard to see how Hartog could dismiss all this and rely instead on Campbell's one line of data. It is hard to resist the conclusion that Campbell's observations reinforced Hartog's prejudices, and *that's* why he went with what Campbell, rather than the other, more conscientious collectors, reported.

A more objective reading of the evidence was obvious: *because of his prejudices against what he thought was low-quality indigenous education,* Campbell didn't find—possibly didn't even look for—many of the schools that the other collectors *did* find. Campbell's behavior seems similar to the behavior of some of my own researchers, who didn't believe that unrecognized private schools existed or were worth finding if they did. My researchers sometimes returned saying there were no private schools in slums or villages. Accompanying these same researchers back to the same villages, they've been surprised at how many schools there actually were, if they had bothered to look for them carefully. My guess is that Campbell, or Campbell's teams, behaved similarly when faced with Munro's request. They didn't believe the schools existed in any great number or if they did, didn't believe they were worth bothering with, so they didn't go out to look, or at least not very carefully.

Hartog's objection to the Madras Presidency data on the quantity of provision was not well-founded. His similar criticisms of the data from Bengal, Bombay, and the Punjab could likewise be questioned. But could Hartog have been on stronger grounds about the *quality* of indigenous private educational provision?

Odd Bedfellows

Critics of Indian education brought together some odd bedfellows. Hartog's criticisms of the low quality of indigenous schools fit in with a prevalent set of criticisms about the low quality of Indian society and culture in general: William Wilberforce reported that Indians were "deeply sunk, and by their religious superstitions fast bound, in the lowest depths of moral and social wretchedness."[19] But it wasn't just British imperialists who shared such views. Karl Marx, writing in the *New York Daily Tribune* in 1853, opined about the perennial nature of Indian misery, concluding "whatever may have been the crimes of England," in India, "she was the unconscious tool of history" in bringing about "India's Westernisation," including through Western education.

But what does Munro's evidence say about the quality of indigenous educational provision? When establishing the terms of reference for his research, judgments concerning the quality of education were not something that Munro asked his collectors to report on— he wanted the facts, not opinions. So it is not negligence that led 14 of the 20 collectors whose evidence is usable to give no subjective comments about quality at all. However, six collectors did add brief subjective comments about this matter. Of them, *three* were *positive* in their comments about both quantity *and* quality of the indigenous system: a typical one noted, "Children are sent to school when they are about five years old and their continuance in it depends in a great measure on their mental faculties, but it is generally admitted that before they attain their thirteenth year of Age, *their acquirement in the various branches of Learning are uncommonly great.*"[20]

Three collectors noted some problems with quality, although one was disappointed that "nothing more is professed to be taught in these day-schools than reading, writing and arithmetic, just competent for the discharge of the common daily transactions of Society"[21]—which, instead of a criticism, could sound like an acknowledgment of what primary school education should realistically aim for.

The other two collectors were more critical, however. One wrote: "For the most part . . . attendance is very irregular. Few of the school masters are acquainted with the grammar of the language which they profess to teach, and neither the master nor scholars understand the meaning of the sentences which they repeat. . . . Education cannot well, in a civilised state, be on a lower scale than it is."[22] And then there is collector A. D. Campbell, from Bellary, who wrote the brief comments quoted earlier.

Given this, we can't make too much of the evidence of the Madras Presidency survey, either way. Those who write about the deficiencies of the system are equally balanced by those who write about its effectiveness. Both sets may have been influenced by their own prejudices and predilections about what schooling should be like. But certainly there is nothing in the presidency survey to support claims about poor quality.

However, when summarizing the submitted evidence in his March 10, 1826, minute, although sanguine about the *quantity* of schooling, Munro was not quite so upbeat about its quality. I looked in detail at his and others' major criticisms—particularly those of Sir Philip Hartog in his damning presentation of the low quality of indigenous education. It was quite uncanny to me the way they paralleled the criticisms made today about private schools for the poor. And the ways in which the government intervened to try to solve these "problems" actually seemed to point to the strengths of the indigenous system, rather than its weaknesses. Again, the parallels with the way government and international agency solutions work today seemed quite remarkable. Have we learned so little?

Low-Paid Teachers?

Munro's only substantive criticism of the quality of indigenous education focused on teachers being underpaid—an exact parallel to the development experts' criticisms of private schools for the poor today. He wrote that teachers "do not earn more than six or seven rupees monthly, which is not an allowance sufficient to induce men properly qualified to follow the profession."[23] The same criticism emerged from William Adam's survey in Bengal, whose disparaging assessment of the quality of indigenous education was used to good effect by Hartog (although Hartog did not endorse Adam's very upbeat assessment of the *quantity* of provision). Adam reported that the benefits of the burgeoning private schools in Bengal "are but small, owing partly to the incompetency of the instructors. . . . The teachers depend entirely upon their scholars for subsistence, and being little respected and poorly rewarded, there is no encouragement for persons of character, talent or learning to engage in the occupation."[24]

Interestingly, Adam conceded a very important point. Teachers' pay, which he considered inadequate, was not low "in comparison with their qualifications, or with the general rates of similar labour in the district." No, for Adam it was low compared "with those emoluments to which competent men might be justly considered entitled."[25] In other words, teachers' pay seemed in line with the market rate, but was low compared with some alternative system to which Adam aspired. This is something I'll return to in a moment.

Low-Quality Buildings?

Another of the criticisms, raised in particular by William Adam, was of the quality of the school buildings, or the total lack thereof: "There are no school-houses built for, and exclusively appropriated to, these schools." Scholars, he observed, met in places of religious worship, or festivals, or village recreation places, or private dwellings, or in the open air, with a "small shed of grass and leaves" erected in the rainy season.[26] This was not good, he noted, pointing to the "disadvantages arising from the want of school-houses and from the confined and inappropriate construction of the buildings or apartments used as school-rooms."[27] Here we have in embryonic form the criticism that would lead, in Gandhi's view, to the promotion of a system that was not based on what could be afforded or efficiently used, but to something imposed from outside that was too expensive to be practical. Instead of a criticism, such comments about the lack of buildings could be used, as Dharampal does, to suggest that the "conditions under which teaching took place in the Indian schools were less dingy and more natural" than in Britain.[28] Again, the parallels with the obsessions of development experts to provide public school buildings that wouldn't be out of place in the West, and their criticisms of present-day private schools for their inadequate infrastructure, jumped out at me.

Low-Quality Teaching Methods?

Perhaps the most revealing of all of the criticisms is of the teaching methods found in the village schools. Adam began his criticism thus: "Poverty still more than ignorance leads to the adoption of modes of instruction and economical arrangements which, under more favourable circumstances, would be readily abandoned."[29] Curiously, the potential strengths of these very same teaching methods are then elaborated at length: Scholars, Adam wrote, are taught effectively to read and write, to learn by rote tables up to 20, and to do commercial and agricultural accounts. Indeed, regarding the method of teaching reading, he says that it is superior to the methods of teaching reading back in Scotland!: "In the matter of instruction there are some grounds for *commendation* for the course I have described has a direct practical tendency . . . well adapted to qualify the scholar for engaging in the actual business of native society. My recollections of the village schools of Scotland do not enable me to pronounce that the instructions given in them has a more direct bearing upon the daily interests of life than that which I find given . . . in the humbler village schools of Bengal." So what was offered was better than that in Scotland for equipping young people with the skills and knowledge needed for everyday life. That seemed an odd basis for criticism to me.

Other British observers, however, were entirely positive about these "economical" teaching methods: A report from the Bombay Presidency in the 1820s held that "young natives are taught reading, writing and arithmetic, upon a system so economical . . . and at the same time so simple and effectual, that there is hardly a cultivator or petty dealer who is not competent to keep his own accounts with a degree of accuracy, in my opinion, *beyond* what we meet with

among the lower orders in our own country; whilst the more splen-
did dealers and bankers keep their books with a degree of ease,
conciseness, and clearness I rather think fully equal to those of any
British merchants."[30]

And, indeed, the supposedly critical Campbell, collector for Bellary, himself seemed to approve of the teaching methods. (He was
also appreciative of the rather stern disciplinary methods in the
village schools: "The idle scholar is flogged, and often suspended
by both hands, and a Pulley, to the roof, or obliged to kneel down
and rise incessantly, which is a most painful and fatiguing, but
perhaps a healthy mode of punishment."[31]) Campbell provided quite a
bit of detail, ending with the following *commendation:* "The economy
with which children are taught to write in the native schools, and
the system by which the more advanced scholars are caused to
teach the less advanced, and at the same time to confirm their own
knowledge is certainly admirable, *and well deserved the imitation it
has received in England.*" What's this? The "economical" teaching
method in the indigenous Indian schools was so much to be praised
that *it had been imitated in England*?

What was this teaching method? And how had it been "imitated"
in England? This seemed to be another very exciting avenue of
exploration opening up to me. Collector Campbell had given a very
thorough description of the method itself: "When the whole are
assembled, the scholars according to their numbers and attainments,
are divided into several classes. The lower ones of which are placed
partly under the care of monitors, whilst the higher ones are more
immediately under the superintendence of the Master, who at the
same time has his eye upon the whole schools. The number of classes
is generally four; and a scholar rises from one to the other, according
to his capacity and progress."

What Campbell was describing is a peer-learning process combined with flexible performance-based grouping of students. The
teacher instructs the brighter or older children, who then convey
the lesson to their younger or less accomplished peers, so that all
are taught. Campbell saw this method in action in Bellary, near
the border between present-day Karnataka and Andhra Pradesh.
Precisely the same method is described for the Malabar Coast—that
part of India stretching from Goa down to its southernmost tip—
by Peter Della Valle *in 1623*, some 200 years earlier! The explorer

wrote how he "entertained himself in the porch of the Temple, beholding little boys learning arithmetic after a strange manner." The method used a combination of four children gathered together "singing musically" to help them remember their lessons, and writing number bonds in the sand, "not to spend paper in vain . . . the pavement being for that purpose strewed all over with fine sand."

In the same way, they were taught reading and writing. Peter Della Valle asked them, "If they happen to forget or be mistaken in any part of the lesson, who corrected them and taught them?" They said they all taught each other, "without the assistance of any Master." For, "*it was not possible for all four to forget or mistake in the same part, and that they thus exercised together, to the end, that if one happened to be out, the other might correct him.*" It was, wrote the explorer, "indeed a pretty, easy and secure way of learning."[32]

The Madras Method

But how did it come to be imitated in England? Dharampal gave a small hint in *The Beautiful Tree* that it had something to do with a Rev. Dr. Andrew Bell. I ordered his books and his biography from the British Library collection at Boston Spa. The beautiful slim, bound folios that arrived carried the exuberant titles so beloved by Regency period writers: his first book was entitled *An Experiment in Education, made at the Male Asylum at Madras; suggesting a System, by which a School or Family may teach itself, under the Superintendence of the Master or Parent.* The title to his magnum opus of 1823 was even more impressive: *Mutual Tuition and Moral Discipline; or Manual of Instructions for Conducting Schools Through the Agency of the Scholars Themselves, For the Use of Schools and Families, with an introductory essay on the object and importance of the Madras System of Education; a brief exposition of the principle on which it is founded; and a historical sketch of its rise, progress, and results.*

Bell's biographer, however, went for the less flamboyant: *An Old Educational Reformer: Dr Andrew Bell.* It's a curiously unfavorable biography, written by an author who oddly had little sympathy for his subject. The first page begins, "Andrew Bell was born in the city of St Andrews on the 27th of March 1753." And that is the last we hear of Bell until page 6, when it is noted, "It is to golf that Andrew Bell most probably owes his moral education." But this is the prelude to pages and pages about the virtues of the golf course at St. Andrew's, not to Andrew Bell's moral education. And it's not very flattering about the poor reverend doctor either: "The fact is, that Dr Bell wrote in a terribly lumbering and painful style, and *no one now can read his books*; but then no one can speak for another as well as the man himself—however clumsily and stupidly he may speak." Or again: "Dr Bell was, at no time of his life, a clear or methodical writer. He said the same thing—*he had only one or two ideas altogether in his head*—over and over again in different ways, in long lumbering sentences, and with a ponderosity of manner that repelled and disenchanted."[33]

I found *I* could read his books. And his "one or two ideas" seemed like dynamite to me. For they vividly showed how the "economical" method of teaching in the private schools for the poor in India became translated into a method that transformed education in Victorian England and beyond. And this borrowing from Indian education struck me as something that could also be relevant to England today.

Dr. Bell had arrived in India in 1787 to take up position as the principal of a school, the Military Male Orphan Asylum, in Fort St. George, now Chennai (previously Madras), to teach the abandoned progeny of British soldiers and native women.[34] He found that the (expatriate) teachers in the asylum "had no knowledge of their duties, and no very great love for them." But then he had his moment of insight: "One morning, in the course of his early ride along the surf-beaten shore of Madras, he happened to pass a . . . school, which, as usual with Indian schools, was held in the open air. He saw the little children writing with their fingers on sand, which, after the fashion of such schools, had been strewn before them for that purpose." He also saw them peer teaching, children learning from one another rather than from their masters. "He turned his horse, galloped home, shouting, 'Heureka! Heureka!' and now believed that he . . . saw his way straight before him."[35]

Bell first tried an experiment. He got one of the older boys who knew his alphabet to teach one of the classes that "the master had pronounced impossible" to teach. But this boy managed to teach the class "with ease." Bell appointed him the class's teacher. "The success exceeded expectation. This class, which had been before worse, was now better taught, than any other in the school." He tried it in other classes, and it worked again. So Bell sacked all his teachers, and the school *"was entirely taught by the boys"* under his supervision.[36]

Bell returned to London in 1797 and published the description of his "Madras Method." Following that, he was in great demand to introduce the system in British schools. First was St. Botolph's, Aldgate in East London, followed swiftly by schools in the north of England. The method was adopted by the new National Society for the Education of the Poor in 1811. By 1821, 300,000 children were being educated under Bell's principles. As it became widely emulated, Bell was asked to write an extended outline of the system, which he published in 1823. His ideas were adopted around Europe, and as far away as the West Indies and Bogotá, Colombia; the educational reformer Pestalozzi was apparently even using the Madras Method.

And Joseph Lancaster, who created the famed Lancastrian schools across Britain—and with whom Bell was to have a furious dispute about who really invented the system—introduced peer learning in his first London school, in Borough Road, in 1801. The system transformed education in the Western world and was arguably the basis by which mass literacy in Britain was achieved. But in its fundamental, "economical" principles, it wasn't invented by either Bell or Lancaster. It was based precisely on what the Rev. Dr. Andrew Bell had observed in India.

Far from being a weakness of the indigenous (private) education system, the cost-effective teaching methods used in the indigenous private schools of 19th-century India were in fact a manifest strength; so much so, as the supposedly critical Campbell noted, they were imitated in Britain, then across Europe and the world, and did so much to raise educational standards.

The Strengths of the Indigenous System

None of the key "problems" with the quality of the indigenous private education system appeared substantial. However, Munro instituted reforms in Madras, with similar reforms copied in the Bengal and Bombay presidencies, to overcome these supposed "problems."' But the way these reforms were instituted does much to show the *strengths* of the indigenous system, rather than its purported weakness. The way the solutions brought their own problems again eerily resonates with what is happening in developing countries today. Again, it didn't seem as though we'd learned much from history.

Munro recommended several reforms. To the problem of the inadequate number of schools—for they didn't reach every child, only as many as in other European countries—he proposed "the endowment of schools throughout the country by Government."[37] That is, creating new state schools. Doing so would also begin to solve the problem of inadequate school buildings, as they would each be in its own modern purpose-built settings, properly funded. The "problem" of inadequate teaching methods would be met with the provision of enough teachers to get rid of the (as it turns out, even by contemporaneous observers, highly effective) pupil-teacher system. And to the major problem that bothered all the critics, the inadequacy of teachers' pay, Munro proposed paying salaries of 9 rupees per month in the village schools to 15 rupees per month in the towns, out of government coffers: "These allowances may appear small," he noted (in fact, they are considerably higher than the contemporaneous salaries), but, supplemented by fees from students, the schoolteachers' situation "will probably be better than that of a parish schoolmaster in Scotland." Quite why this was deemed necessary for poor India was not explained.

Furthermore, he proposed creating a teacher-training college, and to ensure quality, a new Committee of Public Instruction would oversee "the establishing of the public schools" and would fix the curriculum and teaching methods to be used in them.

Finally appointed on June 1, 1826, the Committee of Public Instruction included one A. D. Campbell, the erstwhile Bellary district collector, whose criticisms of the indigenous system had clearly done him no harm. By 1830, however, only 84 schools had been established—14 in the towns and 70 in the villages. These must be contrasted with the 11,575 schools provided by the indigenous system, as reported by Munro. And only four years later, the Committee of Public Instruction was receiving complaints about the system's inadequacies. By 1835, it was recommended that the new schools be abolished, something that was effected in 1836. At the same time, the Committee of Public Instruction was replaced by the Committee for Native Education. In just a decade, Munro's reforms had failed.

The reasons for the failure are edifying—suggesting that the kind of state system being imposed was inferior to the indigenous system that it was brought in to replace. Five reasons for the failure stood out for me.

First, it became apparent that the hoped-for improvement in the quality of teachers, by training them through the expensive teacher-training school and paying them much higher wages, failed. Contrary to what Munro and others had supposed, there simply wasn't a large group of better-educated people willing to become school-masters in the poor villages, whatever the pay. According to statements submitted to the Committee of Public Instruction, the village schools "were rather prematurely introduced before a proper class of teachers for them had been available."[38] Just as in the private schools for the poor today in India and elsewhere, the level of teachers' pay in the indigenous schools reflected teacher availability. The low wages were, if this observation is correct, not low at all, but simply reflected the market rate.

Second, in the new government-funded schools, it soon became apparent that political patronage, not teaching commitment and skill, influenced the way teaching appointments were made. The Committee of Public Instruction heard that "personal or local influence would necessarily often supersede individual qualification or merit under such a mode of election." Now the collectors were reporting that the new state teachers were "inferior on the whole to the common village school masters, and, in general, ignorant also." In other words, the good pay and job security made the positions attractive—not to those who wanted to teach, but to those who could be bought for political patronage. An exactly parallel criticism is raised today of teachers paid by the state, in India and elsewhere.

Third, completely against the committee's explicit intentions, the new schools were excluding everyone apart from the elite, the Brahmins. Why? One source suggested that the government "was uneasy about low-caste people being admitted to the ... Schools. It was feared that, if they were encouraged, the upper classes would show resentment and withdraw their support." So the new public schools became a vehicle to promote caste privilege, rather than a vehicle for improvement of all. Again, it would seem that the indigenous system had unnoticed strengths in promoting education of all, including the lowest castes.

Fourth, one of the great problems reported to the committee was the lack of efficient supervision. *The new state schools became accountable to no one.* The collectors, who should have been supervising them, were reportedly too busy with other business. One collector's assessment is stark: he "doubted the efficiency of the schools which in effect were in no way superior to the already existing private schools." Munro had taken for granted that the success of his public schools could be guaranteed—after all, they would be better funded and equipped than the indigenous private schools. He didn't take into account the problem of supervision and accountability. What he failed to consider was the way that indigenous village schools were already accountable, but not to any central administration. He had failed to note the missing ingredient of accountability in the private system, the same one that so perplexes educational reformers to this day.

Fifth, the new schools were designed to be much larger than the small, "inefficient" private schools—they had to be large because teachers were paid much more, and so economies of scale were required to make them viable. But parents didn't like their size. One collector observed that parents "complained of too great a number of students for the teacher to give proper attention. Hence parents wished to send their children to schools with fewer number [*sic*]. There were 150 private schools in the District." In other words, it was an overlooked hidden strength of the indigenous system that it reflected parental desires for small schools and small classes. The indigenous system had organically evolved to reflect parental choice; the imposed system did not. And because the new schools were designed to be larger, so (theoretically) more efficient, there couldn't possibly be one in every village. One collector reported that "the Schools were very remote from each other," which was a problem for inspection (the collector's concern), but obviously for parents too—the schools were too inaccessible to their children. This conjecture is supported by evidence from elsewhere: "Schools in the district were not in a flourishing condition. Children were unable to attend from a distance." Again, it seems a strength of the indigenous system that schools' small size—based on the reality of low teacher pay—reflected what parents wanted, namely, a school in their own village, not one to which their children had to commute a long distance. Again, we see parallels with what private schools for the poor are providing today, in contrast to what public schools are providing. Then as now, parents preferred small schools close to their homes, not large remote schools designed for the convenience of bureaucrats.

Enter Macaulay

It seemed that there was one final possible criticism of the indigenous private education system. Its quality, whatever its critics claimed, was not suspect—in fact, villagers created schools that adequately reflected the conditions of the villages and used what was available in an economical and efficient manner, so much so, that their successful methods influenced the way education was delivered in Britain and around the world. But it is true, the schools didn't reach *everyone*. While they may have reached as many children as were reached in European countries, including England, and reached children of all castes, coverage was certainly not universal. Could it be that the British style of intervention of publicly funded and provided education was the only way that *universal education* could be achieved?

This counterfactual question of course cannot be answered definitively. But there are interesting indicators as to what the answer might be. For we can see what growth was brought in by the system the British did impose, with its new public schools. And we can look at what happened in England during the same period to gauge what might have happened if the British had not imposed their system in India.

Because of the lack of success of Munro's reforms, a new approach, with a new style of reformer, was introduced. Enter Thomas Babington Macaulay (1800–1859), the British poet, historian, and Whig. Between 1834 and 1838, he took up residence in Calcutta, serving as president of the General Committee of Public Instruction for the British presidency. Everyone in India knows his name. For it is to him more than any other that we owe the public schooling system that still prevails in India today.

Macaulay's famous minute of February 2, 1835, set the seal on a different kind of state intervention in education.[39] He was totally dismissive of Indian indigenous scholarship: "It is, I believe, no exaggeration to say, that all the historical information which has been collected in all the books written in the Sanscrit [*sic*] language is less valuable than what may be found in the most paltry abridgements used at preparatory schools in England." Indian history abounded "with kings thirty feet high, and reigns thirty thousand years long." Indian astronomy "would move laughter in girls at an English boarding school." Indian geography was "made up of seas of treacle and seas of butter." And he totally ignored any contribution that the indigenous private schools might be making to education in India. Instead, he opined, "The great object of the British Government ought to be the promotion of European literature and science among the natives of India, and that all the funds appropriated for the purposes of education would be best employed on English education alone."

Macaulay laid the foundations for the public education system that is still in place in India today—with similar state systems in place across the developing world where the British had influence. He proposed a new centralized system of education, with publicly funded universities in the presidency towns, publicly funded teacher-training institutions, public funds to maintain existing colleges and high schools, establishment of new public middle schools, and the introduction of grants-in-aid to bring some private schools under government control. It set out completely to supersede any existing indigenous provision.

How did it work in practice? Under Macaulay's system, the first publicly funded village school was set up in April 1854; by October, there were 54. Even then, some villagers were reluctant to send their children to the new state schools: "The village priests foreboded evil, and their representatives produced an undefined feeling of dread in the minds of the most indifferent and ignorant people of the lower orders."[40] Possibly from what we saw concerning the Munro schools, this sense of foreboding was justified.

By 1858, this new system had delivered 452 schools and colleges with a total enrollment of 20,874 in the 21 districts of the Madras Presidency. But 36 years earlier, Munro had found a total of 11,575 schools and 1,094 colleges, with 157,195 and 5,431 students, respectively! That is, the new system had led to a huge decline in provision (see Table 4). Now it may be that, just as today, the new inspectors were simply disregarding, either through ignorance or because they weren't considered appropriate, the indigenous private schools in

Table 4.
GROWTH IN SCHOOLING, MADRAS PRESIDENCY, 1822–1900

Year(s)	Population	Number of scholars	% of scholars to population	Number of scholars as % of those in 1822
1822–1825	12,850,941	162,626	1.27	100
1858		20,874		13
1879–1880	31,308,872	268,379	0.86	165
1884–1885	30,868,504	430,851	1.40	265
1895–1896	35,641,828	791,634	2.22	487
1899–1900		862,991		531

SOURCE: Y. Vittal Rao, *Education and Learning in Andhra under the East India Company* (Secunderabad: N. Vidyaranya Swamy, 1979), p. 68.

the villages. In any case, the official figures were certainly nothing to boast about.

By 1879, the official figures had recovered somewhat, but still showed a significantly lower percentage of the population in school than had been found in 1822–1825. Only six years later, in 1885, do we see the figure reaching what it had been *over 60 years before*. And it continued to grow thereafter. So did British education—Macaulay's education—increase the percentage of the population in school? Well, yes, it did, at least it did 60 years later. But should this be a cause of satisfaction and celebration of Macaulay's intervention? The answer to that depends on the crucial question: what would have happened to the numbers in the indigenous system had the British *not* intervened?

The Galloping Horses

There are some indications as to what the answer might be—by looking not to India but to what happened in England itself during that period. My journey here took me to the E. G. West Archives at Newcastle University. The late Professor E. G. West had made his name by suggesting that universal primary education was achieved in the West not through public intervention, as was commonly supposed, but predominantly through private provision. His seminal book *Education and the State* points to a situation that was peculiarly similar to that which we've explored in India before the British took control of education. Before the state got involved, West's research shows that the vast majority of provision was private—by small-scale entrepreneurs (e.g., "dame" schools), churches, and philanthropy. The state intervened with small subsidies to a tiny minority of schools from 1833, but major state involvement came only in 1870. Long before this, in writing that echoed what the British collectors observed in India only a decade later, James Mill, father of John Stuart Mill, wrote in the October 1813 *Edinburgh Review*: "From observation and inquiry . . . we can ourselves speak decidedly as to the rapid progress which the love of education is making among the lower orders in England. Even around London, in a circle of fifty miles radius, which is far from the most instructed and virtuous part of the kingdom, there is hardly a village that has not something of a school; and not many children of either sex who are not taught more or less, reading and writing."[41]

How were such schools funded? Predominantly, it turns out, through school fees. These were very much private schools for the poor, in Victorian England. Mill noted: "We have met with families in which, for weeks together, not an article of sustenance but potatoes had been used; yet for every child the hard-earned sum was provided to send them to school." But we don't have to be satisfied with Mill's anecdotes. Using official census data and reports, West was able to show that, by 1851, there were 2,144,278 children in day schools, of which over 85 percent were in purely private schools, that is, as the census put it, "schools which derive their income solely from (fee) payments or which are maintained with a view to pecuniary advantage" (see Table 5). The remaining 15 percent were subsidized by government, but only to a minuscule extent. And the "mammoth report" of the Newcastle Commission on Popular Education, convened in 1858 and reporting in 1861, estimated that about 95 percent of children were in school for an average of nearly six years. And it was clear where the funding for this schooling came from: even in the minority of schools that received some state funding, two-thirds of the funding came from nonstate sources, including parents' contributions to fees, and church and philanthropic funds. Even here, parents provided *most* of the school fees.

For England and Wales, E. G. West memorably remarked, "When the government made its debut in education in 1833 mainly in the role of subsidiser it was as if it jumped into the saddle of a horse

Table 5.
GROWTH IN SCHOOLING, ENGLAND, 1815–1858

Date	Population	Number of day scholars	% of scholars to population	Number of day scholars as % of those in 1818
1818	11,642,683	674,883	5.80	100
1833	14,386,415	1,276,947	8.88	189
1851	17,927,609	2,144,378	11.96	318
1858	19,523,103	2,535,462	12.99	376

SOURCE: E. G. West, *Education and the State*, 3rd ed. (Indianapolis: Liberty Fund, 1994), p. 187.

that was already galloping." Without government, he suggests, the "horses" (private schools) would have continued to gallop.

For our purposes, what is important to grasp is the huge growth of *private* school enrollment in England, before the state got involved. In the 40 years from 1818 to 1858, enrollment in private schools in England had grown by 318 percent. But in the *60 years* from 1825 to 1885, half of which was taken up with Macaulay's new state system, enrollment in schools in the Madras Presidency increased by less than this, 265 percent. That is, growth was slower in school enrollment under the new British system in India than the equivalent growth in private schools in England. Or to put it another way, suppose that school enrollment in the Madras Presidency had grown at the same rate as in England in an equivalent period. In the 40 years from 1825 to 1865, this would have led to the school population in Madras rising from 162,626 (as found by Munro) to 517,151. But this school population wasn't reached even by 1885 under Macaulay's system, some 20 years later, and was only to be exceeded by 1896, some 71 years later! If the dynamics of the Indian private education system had been anything like those of the parallel system in England, we would have seen a much larger growth in enrollment than had the British not intervened at all.

An Unexpected Ally

Far from bringing education to India, as the British congratulated themselves on doing, they instead crowded out the already-flourishing private education system. The critics of the Indian indigenous education system seem wrong on every count. There is no substantial evidence that it was of low quality—indeed, the opposite seems to be true, that it had found an organic and economical way of educating the population that was good enough in its major principles to be exported, via England, to the rest of the world. It had intrinsic strengths that the British system ignored at its peril, in particular concerning the market rate for teachers and the accountability that came with parents' paying fees.

But the British saw the village schools, and deemed them, as Gandhi put it, "not good enough." No, the British insisted that "every school must have so much paraphernalia, building, and so forth. . . ." So they established the new, centralized state system emanating from Macaulay. And this is the type of system that is the norm in developing countries today. But this system was simply "too expensive for the people." As Gandhi wrote, "This very poor country of mine is ill able to sustain such an expensive method of education."[42] It hasn't led to universal public education even now. In India today, there are still millions of children out of school. Would the indigenous private education system have been better? Based on my own and others' recent research, there is every reason to suppose that the system that depended on parental fees would have been able to expand to cater the increased demand, particularly as the wealth of the people increased.

I bring us back to Gandhi's quote at the beginning of this chapter: "Our state would revive the old village schoolmaster and dot every village with a school both for boys and girls." What I see this means now is that, when Gandhi said that he wished to return to the *status quo ante*, he was saying he wanted to return to a system of *private schools for the poor, funded in the main by fees and a little philanthropy.* Not only has my journey into Indian history provided unexpected evidence of private education for the poor in India before the British took over, it has also provided me with an even more unexpected ally.

The Modern Macaulays

Development experts today, academics, aid agency officials, and the pop stars and actors who encourage them are modern-day Macaulays. They are well intentioned, as was Macaulay. They believe in the fundamental importance of education, as did Macaulay. But they believe that the poor need their help educationally, and can't be trusted to do anything on their own, as did Macaulay. And just as Macaulay denied the significance of indigenous Indian education in the 19th century, during his lifetime apparently failing to take note of what his contemporaries had observed, so too do the Modern Macaulays fall into denial about what the poor are already doing for themselves. Macaulay thought that only one system could help those in India, the model that suited the British upper classes. The Modern Macaulays think the same, only the publicly funded and provided systems that serve Britain and America are good enough for the poor. My journeys—across Africa and India, and into history—lead me to believe that they are as mistaken today as Macaulay was then.

Not Just in India

I've looked at India in some detail. But I could instead have turned to China and found a vibrant private education system dating back to Confucius and before. During the Spring and Autumn and Warring States Periods (770–221 B.C.), when war led to the collapse of officially sponsored schools, the first private schools were launched by fugitive officials, among whom was Confucius. Perhaps the earliest private school was run by Deng Xi, a former senior official in the state of Zheng, who taught students how to engage in the practice of law with his book *Zhu Xing* ("Laws on Bamboo Slips"). And private education flourished, supplemented by the mission schools, well into the 20th century, serving all classes of people, until they were dramatically "crowded out" by Chairman Mao's instruction of June 14, 1952, to nationalize all private schools.[43]

Or I could have turned to Kenya, or elsewhere in Africa—where the lessons to be learned again have extraordinary resonance today. It's true, the Africans didn't have *schools* before the British came, unlike the Indians. But that doesn't mean they didn't educate their children—it's a peculiarly modern and unhelpful mistake to conflate education with schooling. Anthropological studies point to the ways in which children were educated in traditional African society, in their family and kinship groups. Jomo Kenyatta, who was to become the first president of independent Kenya, studied at the London School of Economics under renowned anthropologist Bronislaw Malinowski. In 1938, he published *Facing Mount Kenya*, which described traditional Kikuyu society and criticized some of the disruptive changes brought about by colonialism. Kenyatta was at pains to stress, contrary to what the colonialists were claiming, that African society had its own tradition of universal education that "begins at the time of birth and ends with death. The parents take the responsibility of educating their children until they reach the stage of tribal education. . . . There is no special school building . . . the homestead is the school."[44]

Kenyatta believed that this education system had some advantages over what the British were imposing. It emphasized acquiring practical knowledge in its context, using what he called "the indirect method," where "instruction is given, as it were, incidentally, as a mere accompaniment to some activity," which he believed was superior to the rote-learning methods, removed from reality to the classroom, that the British were imposing. Furthermore, traditional education gave primacy of place "to personal relations," which was far removed from what he saw in British education. In short, he suggested that there was a *fitness of purpose* in traditional education, which "may not have some valuable suggestions to offer or advice to give to the European whose assumed task it is in these days to provide Western Education for the African."

It had a fitness for purpose when it came to traditional African society, but perhaps it wasn't suitable for a modern society like the one Kenya was to become? Perhaps this is true—and perhaps Kenyatta came to realize it on his return to Kenya. But it's particularly interesting to note that the system the British sought to impose on the Africans in Kenya was strongly resisted and the resistance took the form of *creating private schools*.

The European model of schooling was introduced in Kenya toward the end of the 19th century when the Christian Missionary Society opened the first school near Mombassa in 1846. In response to increasing demand for education, the colonial authorities established a Department of Education in 1911. Missionary societies were given government grants to help fund the building of new schools. However, they wanted to give academic education only to European and Asian children—African children were to receive only industrial and agricultural training. Christian teachings became compulsory and African customs and traditions were played down, or banned altogether from the publicly funded schools. African children were also barred from learning English until the last year of primary school.

Suspicious of the aims and motivations of the state, in 1929, the Kikuyu in Central Province began to boycott mission schools and demanded an end to the missions' monopoly on education. After failing to persuade the government to open its own secular schools free from missionary control, the Kikuyu *began to open their own*. During the early 1930s, extensive fund-raising activities took place, private schools were erected, and self-help groups formed. Each private school was governed by a local committee, responsible for recruiting and paying teachers, setting school fees, and conducting other fund-raising events. As private schools became established, joint meetings were organized, culminating in the founding of the Kikuyu Independent Schools Association in August 1934. While KISA emphasized the need to negotiate with the colonial authorities, some school proprietors wanted to remain entirely free from European influence. A rival association, the Kikuyu Karing'a Education Association, was therefore established soon after. By 1939, there were 63 independent Kikuyu schools educating a total of 12,964 pupils.

To help meet the increasing demand for trained teachers, in 1939 both KISA and KKEA agreed to support the opening of a private teacher-training college, Kenya's first ever, public or private, at Githunguri. When Jomo Kenyatta returned to Kenya in September 1946, he was appointed principal of Githunguri, before being elected president of the Kenyan African Union. Over the next five years, Kenyatta would divide his time between these two organizations. Under his leadership, Githunguri would become the private school movement's unofficial headquarters, and KAU would of course develop into the political party that would eventually lead Kenya to independence.

It is interesting to contrast the successful rise of Kenya's independent school movement with comments such as those expressed by the British provisional commissioner for Kikuyu Province in 1929: "It is indisputable that the Kikuyu people, in their present stage of development, are incapable of organising, financing, and running efficient schools without European supervision."[45] On the contrary, the Africans were capable of financing and operating their own schools without government support, and did so well into the first half of the 20th century.

The rest is history. A police investigation of the Mau Mau Uprising early in 1952 sealed the fate of the private schools. When the government declared a state of emergency later that year, both KISA and KKEA schools were closed. In Kenya's struggle against colonial oppression, private schools became the battleground. On becoming president of Kenya in 1964, Jomo Kenyatta championed the *Harambee,* or "self-help" spirit, on which he believed the future development of Kenya would depend. It is clear that at least part of his inspiration for this movement came from his experiences in private education. Private schools were an integral part of the African liberation movement against the British. Perhaps today we can see the emerging private schools as a new liberation movement against the legacy that the British (and other colonial powers) brought to their countries?

Forgotten Lessons

History's lessons can guide us today. The World Bank argues that a country's history has "a bearing on which service delivery arrangements are likely to succeed."[46] My historical journey made me realize that private education has been a norm in many countries, before the Western powers imposed their own systems, and even a part of the liberation struggle against these imposed systems. What was it that Bob Geldof said? That development can succeed when people ignore "the advice of 'the experts,' to find 'their own *culturally appropriate* model.'" Perhaps the vital lesson of history is that a centralized public education system is not the culturally appropriate model for peoples in Asia and sub-Saharan Africa today. In championing private education for the poor, we may well be championing a return to the cultural roots of the people.

12. Educating Amaretch

Easterly's Dilemma

William Easterly begins and ends his latest book, *The White Man's Burden,* with the heart-rending story of 10-year-old Amaretch, an Ethiopian girl whose name means "beautiful one": "Driving out of Addis Ababa," he passes an "endless line of women and girls . . . marching . . . into the city."[1] Amaretch's day is spent collecting eucalyptus branches to sell for a pittance in the city market. But she would prefer to go to school if only her parents could afford to send her. Easterly dedicates the book to her, "and to the millions of children like her." He returns to Amaretch in his concluding sentence: "Could one of you Searchers"—the word he uses to define entrepreneurs of all kinds—"discover a way to put a firewood-laden Ethiopian preteen girl named Amaretch in school?"

The Searchers I've encountered on my journey—the educational entrepreneurs who've set up private schools in places not unlike where Amaretch finds herself—are already finding the way. The accepted wisdom—what everyone knows—is that children like Amaretch need billions more dollars in donor aid to public education before they can gain an education. And the poor must be patient. Although public education is "appalling," "abysmal," "a moral outrage," "a gross violation of human rights"—all epithets commonly used to describe the "government failure" of public education— there is no alternative. The poor must wait until the Modern Macaulays sort it all out for them. It'll take time, but it's the only way. There is no silver bullet.

Behind the scenes, unassisted by donor involvement or government intervention, the poor have found a silver bullet, or at least the makings of one. The route to the holy grail of the development experts—quality education for all—is there for all to see, if only they'll look. By themselves, the poor have found their own viable alternative. The solution is easy: send your children to a private school that is accountable to you because you're paying fees. Perhaps it's all too easy a solution for the development experts (even taking into account some remaining complexities—such as how literally *everyone* can access private education, of a desired *quality*—which I'll come to in a moment). The poor *just did it.*

Sometimes it seems to me, as I reflect on all I've seen on my travels, that what the poor *just did* is invisible to those with power and influence—the development experts, as I've called them throughout this book. Is it invisible because it arose out of the myriad decisions of individuals, rather than through any grand development plan? Individual entrepreneurs, like Reshma and Anwar in the poor areas of Hyderabad, India, or BSE in Makoko, Nigeria, or Theophilus in Bortianor, Ghana, or Xing, in the remote Gansu mountains of China, or Jane in the slums of Nairobi, Kenya, all recognized the desire of poor parents *like them* to have a decent education, saw the problems of public education, and decided that the best way forward might be to start a school. They took a risk, started small, scoured around for teachers and buildings, experimented with what worked, found that parents liked what they were doing—or changed things around until parents did—and their schools grew and grew. Others saw what they were doing and thought it seemed a neat way to help their community and make a little money as well—sometimes conversely. And individual parents—like Victoria's fisherman father and fishmonger mother—anxiously aware that not all was well for their children in government schools, calculated that they could just about afford the private school, gave it a try, found it worked, and told others about their success.

Is that all too simple for the development experts? It's not my place to explore why many with power and influence seem to have difficulty accepting the ease with which the poor have said enough is enough and proceeded with their own, highly workable solution. I'll get on with presenting my findings, in conferences like the one in Oxford, in this book, and wherever else people will listen to me, and try to do the best I can to convey some of what I've found around the world. For what I've found seems to be a cause for celebration. There's no "TV tragedy" here, yet another depressing story out of Africa, nor another dismal tale of how the poor in India and China are sidelined as their countries juggernaut toward development. Instead, the poor are empowering themselves. En masse, they are abandoning public education. It's not good enough for their children. And they've found a superior alternative. That's a good news story, isn't it?

But there's still plenty to be done, for those of us who want to help. The poor have found the makings of their silver bullet, but Amaretch is still out of school. So what is to be done?

There seem to be three problem areas we can usefully address. Reaching Amaretch and children like her—those out of school altogether and also those stuck in dysfunctional public schools—is the first. The second concerns educational quality. Although private schools for the poor, my research has shown, are better than public schools, there is still plenty of room for improvement. Third, there is the genuine information problem currently experienced by parents, an information asymmetry as the economists would put it. How do parents really know whether their school is any good? How can they even more reliably avoid private schools that are not up to scratch?

I'm not about to say, here are Three Big Plans to counter these Three Real Problems. That would be precisely the wrong approach. To borrow from William Easterly: "Has this book found, after all these years, the right Big Plan to achieve quality education for all? What a breakthrough if I have found such a plan when so many other, much smarter, people than I have tried many different plans over fifty years, and have failed. . . . You can relax; your author has no such delusions of grandeur. All the hoopla about having the right plan is itself a symptom of the misdirected approach. . . . The right plan is to have no plan."[2] Agreed. Rather than new Big Plans, I want to point to the general ways in which we can start small and work our way up—and by "we," I mean thousands of small-scale philanthropic and aid agency projects, working hand-in-hand with thousands of small-scale educational entrepreneurs—trying different approaches, building on what works, and rejecting or modifying what doesn't. So many little bits of information are out there in the market, known only to parents, children, and entrepreneurs, that can move the solutions forward. So many different levels of incentives for parents, children, and entrepreneurs can be harnessed to make the solutions work. We don't need an overarching plan at all. But here are some pointers to what might work.

Bringing the Beautiful One to School

Private schools already serve huge numbers of the poor. But not every child is in private school. For some, their parents can't afford the fees, or can't afford the opportunity costs of not having their children working for the family purse. So they either don't send them to school at all (like Amaretch) or must send them to a public school, where they'll likely feel abandoned. Others have parents who aren't particularly bothered about their child's education, with the same effect. We don't really know how many such children there are—the figures from the aid agencies exaggerate the problem because they don't take into account children already attending unrecognized private schools, off the state's radar. But of course, it's nonetheless a significant problem that must be addressed.

But an obvious solution presents itself: many children like Amaretch, from families far too poor to afford it, are *already* benefiting from private education, through the scholarships, free seats, and concessionary places, that private schools are offering. In my research, I found that nearly one in five of all students in the slums of Hyderabad receive free or subsidized tuition based on need. The Searchers who've created private schools are *already* reaching children like Amaretch, but not yet Amaretch herself. It's not rocket science to see how she, too, could be helped, building on what is already being done.

The solution could be to extend what is occurring within the private schools to create *targeted* vouchers for the poorest, for those children whose parents don't care about their education, and, in countries where boys are likely to be favored as I found in India, for girls to use at private schools. I gave a few examples in Chapter 10 of apparently successful schemes that work like this. Easterly also notes the success of the World Bank Food for Education program in Bangladesh—a rare example, he says, of successful aid—that gave cash payments to parents in return for their allowing their girls to go to school (indeed, he notes precisely, "This is the kind of program that could help Amaretch in Ethiopia"[3]). That's great—but it still doesn't capitalize on the full range of incentives that are there for the picking: through these targeted vouchers, true, *parents* have the incentive to send their girls to school, but the schools—presumably public schools—have *no* incentive to educate the girls once they're in school. There's no way the school is accountable to the parents, so teachers still don't have to show up and can still sleep in the classroom. As Easterly pointed out in his earlier work, *The Elusive Quest for Growth*, if people "have the right incentives, development will happen. If they don't, it won't."[4] Harnessing incentives from everyone is the key to successful approaches.

If targeted vouchers are made available for *private* schools in the right way, they have the potential not only to incentivize parents to send their children to school (and if opportunity costs are a problem, these vouchers could include supplements for the parents themselves, as well as to cover school fees), but also to incentivize school management to do its best for the children once in school. The key here is to ensure that parents receive physical vouchers to take to the school of their choice and to use in lieu of school fees, just as if they were cash. The school can then cash in these vouchers from the agency providing them, after suitable checks to prevent fraud. Crucially, as far as the school is concerned, these parents *are* paying fees, just like all the others, and so the school will suffer if they are not satisfied—they can move their children to another school, just as they could if they were paying cash—so the short route to accountability is still maintained. Furthermore, targeted vouchers can also include supplements for textbooks and even midday meals, to allow the poorest to have the education that the wealthier-of-the-poor parents can afford.

If done "in the right way" is the important caveat—which is one reason why I'm not suggesting, even if anyone would listen, a wholesale Big Plan to transfer aid funding straightaway to targeted vouchers for private schools for the poor. I've been experimenting with a small-scale targeted voucher scheme through the Educare Trust in Hyderabad, India, using the physical voucher idea to fund 500 children in private schools. On a small scale, it seems successful. But even on this scale, in schools that I knew fairly well, a case of fraud arose. This problem would grow exponentially with the scale of the intervention, and so we would need to learn countermeasures early on. And even on this small scale, we were aware of small misgivings on the part of one family that was paying fees—why was this other girl being subsidized when they were struggling to pay for their children? In this case, we were able to demonstrate that the girl in question had a bedridden father, and that the fee-paying family should not be deterred from finding funds. But this problem—of moral hazard that bedevils any social welfare scheme, that apparently seems to punish those who virtuously struggle to provide for their children and can seem to reward those who do not—is a real one that any scheme would have to find ways of addressing.

It's easy to see how it could all go wrong. Targeted vouchers handled by the wrong agencies could lead to widespread fraud. I recently did some research for the World Bank in Karnataka, India, one of the most forward-looking, least corrupt Indian states. In Gulbarga, one of the poorest districts, I investigated scholarships, administered through the Ministry of Social Welfare, that were supposedly aimed at some of the most disadvantaged, India's "scheduled castes" and "scheduled tribes," and especially girls from these groups. Parents and school managers told me that most of the scholarships didn't reach the children for whom they were intended. Most were siphoned off as they went through the various levels of the district bureaucracy. And that was in one of India's least corrupt states. Giving funds for targeted vouchers to state agencies like that would seem to be precisely the wrong way forward. But if reputable nongovernmental organizations or microfinance banks with good track records for genuinely reaching the poor could manage the funds, then there might be some hope of reaching a multitude of children.

And there's nothing ideological here: if an experiment showed that having vouchers available for public schools also worked, that would be fine too. The public schools would probably need to be properly incentivized. Thus, if the school's—and teachers'—income depended on getting the vouchers, and so they really had to compete for them, then they would not abandon the children using them in the classrooms.

But surely finding the funds for a large number of targeted vouchers would be a problem? I don't think it would. Even *as things stand now*, with current levels of aid funding and *without touching any government funds currently being spent on public education*, so with no need to reform public education and public finance, I reckon we could afford to send *every* out-of-school child to private school. (In what follows, please, I'm not suggesting that all these funds be immediately diverted to do this. I'm just showing, in case anyone was worried about this point, that the required funding is already available.)

Take Ghana for instance. The British aid agency, Department for International Development, *alone* gives about $27 million per year to Ghanaian state education. In the poor areas of Ga, where my research was conducted, a typical private school for the poor might charge about $30 per year. In remoter rural areas, the cost will be even lower. If all those funds spent by DfID alone in Ghana were spent on scholarships to fund 100 percent of these private school fees, it would provide places for at least 900,000 children annually. Suppose, more realistically, that there are some costs associated with voucher administration, say 6 percent of the funding. It would still provide funding for nearly 850,000 out-of-school children. No one really knows how many children are currently out of school in Ghana. The government estimates about 1 million, but some of them are not out of school at all, but in private unregistered schools. If around 15 percent of the out-of-school children are currently in such private schools, then *the education aid budget for Ghana from DfID alone would provide all the funds for targeted vouchers for those currently out of school to attend private schools.* Add in the education aid budgets for Ghana, from the U.S. Agency for International Development, Oxfam, the Nordic countries, Germany, the Netherlands, and so forth, and it soon becomes clear that children currently in govern-ment schools could also attend private school.

A second objection might be that this is all well and good for urban areas, where we know there's already a huge supply of private schools, but what about remoter rural areas, where there might be only a few schools, or even *none*? Even if we could, in theory, fund the schooling of all these rural children, this would still be useless if there were no private schools for them to attend. But it is surely plausible that a major reason for the lower number of private schools in rural than urban areas is because fewer parents can afford the fees. If so, then targeted vouchers could also lead to an increase in the number of private schools in rural areas, just as their numbers are higher in urban or small-town areas where fee-paying capacity is higher. Based on what I have seen in my journeys, it seems likely that private entrepreneurs would respond to this kind of incentive. And if the reason why entrepreneurs are not establishing schools in some remote villages—cases in rural Gansu, China, spring to mind—has less to do with finance than with the lack of availability of suitable teachers, then incentives can be worked into the targeted vouchers to solve this problem too. Perhaps targeted vouchers in these kinds of remote rural areas could include additional amounts for teacher recruitment, training, and/or accommodation. As long as everyone is suitably incentivized, there would seem to be no reason why a process of judicious experimentation couldn't discover ways of making this work, even in apparently inhospitable places.

Quality Matters

Getting Amaretch into private school is one, solvable, challenge. But what about the quality of education when she gets there? At a recent conference, Professor Keith Lewin said to me that there should be "a plague on both your houses." Candidly he agreed that government schools for the poor are appalling. But so too are private schools for the poor: "You might have shown that they're better than public schools," he chided, "but they're still rubbish."

Perhaps he had in mind problems such as poor infrastructure, lack of proper latrines, leaky roofs, and so on. Of course, he's right. These can be improved. How can we get Amaretch's private school to be of a higher infrastructural standard? Here a creative new frontier for investors and philanthropists is dramatically revealed, where the investment community can potentially make a huge difference in the lives of poor people. The key relevant finding of the research is that the vast majority of the private schools in the poor areas are *businesses*, not charities, dependent more or less entirely on fee income and, very importantly, making a reasonable profit.

I explored this with 10 to 15 case study schools in each of the countries, to gain a deeper insight into finances. In every instance, the case study schools showed a viable return for the proprietor. For example, in the shantytown of Makoko in Lagos State, a typical case study school had 220 pupils and 13 teachers, and average fees of 1,800 naira ($12.41) per term, with 9 percent of students on free scholarships. Teacher salaries averaged 4,388 naira ($30.26) per month, with other recurrent expenditures at 7,450 naira ($51.38) per month, plus the proprietor's monthly salary of 8,000 naira ($55.17). Such a school made a surplus of about $1,456 per annum, or about 20 percent of its income.

Because the private schools for the poor are run as businesses, a pretty easy solution is available to help school proprietors improve their infrastructure: microfinance loans could be provided, through existing or purpose-created microfinance organizations. Again, through the Educare Trust in Hyderabad, and Educare in Makoko, Nigeria, I set up two small pilot loan schemes, each funded by donations of $25,000, that offered loans of between $500 and $2,000, at commercial interest rates to private school managers who wanted to improve their infrastructure. The entrepreneurs submitted detailed proposals, which were vetted, along with their (usually informal) accounts, to ensure that the plans were reasonable and the repayments—typically over three years—were affordable. Typical projects included building proper latrines, refurbishing classrooms or building new ones, buying land, or on the lower end, buying a school bus and desks and chairs. I've also seen the need for a bit of financial management advice and training, to help school proprietors manage their budgets more effectively. All this can be provided with philanthropic funding.

I've found a hunger for this kind of money, available to schools that couldn't usually access other funds, perhaps because they didn't have formal property rights or were operating only semilegally— the kind of small businesses highlighted by Hernando de Soto in *The Mystery of Capital*. This hunger showed that critics' claims of private school proprietors' profiteering from the poor—the "hidden curriculum" condemnation I heard, that if schools don't provide latrines, for instance, it shows the proprietor only cares about profit, not the children in his care—are completely misplaced. As soon as funds were made accessible, the private school proprietors showed themselves eager to invest in improvements. In these small-scale projects, we've had no problem with defaulters, using some of the mechanisms common to microfinance programs, such as peer pressure, in our case through private school associations. If larger microfinance agencies can embrace such loans, then it could be taken to a much larger scale. Easier access to financing could mean that problems with poor private school infrastructure are also relatively easily solvable. Amaretch's school is already looking much better.

But perhaps Professor Lewin had in mind other, deeper problems with budget private schools, concerning teaching methods and curriculum? Suppose Amaretch is a really bright girl. Will she then be stuck in a class, learning by rote, week after week, topics that she could easily assimilate in a few hours? Or suppose she's not so quick herself, perhaps because of her lack of schooling. Will she then be stuck in a class falling further behind the others and eventually fail altogether? And what will she be taught? Will she be forced to digest subject after subject of the state national curriculum that she'll only pass in exams through extensive cramming and that will make her wonder what the point of all that cramming is? And will she wish that she had covered other topics in school that would seem much more immediately relevant to what she would need in her adult life? If she became the proprietor of a small business, would she wish she'd had training in business skills, entrepreneurship, or accounting methods? If she got a job in a product-support call center, would she wish she'd had an advanced course in English pronunciation? In short, even when she gets to private school, can we really say that she is receiving the *education* that she deserves, rather than a certain amount of dubious *schooling*?

I have to admit, for what it's worth, that I find this kind of objection quite compelling. I'm not totally satisfied by what I see in the private schools for the poor, in terms of their teaching and learning styles, and the curriculum. It always makes me sad when I see the brightest kids treading water, struggling to maintain enthusiasm for rote learning a passage that they understood at the first reading; some become disruptive, even drop out of school altogether, as a result of their boredom. Conversely, it breaks my heart to see less-gifted children (described in India as "dull," which always makes me cringe) struggling to keep pace with their class, left behind because they've not mastered basic reading and arithmetic, and who now will never do so, because the rest of the class has moved on. And the children in between too, I often wonder whether their learning couldn't be made more engaging, more liberating, less passive.

For it's true, in general, that the private schools I've visited are generally steeped in the same learning styles—usually rote learning—as the public schools, and they tend to follow the state curriculum. Regarding the latter, they more or less must. The government inspectors aren't too keen on letting them deviate from it, and more to the point, parents want their children to pass the state exams, currently the only route to higher education and employment. And the teaching styles—well, they are ones that everyone is used to and feels comfortable with, the way that proprietors and teachers themselves were taught, and parents accept as being the right ones.

In short, I'm as bothered by pedagogy and curriculum as many development experts are. Now, development agencies have plowed millions upon millions of dollars into trying to get teachers to change their methods, and children to rise above passivity. Millions of dollars have been spent on training teachers in child-centered methods (the District Primary Education Project is a notable example in India), or in using high-technology solutions, such as television, interactive radio, or information technology, to bypass teachers altogether, or to train them in "modern" methods, or to supplement classroom teaching with these beamed-in add-ons.[5]

But the stark fact is, little or none of this really works—the child-centered methods introduced (which are themselves often the subject of criticism in the donor countries promoting them) just don't gel with teachers, who tend to revert to their preferred methods once the aid workers have bid farewell. Expensive high-tech solutions, the television, interactive radio, and information and communications technology projects that hit the headlines, might work well while they're being funded. However, as soon as the aid funding is withdrawn, the intervention ends. Presumably, aid agencies engaged with these kinds of projects assume that, once they've shown how brilliant they are, then governments will pick up the tab. Unfortunately, the evidence shows that this doesn't happen. Once the aid agencies disappear, everything reverts to the *status quo ante*. Such projects do not manage to harness any *incentives* for poor people to continue with, or invest in, the intervention, and it is hard to see how *any* of the proposed solutions can overcome these combined problems.

But is the correct response then to simply let things continue as they have and avert our gaze whenever we go into these classrooms and see what is taking place? I don't think it need be. For again, the private school market provides the basis for a possible way forward.

First, it becomes quickly apparent from any visit to private schools in poor areas that very often the proprietors themselves are eager to learn of different ways of teaching and learning, and of new curriculum areas, from overseas visitors. I found it rather embarrassing on my first visit to the slums of Hyderabad back in 2000, that I was asked to speak at a meeting of private school proprietors and was bombarded with questions about what they could do better with teaching and curricula. I was from overseas, where everything was much better, what could I advise them to do? And going around each school, the proprietor would sit me down in his or her tiny office after I'd visited the classes, and ask: "How can I improve my teaching? Tell me, what can I do better?" I used to hide behind the idea that I was there to learn from them, that they had so much to teach us in the West. I still think that's true: the very fact that private school proprietors are there at all in these seemingly inhospitable environments is something that we can learn from and gain inspiration.

But I think now that it was a bit of a cop-out to say that I had nothing to contribute, only things to learn, about the way they handled their curricula and teaching. That was certainly *their* reaction, as attested by the many disappointed faces when I trotted out the "I'm only here to learn" line. But we don't have to go the route of the failed—or soon discontinued—aid interventions to effect real change. Private school proprietors' eagerness for new ideas is the key reason why not—and why they are motivated, incentivized, to want to explore new ideas in a completely different way from those handing out or receiving aid funds.

A couple of years ago, I collaborated on a small-scale project in a private school in the slums of Hyderabad with Dr. Sugata Mitra, who, before he moved to Newcastle University, was chief scientist at NIIT Ltd., one of India's largest computer education companies. Mitra has experimented with peer-group learning using information technology—dubbed "the hole in the wall" by the media. Now, Hyderabad is flooded with call centers; many alumni of private schools for the poor seek employment with them but are stymied by their low standard of English pronunciation—their teachers can't help because they don't speak English well enough either. I invited Mitra to try the hole-in-the-wall approach here: could children *teach themselves* to improve their English pronunciation?

We conducted the experiment in Wajid's Peace High School. The details—based on a speech-to-text recognition program[6]—need not concern us here. The experiment showed that this method was successful in improving English pronunciation. But what happened *after* the experiment was most relevant. Wajid is closely connected to many other private school proprietors through various federations and informal associations. Many came to see what was happening in his school. Many came to learn of our findings. And they wanted what Wajid had in *their* schools. And they were prepared to pay for it, of course; they didn't simply want it handed to them. Previously, his preferred investment in computer technology was, once suitable surpluses had been accrued, to acquire as many secondhand computers as possible, and a computer teacher. Now proprietors like Sajid-Sir were saying to us: "Perhaps we don't need a computer teacher. We need the hole in the wall."

The school proprietors were hungry for innovation. Why? First, whatever the critics of private schools for the poor may claim, the proprietors simply care about their children's education and want the best for them. Even on its own, that might be enough for some of them to invest some of their surpluses in new methods and technology. But the power of the market is that the proprietors' good intentions are coupled with another major incentive that makes it even more likely that they will seek to invest: they know that they face increasing competition. School proprietors need to differentiate themselves within the marketplace. To maintain or even increase market share, they need parents to know that their school is special. If a method of learning seems to have demonstrably better outcomes, they'll want it for their schools.

Importantly, the situation in these poor areas is completely different from the situation in private schools in the West: there is a *genuine market* operating in these countries. In some of the poorest areas of the world, private education makes up the *vast majority* of school enrollment. In the West, however, private education is only a small fraction of total enrollment, around 7 percent in the United Kingdom, for instance. This is true, even if one focuses instead on urban areas, which have a particularly high concentration of private education: in central London, for instance, private school enrollment is only about 13 percent, and overwhelmingly organized along non-commercial, nonprofit lines. Such private education "markets" are unlikely to illustrate real competitive behavior, are more likely to exhibit complacency or even anti-competitive cartels (as has recently been reported in the UK[7]), because the "market" is very small, has a largely captive audience, and is competing against a near-monopoly state provider.

In poor areas of developing countries, however, private education forms the majority of provision. In these areas, parents have genuine choices of a number of competing private schools within easy reach and are sensitive to the price mechanism (schools close if demand is low, and new schools open to cater to expanded demand); in these genuine markets, educational entrepreneurs respond to parental needs and requirements.

So let's return to concerns about the quality of education for Amaretch, and what outsiders could usefully offer by way of improvements. We don't have to be afraid of imposing solutions that are not deemed practicable by parents. We don't have to worry about finding solutions that are not sustainable because no one can afford to follow them through once the aid money dries up. Instead, if we're concerned about teaching and learning and curricula, we can try small-scale experiments—like the one in Hyderabad with Sugata Mitra—to see if something works. If it does, we won't keep it to ourselves but will make sure everyone knows about it. (The same is true if it doesn't work, so that people can avoid repeating that mistake.) The only way that we can really help is to ensure that the improved technology—whether in curriculum, teaching methods or learning methods—is available, suitably packaged, as inexpensive as possible, through some commercial enterprise. If private schools think it's desirable, they'll buy into it—perhaps using loan funds to help. The problems of sustainability and scalability that so bedevil any aid intervention are solved. Testing new methods in the market is where venture philanthropy can make its mark. If a new method works, then let the market take it up. If it doesn't, then we'll know that our aspirations for educating the poor with that method were misplaced, but we can always try another.

The Brand-Conscious Poor

In *The Fortune at the Bottom of the Pyramid*, C. K. Prahalad challenges the "dominant assumption" that the poor don't care about brand names: "On the contrary," his findings suggest, "the poor are very brand-conscious."[8] In private education, brand names could be important in helping solve the genuine information problem that exists—and they provide a *third* major opportunity for outsiders to assist with the education market. How can poor parents judge whether one private school in their community is better than another and whether it adequately serves the educational needs of their children? Typically, my research showed that parents use a variety of informal methods, such as visiting several schools to see how committed the teachers and proprietor appear. Or they talk to friends, comparing notes about how frequently exercise books are marked and homework checked. Importantly, I found that if parents choose one private school but subsequently discover that another seems better, they have little hesitation in moving their child to where they think they will get a better education. Even parents who don't bother with these kinds of judgments or exploring the different options benefit because some (perhaps most?) parents *do* bother. The less concerned can free ride on the choices of the more concerned. And since school proprietors know this, they ensure that teachers show up and teach, and they invest any surpluses in school improvement, to ensure parental satisfaction. Although not all parents discharge their educational responsibilities with care and wisdom, private school managers must cater to those who do. This is another way in which the market deals with a problem—apathetic parents— that bedevils public school systems (since public schools provide no economic incentive for their principals to cater to the demands of well-informed parents).

Some might think that this is all well and good, but parents, even concerned parents, don't know *what education is*—they themselves may be illiterate, for instance—so can't possibly judge what their children are getting. But I think this is misguided. Particularly at the primary school level—the level of most concern in this book— the nature of what constitutes a desirable education isn't that hard to understand. Parents believe it should be about becoming literate and numerate, well-behaved, and well-equipped for adult life, employment, and future studies, and for fine things like democracy. All these elements can be relatively readily discerned using the informal methods described above.

So there *is* an information problem, but there are plenty of ways of circumventing it.

But this solution doesn't quite satisfy me. Because I know that in markets I'm faced with all the time—markets with as great or even greater information asymmetries—I can rely not only on these kinds of informal methods of judgment, but can fall back on a much stronger tool in making my consumer decisions. I don't know anything about computer software or hardware, Internet searches, digital cameras, commercial airlines, or car maintenance, or even much about food and clothing, to name a few market decisions I've been faced with in recent days, and so for which the information problem rears its ugly head. Of course, I could become deeply informed about each of these areas, but life is too short. I could look at consumer guides like *Which?* magazine or the specialized press in each of these areas. But I don't. But still, in general, I manage to purchase all the necessary goods and services in a way that usually works fine for me, without much effort to overcome the information asymmetry.

How? I *buy trusted brands*. I have a Sony computer and digital camera and Microsoft software; I use Google for my computer searches, fly by British Airways or KLM/Air France, use Northern Motors to maintain my Nissan, and shop at Tesco and Marks & Spencer for food and clothing. (Some might argue that these brands only function because of government regulation. I doubt that it is the fear of health and hygiene inspectors that keeps Tesco from offering me rotten fruit and vegetables. I think they fear losing my custom far more, and that's why they offer fresh produce.) Buying trusted brands would be another way of overcoming the information problem for poor parents wanting the best education for their children.

Assisting the market in the creation of educational brand names that will help parents make more informed decisions is another possible area for outside action—for philanthropy, investment, and aid if required to satisfy investors of the viability of the market, or to provide technical assistance on legal and financial matters to educational entrepreneurs. One possibility would be for investors to assist expansion-minded proprietors in accessing loan capital, in the way already outlined above. Or it could involve creating a specialized education investment fund to provide equity to education companies that run chains of budget private schools. Suitable exit strategies could be worked out for the investment fund, perhaps by giving advice on how to list on local stock exchanges or to get other investors on board.

A further possibility could involve investors' engaging in a joint venture with local educational entrepreneurs to set up a chain themselves. Investment in initial research and development would be required to create the standards for a demonstrable and truly replicable model of education for the poor. This might be best accomplished within existing schools that would then demonstrate the efficacy of the model to parents, investors, and potential franchisees—if a franchise model was deemed appropriate—and be used to train new school managers and teachers.

Such research and development would explore the technology, curriculum, pedagogy, and teacher-training requirements for the successful *educational* model, and the quality control, financial, and regulatory requirements for the brand-name chain. Establishing a chain of "budget" private schools, serving poor communities, would seem an extraordinarily exciting and innovative project for investors and philanthropists to engage in.

Why would private school owners wish to become part of a chain of schools, either as franchise holders or managers? Competition would be a chief spur: School proprietors realize a key problem now is the powerful competition from other private schools—from the roof of one school in the slums of Hyderabad, seven other private schools are visible, all competing for the same children. School proprietors are eager to differentiate themselves in this market, and a key concern of parents is educational quality. By becoming part of the brand name, managers could show that they emphasize quality more than their competitors and so would attract more children.

Parents would prefer that their children attend a brand-name school because it would solve their information problem in a neat way. Children, too, might prefer to be in a brand-name school to benefit from the improved curriculum, pedagogy, technology, and teacher training. They would be part of a much larger organization and would benefit from the networks and opportunities that creates. And as the brand name became well-known, prospective employers and higher education institutions would trust where children have been educated, giving the pupils an edge for the future.

What of schools that don't become part of the chain? In the short term, they could suffer, perhaps even go out of business—but only as a result of parents' shifting their children to the school that they perceive as having higher-quality education. But in the dynamic market of education, two things would likely happen. First, individual educational entrepreneurs would seek to improve what they offer in order to retain children or win back those who have left. Second, most fundamentally, if the financial and educational viability of an educational brand name was demonstrated, others would soon enter the market, establishing competing brand names that offer quality education at a low cost.

Prahalad observes that the founder of Aravind Eye Care System—which provides cataract surgery for large numbers of the poor—was "inspired by the hamburger chain, McDonald's, where a consistent quality of hamburgers and French fries worldwide results from a deeply understood and standardised chemical process."[9] There seems every reason to think that a similarly "deeply understood and standardised" learning process could become part of an equally successful model of private school provision, serving huge numbers of the poor.

261

And perhaps you don't even have to start with the poor. I've a friend who's starting a chain of private schools in China for the middle classes. Just as mobile phone and computer technology all began with the advantaged, and eventually diffused, lower and lower, into the socioeconomic substrata, so too might educational brand names.

This kind of brand experimentation in the market could even take on what is currently strongly felt to be the justified monopoly of the state—the examination and assessment system itself, and the associated curriculum leading up to it. In information technology, NIIT Ltd. started out offering courses to a few people who thought they might be beneficial. In time, it has emerged to create its own brand of certification. A graduate of NIIT—a GNIIT—is now accepted as possessing an internationally recognized qualification. Search through the matrimonial pages in the *Times of India* (a sort of "lonely hearts" section in which parents seek matches for their children) and you'll see that being a GNIIT is as much a signifier of quality in a potential partner as the possession of other, better-known standards in the West, such as a BA or MSc. And this is so even though these standards have emerged totally independently of government—and even against government's wishes: I had a particularly harrowing afternoon in the office of the deputy director of the All-India Council for Technical Education. During our interview, a large and malevolent-looking rat ran around the office; at one point, I had to lift my feet as it passed under me. The deputy director called in his secretary and told him to set the traps that evening. As the rat continued its peregrinations around his office, he told me, "I sometimes get phone calls from ministries around the world, in Dubai or Saudi, asking about NIIT qualifications." Presumably, potential employees had these on their resumés, and the authorities were wondering about their value. "I tell them they are not worth the paper they are written on" because they were not accredited by his organization. But whatever he thought from his rat-infested office, that's not what millions of employers in India and elsewhere think of NIIT certificates. The brand name has become so well-known and respected that, just as Americans often ask for a Kleenex after sneezing, referring to a facial tissue, or make a Xerox when they mean a photocopy, or offer to FedEx an urgent document when they mean send it by courier, so Indians talk of doing an NIIT, when they mean undertaking a computer course, even when they do it at one of NIIT's top rivals.

Just as NIIT has conquered the world of computer education certification, so I believe there is nothing to stop some educational entrepreneurs, perhaps assisted by forward-looking philanthropy, in creating brand-name certification for budget private schools that will signify quality and relevance to employers and higher education admissions officers. Of course, just as NIIT did, the Searchers could start small and find what suits parents, children, employers, and college and university registrars, conducting market research and testing what they're offering customers. But as the brand grew, there seems to be no reason at all—apart from government regulations that could outlaw it—that the new education certificate could not become nationally and internationally respected, providing an alternative for budget private schools to offer that would satisfy all those using them. Importantly, such a brand name could go a long way toward solving the problem of overloaded and irrelevant curricula, using outmoded pedagogy, that currently bedevil public education systems in developing countries.

A Solvable Problem

Private schools for the poor are burgeoning across the developing world. In many urban areas they are serving the majority of poor schoolchildren. Their quality is higher than that of government schools provided for the poor—perhaps not surprisingly given that they are predominantly businesses dependent on fees to survive and, hence, are directly accountable to parental needs. Those worried—like Easterly—about how to extend access to education for the poor could usefully look to the private education sector as a way forward. By increasing what private schools for the poor already offer, such as additional free and subsidized places for the poorest, sensitively applied targeted vouchers could broaden access on a large scale. Crucially, because the private schools serving the poor are businesses, making a reasonable profit, they provide a pioneering way forward for investor involvement too. Investing in microfinance-style loan programs so that private schools can improve their infrastructure is one way forward. Providing investment for innovation in curriculum and learning, which, if successful, could be rolled out on a commercial basis, is a second possibility. And investing in a chain of schools—either through a dedicated education investment fund or through joint ventures with educational entrepreneurs—could help solve the information problem for poor parents and improve the existing educational opportunities. Educating Amaretch is a solvable problem. The Searchers who have created private schools for the poor are hungry for investment; investors can assist them in pursuing their central role in providing quality "education for all."

And Finally: Implications for the West?

Does this discussion have any implications for education in the West? I don't mind if it doesn't, apart from the implications for aid and development that I've already discussed. But I've often been pressed on this when lecturing in America or Britain, especially to sympathetic audiences. Does it have any relevance for us? In this concluding section, I'll point to two possible ways in which the evidence might be relevant.

You're Not a Hypocrite if You Go Private

First, I think the evidence presented in this book can help us deal with what has been called "middle-class angst" in the West: when their children reach school age, middle-class parents are faced with the dilemma of sending their children to the assigned state school or a private alternative. For many, this decision brings a terrible moral dilemma. In Britain, we've been inundated in recent years with pundits milking this one for all its worth. Fiona Miller—the girlfriend of then Prime Minister Tony Blair's former adviser Alistair Campbell and herself a former adviser to Cherie Blair—argued in a Channel 4 documentary that pushy middle-class parents who were abandoning the local comprehensive state school were the biggest threat to public education. And Teacher of the Year Philip Beadle took the same line in a 2006 Channel 4 documentary, "We Don't Need No Private Education," even manipulating the words, in my view, of an upwardly mobile black father to suggest that the quality of private schools in Britain was inferior to those of state schools. Stealing this particular limelight above all, Oxford don Adam Swift made his name telling middle-class parents that sending their children to private school damaged the egalitarian project of public education in his book *How Not to Be a Hypocrite.*

The title of his book conveys the dilemma facing parents. For if you send your children to private school, you are saying that the state system is not good enough for your children—it must be thus, for the state system is free, but you have to fork out considerable sums to send your child to the private alternative. But by saying this, you are removing yourself, an educationally concerned middle-class parent, says Swift, from the state system and, hence, consigning it to a vicious cycle of mediocrity. But of course if you choose to follow what you believe to be morally right, by supporting the state schools that the majority must attend, then you run the risk of jeopardizing your own dear child's future. So what to do?

Swift's dilemma—of middle-class angst—may seem minor compared with those problems facing parents in poorer countries. But I think the solution that poorer parents have embraced can help soothe the consciences of middle-class parents too. The evidence from around the world shows us, first, that most people, poor as well as rich, care deeply about their children's education; there is no middle-class monopoly on this. And second, because of the universality of parental concern, there's nothing intrinsically socially divisive about private education either. It may be true today that private education in the West is patronized largely by the middle and upper classes. But they do so for a mixture of reasons, including the intervention of strong government over a period of a hundred years or more. It wasn't always the case—before the state got involved (in Britain in 1870), provision was, of course, overwhelmingly private. Indeed, the *less* middle-class parents patronize private education, the *more* socially divisive they allow it to become. Conversely, the more middle-class parents stop worrying and use private education, the more chances there will be of effective *chains* of private schools emerging. And the more these brand names emerge, the greater the chance of a larger number of people being able to free ride on the informed choices of the middle classes, as competing chains lower fees, making their schools accessible to a still larger number of children. Moreover, when more parents begin using private education, the politicians and opinion makers are more likely to face up to the idiocy of parents' paying twice for their children's education—once through taxes and again through private school fees. The more policymakers are forced to confront this double payment, the greater the likelihood of reforms also emerging in the

West, like tax credits for school fees and targeted vouchers for those who can't afford private education. Thus, such reforms would lead to the end of the less-well-off having to acquiesce in state inferiority.

In other words, forget Swift's accusations of hypocrisy. There's only a virtuous circle waiting to be conscribed, if you as a middle-class parent follow your desires and use private schools.[10]

Far Too Modest a Proposal

Proponents of school choice in America usually favor vouchers as the solution to the problem of poorly performing public education. The kinds of schemes working in America, such as the nearly 20-year-old voucher system in Milwaukee, are like the targeted vouchers described earlier, allowing particular groups of disadvantaged parents to send their children to private schools. However, under these reforms the majority of children stay in the public schools that aren't quite as bad as those from which parents are permitted to exit. However, some argue for universal vouchers, aimed at allowing everyone to choose the school they send their children to, whether public or private. The evidence of this book suggests—although by no means proves—that American education reformers may have hit on far too modest a proposal for raising educational standards. Less controversially, the evidence accrued here certainly shows that some of the objections to universal vouchers are not as strong as their critics like to make out.

The late Milton Friedman is usually regarded as the godfather of vouchers. Just over 50 years ago, he wrote an essay entitled "The Role of Government in Education," in which he outlined his school voucher proposal for the first time. With his wife, Rose, he further elaborated these ideas in 1980 in *Free to Choose*, where they also outlined some of the major objections that were emerging to the proposal for universal education vouchers in America, which remain fundamentally some of the main objections today. One of those objections they characterized as "doubt about new schools."[11] Given that private schools were then either religious (parochial) schools or elite academies, critics of the voucher proposal wanted to know what reason there was "to suppose that alternatives will really arise?" The Friedmans were convinced that "a market would develop where it does not exist today," attracting "many entrants, both from public schools and from other occupations." Their conviction came from talking to many people about vouchers. Many people they spoke to said something like: "I have always wanted to teach (or run a school) but I couldn't stand the educational bureaucracy, red tape, and general ossification of the public schools. Under your plan, I'd like to try my hand at starting a school."

The evidence from developing countries today supports their confidence in the entrepreneurial spirit: educational entrepreneurs *do* emerge to provide educational opportunities, including among some of the poorest members of society. They emerge because parents and poor communities are concerned about education; it is a fundamental priority. When they have (well-founded) doubts about the efficiency and effectiveness of public schools, they'll create alternatives of their own—at least when not discouraged or prevented from doing so by prevailing tax, regulatory, and welfare policies.

Our evidence also helps challenge another of the fundamental objections to vouchers in America, that prosperous families would "top up," or supplement, the state provision with their own funds, which would penalize poor parents who wouldn't want to spend their resources on education. The Friedmans replied: "This view . . . seems to us another example of the tendency of intellectuals to denigrate parents who are poor. Even the very poorest can—and do—scrape up a few extra dollars to improve the quality of their children's schooling, although they cannot replace the whole of the present cost of public schooling."[12] The evidence from developing countries supports this argument: if some of the poorest parents on this planet will scrimp and save to pay for their children's education, is it plausible that the poor in America today—a more affluent group than the poor of the Third World—would not be able to "top up" vouchers too?

However, our evidence suggests we go further than this. It suggests that many poor parents can in fact pay for *all* their children's schooling, without any government assistance. Indeed, by 1980, the Friedmans were also aware of other compelling evidence, this time from history, that suggested they were being far too moderate in their universal voucher proposal. By this time, they'd reviewed the history of education in Victorian England, which we briefly touched on in the last chapter, and parallel evidence from 19th-century America, and realized that schooling was "well-nigh universal in the United States before attendance was required," whereas in the

United Kingdom, it was "well-nigh universal before either compulsory attendance or government financing of schooling existed."[13] This evidence challenged the desirability of compulsory schooling laws, and hence, as compulsion was the prime justification for public funding, the raison d'être of this began to disentangle too. Although still viewing the education voucher as a useful stepping stone, by 1980 the Friedmans were inclined toward something more radical: "We regard the voucher plan as a partial solution because it affects neither the financing of schooling nor the compulsory attendance laws. *We favor going much farther.*" "Farther," in this case, was a move away from the desirability of universal vouchers to an emphasis on, at most, targeted vouchers for the poorest: "Public financing of hardship cases might remain, but that is a far different matter than having the government finance a school system for 90 percent of the children going to school because 5 or 10 percent of them might be hardship cases." By 1980 then, the Friedmans favored a more complete privatization of education, with the government's abandoning compulsory schooling laws and withdrawing from funding education, except for, at most, a small minority of parents who are "hardship cases." The Friedmans did not further elaborate on the theme of privatization, acknowledging that their views "on financing and attendance laws will appear to most readers to be extreme"; hence their pragmatic "return to the voucher proposal—a much more moderate departure from present practice."

Perhaps the evidence accumulated throughout this book suggests that their more radical departure might be the more sensible approach for America, and by extension for other countries in the West too. For what we are seeing in Africa and Asia, in effect, is a grassroots privatization of education. This evidence raises the possibility that we may not be too radical but rather too cautious if we look only to state intervention through vouchers to assist the disadvantaged in the West too. The poor in Asia and Africa don't sit idly by, dispossessed and disenfranchised—adjectives used by the liberal elite to describe the disadvantaged in America—acquiescent in their government's failure until outsiders step in to improve their lot. Instead, some of the most disadvantaged people on this planet engage in "self-help," vote with their feet, exit the public schools, and move their children to private schools set up by educational entrepreneurs from their own communities to cater to their needs, without any outside help. Could it be that the government intervention we take for granted in America and the West *crowds out* parallel educational enterprise that could help the poor help themselves, as they are doing in places like Kenya and India? Could it be that real privatization could emerge in the same way that it has emerged in developing countries, from the bottom up?

Perhaps the situations in the West and developing countries are too different to make this conclusion justifiable? Perhaps public education—although almost universally chastised for being of low quality in the West—is not nearly as bad as what the poor in developing countries face every day? So resistance to it is not nearly as great or as obvious. Perhaps the "poor" in the West have been so ingrained with the dependency culture of relying on the state for education, as James Bartholomew suggests in his book *The Welfare State We're In*, that they won't be prepared to embrace the private sector as the poor do in the countries I visited? I don't know the answers to these questions. If they're in the affirmative, then this radical solution probably wouldn't be sustainable in the West. If they're in the negative, then perhaps it could. I'm sorry not to be more specific. But my reading of the runes is that what's happening in India, China, and Africa now, the grassroots privatization of education, might just take purchase in the West too.

If India Can, Why Can't We?

In 1980, the *NBC News White Paper* "If Japan Can, Why Can't We?" sent shock waves through American corporations. The program revealed how the Japanese captured world auto and electronics markets by reorganizing from first principles. This was also the wake-up call to the British manufacturing industry. My research leads me to think that a similar wake-up call is due here *in education*—not from Japan, but from India this time. And China. And perhaps Nigeria, Ghana, and Kenya too.

In the fissures of crumbling public education systems, a vibrant and confident education industry is beginning to emerge. It is serving the poor as well as the rich. It is bringing much higher standards than appear possible under public education. And with judicious support, it can engage to meet the needs of all, and can innovate through competition to improve teaching and learning and expand the curriculum, in ways that are unimaginable under public systems.

If strong chains of budget private schools start to emerge in these countries, perhaps especially if they should emerge in the new economic tigers of India and China, then these educational giants could begin to challenge the monopolies of public education in the West. Just as the Americans in particular are afraid of competition from low-cost industries in India and, especially, China, so too could they become worried by competition from educational chains emerging there.

My hunch, for what it's worth, is that the educational enterprise will go from strength to strength in India and China, and in Africa too. And if for India, why not for us? There is an obvious historical precedent for this reading of events. In the 19th century, the solution to how to improve educational opportunities in England, and throughout the West, was found by copying—no doubt enhancing them along the way—the methods found in the private schools in India. Through the Rev. Dr. Andrew Bell's Madras Method and later Joseph Lancaster's eponymous techniques, the West copied what was occurring in India and transformed the educational experience here. Perhaps budget private schools, the grassroots privatization we see in the developing world, will one day be copied here too, transforming the educational opportunities that we give our children?

That's my best guess. But whether or not that happens, budget private schools in Africa and Asia appear to be here to stay. Poor parents know what they are doing. They want the best for their children, and they know private schools are the way forward. The poor have found their silver bullet. It's time for policymakers and opinion leaders to catch up with them.

The Eclipse

I certainly couldn't have planned it. During the last week of the research project, I was in Ghana to speak at a conference and to wrap things up there. And the day I was due to fly back to England, Wednesday, March 29, 2006, the last day of my journey, there was to be a total eclipse of the sun. It would be visible only within a very narrow corridor across the earth's surface, starting in Brazil and ending at sunset in western Mongolia, and including Ghana en route!

On Saturday, March 25, 2006, the *Daily Graphic* carried a one-word front-page headline: "Eclipse." "Six regions in the country have been listed along the path to be covered by the total solar eclipse expected in the country between 8.30 am and 9.30 am next Wednesday," read the story. All the agencies of state, complete with acronyms, were getting mobilized: The executive director of the Centre of Remote Sensing and Geographic Information Services (CRSGIS) "urged all Ghanaians to be interested in the eclipse," the *Daily Graphic* enthused. The chairman of the National Planning Committee for Solar Eclipse said, "Special arrangements were being made with the Ghana Post to sound its sirens nationwide to announce the time of the eclipse." And he called on "churches and mosques" to "use their bells and microphones to announce the occurrence." Six million sunshades had been imported from Germany, with the Ministry of Tourism and Modernisation of the Capital City "making arrangements with private importers to bring in more." The National Disaster Management Organisation (NADMO) reported that "it was working in collaboration with the CRSGIS to draw the attention of the public to the hazards associated with the appearance of the total eclipse of the sun." Under Act 517, it reported, it was mandated "to prepare national disaster plans for preventing and mitigating the consequences of disaster and also to provide public awareness warning systems and general preparedness for the general public." It was "doing just that," it added. The deputy national coordinator in charge of relief and reconstruction at NADMO counseled that "during the period when the sudden darkness came, the behaviour of pets, nocturnal creatures and other animals might change."

On the Monday before the eclipse, I was in the fishing village of Bortianor, listening to the school proprietor of Supreme Academy, Theophilus Quaye, relating all that he'd read in the weekend's *Daily Graphic* to his students at morning assembly. But they knew already; the whole village was abuzz with excitement. On the beach, women waiting for their fishermen husbands to return had asked me to bring the imported sunglasses for their children. I'd bought a bagful in the city, at 10,000 cedis apiece (about $1, a price that was to rise to 25,000 cedis [about $2.50] as demand grew and supplies became scarce), and solemnly handed them over to Theophilus to distribute.

On Tuesday, I presented my findings at a conference. And on Wednesday morning, at my hotel in East Legon, Accra, I packed my bags, ate breakfast, and went outside at around 8:15. The next hour was to be quite extraordinary.

The sun had been up for an hour or more; the day had got under way as normal. As the moon slowly, imperceptibly at first, began to move in front of the sun, one by one the hotel staff congregated outside where I was standing. Sharing our imported German sunglasses, we stared up at the sun and saw the tiny speck of dark moon slowly moving across it. The young female hotel staff, in their neat black short skirts and cream blouses, begin to get excited: "CNN mentioned Ghana," a newcomer tells us, and her friend emits in delight, "Ghana is the gateway to Africa, CNN mentioned Ghana!"; they jump around with joy. A couple of young men gather in the shade of the outside bar. They are talking about science and how great it is that scientists have predicted this: "How did they know it would happen today? They said it would, and it did, exactly as they said!" Slowly it gets darker and slightly cooler. "It's as if it's going to rain," says one of the young men, "but the sky has no clouds."

The mood among the staff becomes increasingly excited as it becomes cooler and darker. One staring at the sun captures what all appear to be thinking—"God is great! Thank you, Jesus"—for they all join in; Ghana is a very religious country. The young men discussing science turn to this theme: "Scientists don't usually believe in God," says one, but his friend corrects him, "What about Sir Isaac Newton!" Yes, they agree, Sir Isaac Newton was a top scientist, and he believed in God.

And at the moment of total eclipse, when you can look directly at the sun without sunshades and see only darkness, with just the thinnest outline of light around the encompassed moon, the staff go wild, cheering, shouting, "God is great, Jesus is wonderful, thank you, God"; they cheer and dance, and ululate. And it's not just "pets, nocturnal creatures and other animals" whose behavior changes. Inexplicably, I find myself weeping, moved by my fellow watchers' response, acknowledging the somber beauty of these immense but predictable movements in the heavens. It's suddenly dark and still— but everywhere people are alive with excitement. And then it's all over, in exactly a minute, the light appears again suddenly—you can no longer look at the sun, but when you do in your dark glasses, you see that only the smallest sliver of sun has actually appeared— no matter, this tiny piece of sun has made it light again. It is totally memorable.

Later that day, I catch the flight home from Ghana, my journey over. And I think about the eclipse. As I eat my airline meal and drink the accompanying wine, I can't help feeling that there is a metaphor here for what I'd found over the years of my travels. At first I think it is obvious: the sun is like public education; the moon like private education moving slowly, imperceptibly at first, eventually blotting out the sun, eclipsing the state. But that wouldn't do, because of course then the moon moves away and the sun regains its preeminence. That metaphor didn't seem quite right. That was not what I thought I was seeing, a revival of private education that would eventually give way to the state again. A few drinks later, a different interpretation occurs to me. Wasn't the sun like the entrepreneurial spirit that I saw among the people, the spirit of self-help? And wasn't the moon like the state, apparently succeeding in blotting it out, stopping its light from shining through? It succeeds, but only for a brief moment in time. Eventually, the power of the sun, the power of the spirit of self-help, breaks through again to reign supreme.

These thoughts filled my mind on the journey home, and I wrote them in my notebook, hoping that they wouldn't seem too cheesy in the light of day—and without the accompaniment of a few glasses of wine. Probably they do, but perhaps it's still an apt metaphor. Public schooling seems to many to be a permanent, timeless feature of human civilization. But it's a temporary aberration; the revolution that is taking place in developing countries is seeing to that. The power and spirit of free enterprise are shining through again in the field of education. Will it eventually replace public schooling? I think the evidence shows that to be very likely. But will the state come around again, threatening to crowd it out, just as the moon will return to eclipse the sun? Perhaps it will. But the market in education is powerful. It builds on something that no central planner can possibly embrace, the strength of millions of decisions by individual families, the millions of bits of information grasped by the Searchers who relentlessly create and innovate, modify and develop what the people want. The power of educational self-help is strong, and you won't need special glasses to observe its effects.

Postscript

Just as I was finishing writing the book, I heard about the First Annual Private-Sector Development Competition, jointly organized by the *Financial Times* and the International Finance Corporation. They were looking for essays based on research that would help move forward understanding of how the private sector could assist development, and how this might open up opportunities for investors. And they had assembled an impressive array of judges, including the authors of influential books on development, such as Martin Wolf (*Why Globalisation Works*), Hernando de Soto (*The Mystery of Capital,*) and C. K. Prahalad (*The Fortune at the Bottom of the Pyramid.*) My team leader in Nigeria, Lanre, e-mailed me and said I should enter. So I thought I'd give it a go, with little expectation of success.

I condensed the last chapter of this book and my research findings into an essay, "Educating Amaretch: Private Schools for the Poor and the New Frontier for Investors." While harvesting potatoes and onions in my garden in rural Northumberland in late August 2006, I received a phone call from the International Finance Corporation office in Washington. I had to get Thomas Davenport to repeat his message several times before I could believe what I'd heard: I'd won the gold prize! I was flabbergasted, excited, humbled. For a couple of nights I could hardly sleep, I felt so elated that these ideas on private schools had found a sympathetic audience. No longer was I to plow a lonely furrow.

I was flown to Singapore for a long weekend in September 2006 to pick up the prize at the annual Governors' Meeting of the World Bank and International Monetary Fund. I was honored to meet with the judges, to discuss their ideas, and to hear about the other prize-winning entries. The day after the presentation, the *Financial Times* published an edited version of my essay, under the title "Private Schools for the Poor Seek Investors." A day later, a message was waiting for me on my answer machine: "Professor Tooley, I've read your article in the *Financial Times* . . . well, I'm your investor." It was Richard Chandler, the New Zealander founder and chairman of the Singaporean private investment company Orient Global. Over the course of the next two months, we met, in Newcastle and Dubai, exploring ways in which we could collaborate on our shared vision of how to improve lives and increase prosperity through market-based solutions. It was such an incredible opportunity, to do something practical based on all the ideas I had accumulated during the course of my journey.

In April 2007, I joined Orient Global as president of its newly created $100 million Education Fund, aimed at investing in private education in emerging economies. The Fund has given grants to several of the organizations and people mentioned in this book: to George Mikwa and the new Kenya Independent Schools Association, working in the slums of Nairobi; to AFED, the Association of Formidable Educational Development, serving low-cost private schools in the shantytowns of Nigeria; to Joy's school in Zimbabwe after Mugabe's troops bulldozed the shantytowns where her parents lived; and to scholarship schemes serving the remote village private schools in rural Gansu, China.

Most significantly, through the Fund I've laid the foundation for a chain of low-cost private schools. Closely following ideas set out in the last chapter. I've guided the initial research and development for curriculum, technology, and learning methods, acquired the first schools and built a strong team to carry the vision forward. The education entrepreneurs I've known longest are based in Hyderabad. So it is there for the last two years I made my home, and where I am writing this conclusion, working closely with Anwar, Wajid, and Reshma, all people I first met back in 2000, when my journey started.

And so this story ends in Hyderabad, where it began. The story of private schools serving the world's poor is only beginning.

References

Action Aid. 2003. "Response to World Development Report 2004." Submission to the *World Development Report 2004: Making Services Work for Poor People*. Washington: World Bank.

Adam, William. 1841. "State of Education in Bengal, 1835–38." In *The Beautiful Tree: Indigenous Indian Education in the Eighteenth Century*, by Dharampal, pp. 265–352. Coimbatore: Keerthi Publishing House, 1995.

Adelabu, M., and P. Rose. 2004. "Non-State Provision of Basic Education in Nigeria." In *Nigeria: Study of Non-State Providers of Basic Services*, ed. G. Larbi, M. Adelabu, P. Rose, D. Jawara, O. Nwaorgu, and S. Vyas. Commissioned by Policy Division, Department for International Development (DfID), UK, Country Studies, International Development Department, University of Birmingham.

Andhra Pradesh Education Act 27 of 1987. In *Law of Education in Andhra Pradesh*, 2nd ed., vol. 1, by V. J. Rao. Hyderabad: J. D. Gogia for S. Gogia & Company, 2000.

Asia Development Bank. 2003. "Technical Assistance to the People's Republic of China for Preparing the Gansu Roads Development Project." TAR:PRC 33470. www.adb.org/Documents/TARs/PRC/tar_prc_33470.pdf.

Bartholomew, J. 2004. *The Welfare State We're In*. London: Politicos.

Bashir, S. 1997. "The Cost Effectiveness of Public and Private Schools: Knowledge Gaps, New Research Methodologies and an Application in India." In *Marketizing Education and Health in Developing Countries: Miracle of Mirage?* ed. C. Colclough, pp. 124–64. Oxford: Clarendon Press.

Bell, A. 1797. *An Experiment in Education, Made at the Male Asylum at Madras*. London.
———. 1823. *Mutual Tuition and Moral Discipline; or Manual of Instructions for Conducting Schools through the Agency of the Scholars Themselves*. 7th ed. London: Hatchard and Son.

Brown, G. 2006. "Our Final Goal Must Be to Offer a Global New Deal." *Guardian* (UK), January 11.

Campbell, A. D. 1823. "Collector, Bellary to Board of Revenue: 17-8-1823 (TNSA:BRP: Vol. 958, Pro. 25-8-1823, pp. 7167–85, Nos. 32–33)." In *The Beautiful Tree: Indigenous Indian Education in the Eighteenth Century*, by Dharampal, pp. 178–89. Coimbatore: Keerthi Publishing House, 1995.

Census of India. 2001. "Primary Census Abstract: Andhra Pradesh, Karnataka and Lakshadweep." CD-ROM, Office of the Registrar General, New Delhi.

China Education and Research Network. 2005. "China Education and Research Network (2005) Outline and Actions of China's Education Reform and Development in 2005."

Commission for Africa. 2005. "Our Common Interest: Report of the Commission for Africa." www.commissionforafrica.org/english/report/introduction.html.

Cooke, William. 1823. "Principal Collector, North Arcot District, to Board of the Revenue: 3.3.1823 (TNSA:BRP: Vol. 944, Pro. 10.3.1823, pp. 2806–16, Nos. 20–21)."

In *The Beautiful Tree: Indigenous Indian Education in the Eighteenth Century,* by Dharampal, pp. 128–43. Coimbatore: Keerthi Publishing House, 1995.

Coulson, A. J. 1999. *Market Education: The Unknown History.* New Brunswick, NJ: Transaction Publishers.

Dabalen, A., and B. Oni. 2000. "Labor Market Prospects of University Graduates in Nigeria." World Bank, Washington.

Dalrymple, William. 2002. *White Mughals: Love and Betrayal in Eighteenth-Century India.* London: Harper-Collins.

Deng, Peng. 1997. *Private Education in Modern China.* Westport, CT: Praeger.

Dent, J. 1825. "Board of Revenue to Chief Secretary to Government, 21-2-1825 (TNSA: BRP: Vol. 1011, Pro. 21-2-1825, pp. 1412–26, No. 46)." In *The Beautiful Tree: Indigenous Indian Education in the Eighteenth Century,* by Dharampal, pp. 227–31. Coimbatore: Keerthi Publishing House, 1995.

DfID (Department for International Development). 2001. "The Challenge of Universal Primary Education." London.

Dharampal. 1995. *The Beautiful Tree: Indigenous Indian Education in the Eighteenth Century.* Coimbatore: Keerthi Publishing House. (Orig. pub. 1983.)

Drèze, J., and A. Sen. 2002. *India: Development and Participation.* 2nd ed. New Delhi: Oxford University Press.

Easterly, W. 2001. *The Elusive Quest for Growth: Economists' Adventures and Misadventures in the Tropics.* Cambridge, MA: MIT Press.

———. 2006. *The White Man's Burden: Why the West's Efforts to Aid the Rest Have Done So Much Ill and So Little Good.* New York: Penguin Press.

Education Committee, UK National Commission for UNESCO. 2003. *Education for All: United Kingdom Perspectives.* Slough: NFER.

Fraser, T. 1823. "Collector, Nellore to Board of Revenue: 23.6.1823 (TNSA:BRP: Vol. 952 Pro. 30.6.1823, pp. 5188–91, No. 26)." In *The Beautiful Tree: Indigenous Indian Education in the Eighteenth Century,* by Dharampal, pp. 152–56. Coimbatore: Keerthi Publishing House, 1995.

Friedman, Milton. 1955. "The Role of Government in Education." In *Economics and the Public Interest,* ed. Robert A. Solo, pp. 123–44. New Brunswick, NJ: Rutgers University Press.

Friedman, Milton, and Rose Friedman. 1980. *Free to Choose.* Harmondsworth UK: Penguin.

Ga District Assembly. 2002. "Ghana Poverty Reduction Strategy: Three-Year Medium Term Development Plan 2002–2004." District Planning Co-Ordinating Unit. Amasaman, Ghana.

———. 2004. "Poverty Profile, Maps and Pro-Poor Programmes." Amasaman, Ghana.

Gansu Statistics Bureau. 2001. "The Fifth Gansu Population Census Report" (in Chinese). www.stats.gov.cn/tjgb/rkpcgb/dfrkpcgb/t20020331_15402.htm.

———. 2004. *2004 Gansu Yearbook.* Beijing: China Statistics Publishing House.

Geldof, B. 2004. Foreword to *The Rough Guide to a Better World,* by M. Wroe and M. Doney, pp. 5–7. London: Rough Guides in association with DfID.

Glewwe, P., N. Illias, and M. Kremer. 2004. "Teaching Incentives." Working paper, National Bureau of Economic Research, Cambridge, MA.

Government of Andhra Pradesh. 1997. "Census of India 1991, Series 2, Andhra Pradesh: District Census Handbook Hyderabad."

Halpin, Tony. 2006. *Times Educational Supplement,* February 5. www.timeson line.co.uk/tol/news/uk/article734920.ece.

Hanushek, E. A. 2003. "The Failure of Input-Based Schooling Policies." *Economic Journal* 113 (485): F64–F98.

Harris, T. 1822. "Principal Collector, Canara, to Board of Revenue: 27.8.1822 (TNSA: BRP: Vol. 924 Pro. 5.9.1822, pp. 8425–29, Nos. 35–36)." In *The Beautiful Tree: Indigenous Indian Education in the Eighteenth Century,* by Dharampal, pp. 88–90. Coimbatore: Keerthi Publishing House, 1995.

Hartog, Philip. 1939. *Some Aspects of Indian Education Past and Present.* University of London, Institute of Education, Studies and Reports no. VII. London: Oxford University Press, Humphrey Milford.

He, Zhiyi. 2001. *The Socio-Economic Study on Private Education in Guangdong.* Guangzhou, China: Guangdong People's Publishing House.

Hyde, C. 1823. "Principal Collector of South Arcot to Board of Revenue: 29-6-1823, Cuddalore (TNSA:BRP: Vol. 954, Pro. 7-7-1823, pp. 5622–24, Nos. 59–60)." In *The Beautiful Tree: Indigenous Indian Education in the Eighteenth Century,* by Dharampal, pp. 144–46. Coimbatore: Keerthi Publishing House, 1995.

Jimenez, E., M. E. Lockheed, E. Luna, and V. Paqueo. 1991. "School Effects and Costs for Private and Public Schools in the Dominican Republic." *International Journal of Educational Research* 15 (5): 393–410.

Jimenez, E., M. E. Lockheed, and V. Paqueo. 1991 "The Relative Efficiency of Private and Public Schools in Developing Countries." *World Bank Research Observer* 6 (2): 205–18.

Jimenez, E., M. E. Lockheed, and N. Wattanawaha. 1988. "The Relative Efficiency of Public and Private Schools: The Case of Thailand." *World Bank Economic Review* 2 (2): 139–64.

Kenyatta, J. 1938. *Facing Mount Kenya.* London: Vintage Books.

Kikuyu Province Annual Report, 1929, see note 45 in chap. 11.

Kingdon, G. 1996. "The Quality and Efficiency of Private and Public Education: A Case Study in Urban India." *Oxford Bulletin of Economics and Statistics* 58 (1): 57–81.

Krueger, A. B. 2003. "Economic Considerations and Class Size." *Economic Journal* 113 (485): F34–F63.

LASEEDS (Lagos State Economic and Empowerment Development Strategy). 2004.

Lassibille, G., and J. Tan. 2001. "Are Private Schools More Efficient than Public Schools? Evidence from Tanzania." *Education Economic* 9 (2): 145–72.

Lauglo, J. 2004. "Basic Education in Areas Targeted for EFA: ASAL Districts and Urban Informal Settlements in Kenya." World Bank, Washington.

Leach, J. 2005. "DEEP Impact: An Investigation of the Use of Information and Communication Technologies for Teacher Education in the Global South." Education Paper no. 58, DfID. www.dfid.gov.uk/pubs/files/ict-teacher-education-no58.asp.

Lee, Thomas H. C. 2000. *Education in Traditional China: A History.* Leiden, Neth.: Brill.

Leitner, G. W. 1883. "History of Indigenous Education in the Punjab since Annexation and in 1882." In *The Beautiful Tree: Indigenous Indian Education in the Eighteenth Century,* by Dharampal, pp. 347–52. Coimbatore: Keerthi Publishing House, 1995.

Lin, Jing A. 1999. *Social Transformation and Private Education in China.* Westport, CT: Praeger.

Macaulay, T. B. 1835. "Minute of 2 February 1835 on Indian Education." In *Macaulay, Prose and Poetry,* selected by G. M. Young, pp. 721–29. Cambridge, MA: Harvard University Press, 1957.

Meiklejohn, J. M. D. 1881. *An Old Educational Reformer: Dr Andrew Bell.* Edinburgh: William Blackwood and Sons.

Mingat, A., and C. Winter. 2002. "Education for All by 2015." *Finance and Development* 39 (1): 1–6.

Mitra, S., J. Tooley, P. Inamdar, and P. Dixon. 2003. "Improving English Pronunciation: An Automated Instructional Approach." *Information Technologies and International Development* 1 (1): 75–84.

Municipal Corporation of Hyderabad. 2004. "City Development Strategy." Conference on City Development Strategies: From Vision to Growth and Poverty Reduction, November 24–26, Hanoi.

Munro, Thomas. 1822. "Minute of Governor Sir Thomas Munro Ordering Indigenous Education: 25.6.1822. (TNSA: Revenue Consultations: Vol. 920: dated 2.7.1822)." In *The Beautiful Tree: Indigenous Indian Education in the Eighteenth Century*, by Dharampal, pp. 83–84. Coimbatore: Keerthi Publishing House, 1995.

———. 1826. "Minute of Sir Thomas Munro, March 10, 1826 (Fort St George, Revenue Consultations), 10 March 1826." In *The Beautiful Tree: Indigenous Indian Education in the Eighteenth Century*, by Dharampal, pp. 248–51. Coimbatore: Keerthi Publishing House, 1995.

Murphy, P., S. Anzalone, A. Bosch, and J. Moulton. 2002. *Enhancing Learning Opportunities in Africa: Distance Education and Information and Communication Technologies for Learning*. Washington: World Bank.

Murray, L. G. K. 1822. "Collector, Madras, to Board of Revenue: 13.11.1822 (TNSA:BRP: Vol. 931. Pro. 14-11-1822, pp. 10, 512–13, Nos. 57–58)." In *The Beautiful Tree: Indigenous Indian Education in the Eighteenth Century*, by Dharampal, pp. 113, 126–27. Coimbatore: Keerthi Publishing House, 1995.

Nambissan, G. B. 2003. "Educational Deprivation and Primary School Provision: A Study of Providers in the City of Calcutta." IDS Working Paper no. 187, Institute of Development Studies, University of Sussex, Brighton.

National Bureau of Statistics. 2006. "Important Data of Population Census of Gansu Province." www.gansu.gov.cn/Upload/ZH/G_ZH_0000000899_22.htm.

Nilekani, Nandan. 2008. *Imagining India: Ideas for the New Century*. New Delhi: Allen Lane, Penguin.

Oxfam International. 2005. *Paying the Price: Why Rich Countries Must Invest Now in a War on Poverty*. Oxford: Oxfam International.

Potter, C., and A. S. F. Silva, eds. 2002. *Teachers in Action: Case Studies of Radio Learning in South African Primary Schools*. Johannesburg: Open Learning Systems Education Trust.

Prahalad, C. K. 2004. *The Fortune at the Bottom of the Pyramid*. Upper Saddle River, NJ: Wharton School Publishing.

PROBE Team. 1999. *Public Report on Basic Education in India*. Oxford: Oxford University Press.

Rao, V. J. 2000. *Law of Education in Andhra Pradesh*. 2nd ed., vol. 1. Hyderabad: J. D. Gogia for S. Gogia & Company.

Rao, Y. Vittal. 1979. *Education and Learning in Andhra under the East India Company*. Secunderabad: N. Vidyaranya Swamy.

Rhodes, R., and S. Rasmussen-Tall. 2005. "Teacher Training via Radio Is Launched in Mali." www/usaidmali.org/article.php?id = 0079_EN&lan = en&skin.

Rose, P. 2002. "Is the Non-State Education Sector Serving the Needs of the Poor? Evidence from East and Southern Africa." Paper prepared for DfID seminar in preparation for *2004 World Development Report: Making Services Work for Poor People* (cited with the author's permission, p.m.rose@sussex.ac.uk).

Sachs, J. D. 2005. *The End of Poverty: Economic Possibilities for Our Time.* London: Penguin Books.

Save the Children. 2004. Submission to the *World Development Report 2004: Making Services Work for Poor People.* Washington: World Bank.

Save the Children UK. 2002. "Private Sector Involvement in Education." Submission to "The Private Sector as Service Provider and Its Role in Implementing Child Rights," Office of the High Commissioner for Human Rights, Geneva.

Save the Children UK, South and Central Asia. 2002. "A Perspective from Nepal and Pakistan." Submission to "The Private Sector as Service Provider and Its Role in Implementing Child Rights," Office of the High Commissioner for Human Rights, Geneva.

Sen, A. 1999. *Development as Freedom.* New York: Knopf.

Sivaramakrishnan. 1995. Afterword to *The Beautiful Tree: Indigenous Indian Education in the Eighteenth Century,* by Dharampal, pp. 436–50. Coimbatore: Keerthi Publishing House, 1995.

Smalley, S. 1823. "Collector of Chingleput to Board of Revenue: 3.4.1823 (TNSA:BRP: Vol. 946, Pro. 7-4-1823, pp. 3493–96, No. 25)." In *The Beautiful Tree: Indigenous Indian Education in the Eighteenth Century,* by Dharampal, pp. 144, 146–47. Coimbatore: Keerthi Publishing House, 1995.

Sullivan, J. 1822. "Principal Collector, Coimbatore to Board of Revenue: 23.11.1822 (TNSA:BRP: Vol. 932, Pro. 2.12.1822, pp. 10939–943, No. 43)." In *The Beautiful Tree: Indigenous Indian Education in the Eighteenth Century,* by Dharampal, pp. 100–7. Coimbatore: Keerthi Publishing House, 1995.

Swift, Adam. 2003. *How Not to Be a Hypocrite: School Choice for the Morally Perplexed Parent.* London: Routledge.

Tomasevski, Katarina. 2003. *Education Denied: Costs and Remedies.* London: Zed Books.

Tooley, J. 2000. *Reclaiming Education.* London: Continuum.

———. 2008. "From Adam Swift to Adam Smith: How the 'Invisible Hand' Overcomes Middle Class Hypocrisy." *Journal of Philosophy of Education* 41 (4): 727–41.

Tooley, J., and P. Dixon. 2005a. "An Inspector Calls: The Regulation of 'Budget' Private Schools in Hyderabad, Andhra Pradesh, India." *International Journal of Educational Development* 25: 269–85.

———. 2005b. "Is There a Conflict between Commercial Gain and Concern for the Poor? Evidence from Private Schools for the Poor in India and Nigeria." *Economic Affairs* 25 (2): 20–27.

———. 2005c. *Private Education Is Good for the Poor: A Study of Private Schools Serving the Poor in Low-Income Countries.* Washington: Cato Institute.

Tooley, J., P. Dixon, and I. Amuah. 2007. "Private and Public Schooling in Ga, Ghana: A Census and Comparative Survey." *International Review of Education* 53 (3–4): 389–415.

Tooley, J., P. Dixon, and S. V. Gomathi. 2007. "Private Schools and the Millennium Development Goal of Universal Primary Education: A Census and Comparative Survey in Hyderabad, India." *Oxford Review of Education* 33 (5): 539–60.

Tooley, J., P. Dixon, and O. Olaniyan. 2005. "Private and Public Schooling in Low-Income Areas of Lagos State, Nigeria: A Census and Comparative Survey." *International Journal of Educational Research* 43 (3): 125–46.

Tooley, J., P. Dixon, and J. Stanfield. 2008. "The Impact of Free Education in Kenya: A Case Study in Private Schools in Kibera." *Educational Management, Administration and Leadership* 36 (4): 449–69.

Tooley, J., L. Qiang, and P. Dixon. 2007. "Private Schools for the Poor in Gansu Province, China" (in Chinese). *Private Education Research* 6 (2): 25–28.

Tooley, J., and J. Stanfield, eds. 2003. *Government Failure: E. G. West on Education*. London: Profile Books.

UNDP (United Nations Development Programme). 2003. *Human Development Report 2003*. New York: UNDP.

UNESCO (United Nations Educational, Scientific, and Cultural Organization). 2000a. "Education for All: Meeting Our Collective Commitments. Expanded Commentary on the Dakar Framework for Action." Paris. www.unesco.org/education/efa/wef_2000/expanded_com_eng.shtml.

———. 2000b. "Preparation of National Plans of Action, Education for All, Country Guidelines." http://unesdoc.unesco.org/images/0012/001219/121911e.pdf.

———. 2002. *Education for All: Is the World on Track?* EFA Global Monitoring Report 2002. Paris: UNESCO.

———. 2004. *Education for All: The Quality Imperative*. EFA Global Monitoring Report 2005. Paris: UNESCO.

UNICEF (United Nations Children's Fund). 2002. Submission to "The Private Sector as Service Provider and Its Role in Implementing Child Rights." Office of the High Commissioner for Human Rights, Geneva.

Vaughan, J. 1823. "Principal Collector, Malabar to Board of Revenue: 5-8-1823 (TNSA:BRP: Vol. 957, Pro. 14-8-1823, pp. 6949–55, Nos. 52–53)." In *The Beautiful Tree: Indigenous Indian Education in the Eighteenth Century*, by Dharampal, pp. 199–203. Coimbatore: Keerthi Publishing House, 1995.

Vibart, H. 1822. "Assistant Collector, Seringapatnam to Board of Revenue, 29.10.1822 (TNSA:BRP: Vol. 929, Pro. 4-11-1822, pp. 10260–2, Nos. 33–34)." In *The Beautiful Tree: Indigenous Indian Education in the Eighteenth Century*, by Dharampal, pp. 94, 96–97. Coimbatore: Keerthi Publishing House, 1995.

Watkins, K. 2000. *The Oxfam Education Report*. Oxford: Oxfam in Great Britain.

———. 2004. "Private Education and 'Education for All'—or How Not to Construct an Evidence-Based Argument." *Economic Affairs* 24 (4): 8–11.

West, E. G. 1994. *Education and the State*. 3rd ed. Indianapolis: Liberty Fund. (Orig. pub. 1965.)

———. 1983. "Nineteenth-Century Educational History: The Kiesling Critique." *Economic History Review* 36: 426–34.

World Bank. 2003. *World Development Report 2004: Making Services Work for Poor People*. Washington: World Bank.

World Education Forum. 2000. *The Dakar Framework for Action, Education for All: Meeting Our Collective Commitments*. Paris: UNESCO.

Zymelman, M., and J. Destefano. 1989. "Primary School Teachers Salaries in Sub-Saharan Africa." Division Paper no. 45, World Bank, Washington.

Notes

Chapter 2

1. Quotes are, in order, from J. Drèze and A. Sen, *India: Development and Participation*, 2nd ed. (New Delhi: Oxford University Press, 2002), pp. 286, 172–73, 59, 172, 161, and fn. 72, p. 172.

2. Quotations are, in order, from PROBE Team *Public Report on Basic Education in India* (Oxford: Oxford University Press, 1999), pp. 103, 47, 48, 63, and 102.

3. Ibid., p. 64 (emphasis added).

4. Drèze and Sen, *India: Development and Participation*, p. 173.

5. Quotations are, in order, from K. Watkins, *The Oxfam Education Report* (Oxford: Oxfam in Great Britain, 2000), pp. 1, 333, 346, 230, 229, 6, 230, and 106.

6. Data on Hyderabad and Mahbubnagar are from Municipal Corporation of Hyderabad, "City Development Strategy," Conference on City Development Strategies: From Vision to Growth and Poverty Reduction, November 24–26, 2004, Hanoi; and Government of Andhra Pradesh, "Census of India 1991, Series 2, Andhra Pradesh: District Census Handbook Hyderabad," Government of Andhra Pradesh, 1997. Data on Delhi are from Census of India, "Primary Census Abstract: Andhra Pradesh, Karnataka and Lakshadweep," CD-ROM, Office of the Registrar General, New Delhi, 2001.

Chapter 3

1. Data are from LASEEDS, 2004, pp. 29, 5, and 7.

Chapter 4

1. A native or inhabitant of Newcastle upon Tyne, England, or its environs.

2. Data are from Ga District Assembly, "Ghana Poverty Reduction Strategy: Three-Year Medium Term Development Plan 2002–2004," District Planning Co-Ordinating Unit, Amasaman, Ghana, 2002; and Ga District Assembly, "Poverty Profile, Maps and Pro-Poor Programmes," Amasaman, Ghana, 2004.

3. For further information on all the research data here and in following chapters, see J. Tooley and P. Dixon, "An Inspector Calls: The Regulation of 'Budget' Private Schools in Hyderabad, Andhra Pradesh, India," *International Journal of Educational Development* 25 (2005a): 269–85; J. Tooley and P. Dixon, "Is There a Conflict between Commercial Gain and Concern for the Poor? Evidence from Private Schools for the Poor in India and Nigeria," *Economic Affairs* 25, no. 2 (2005b): 20–27; J. Tooley and P. Dixon, *Private Education Is Good for the Poor: A Study of Private Schools Serving the Poor in Low-Income Countries* (Washington: Cato Institute, 2005c); J. Tooley and P. Dixon, "'De Facto' Privatisation of Education and the Poor: Implications of a Study

from Sub-Saharan Africa and India," *Compare* 36, no. 4 (2006): 443–62; J. Tooley and P. Dixon, "Private Schooling for Low-Income Families: A Census and Comparative Survey in East Delhi, India," *International Journal of Educational Development* 27, no. 2 (2007): 205–19; J. Tooley, P. Dixon, and I. Amuah, "Private and Public Schooling in Ga, Ghana: A Census and Comparative Survey," *International Review of Education* 53, no. 3–4 (2007): 389–415; J. Tooley, P. Dixon, and S. V. Gomathi, "Private Schools and the Millennium Development Goal of Universal Primary Education: A Census and Comparative Survey in Hyderabad, India," *Oxford Review of Education* 33, no. 5 (2007): 539–60; J. Tooley, P. Dixon, and O. Olaniyan, "Private and Public Schooling in Low-Income Areas of Lagos State, Nigeria: A Census and Comparative Survey," *International Journal of Educational Research* 43, no. 3 (2005): 125–46; J. Tooley, L. Qiang, and P. Dixon, "Private Schools for the Poor in Gansu Province, China" (in Chinese), *Private Education Research* 6, no. 2 (2007): 25–28; and J. Tooley, P. Dixon, and J. Stanfield, "The Impact of Free Education in Kenya: A Case Study in Private Schools in Kibera," *Educational Management, Administration and Leadership* 36, no. 4 (2008): 449–69.

Chapter 5

1. Statistics are from Asia Development Bank, "Technical Assistance to the People's Republic of China for Preparing the Gansu Roads Development Project," TAR:PRC 33470, 2003, pp. 2–3, www.adb.org/Documents/TARs/PRC/tar_prc_33470.pdf; Gansu Statistics Bureau, "The Fifth Gansu Population Census Report" (in Chinese), 2001, www.stats.gov.cn/tjgb/rkpcgb/dfrkpcgb/t20020331_15402.htm (2001); and National Bureau of Statistics, "Important Data of Population Census of Gansu Province," 2006, www.gansu.gov.cn/Upload/ZH/G_ZH_0000000899_22.htm.

2. For further details of the research method and findings, see James Tooley, Liu Qiang, and Pauline Dixon, "Private Schools for the Poor in Gansu Province, China" (in Chinese), *Private Education Research* 6, no. 2 (2007): 25–28.

3. Gansu Statistics Bureau, "Fifth Census Report," p. 738.

4. Katarina Tomasevski, *Education Denied: Costs and Remedies* (London: Zed Books, 2003).

5. China Education and Research Network, "China Education and Research Network (2005) Outline and Actions of China's Education Reform and Development in 2005," 2005.

Chapter 6

1. Peter Jennings, *Primetime*, ABC Television, November 18, 2004.

2. References for this paragraph are G. Brown, "Our Final Goal Must Be to Offer a Global New Deal," *Guardian* (UK), January 11, 2006; and J. Lauglo, "Basic Education in Areas Targeted for EFA: ASAL Districts and Urban Informal Settlements in Kenya," World Bank, Washington, 2004.

3. References for the quotations in this paragraph are, in order, J. D. Sachs, *The End of Poverty: Economic Possibilities for Our Time* (London: Penguin Books, 2005); UNDP, *Human Development Report 2003* (New York: UNDP, 2003), p. 115; Oxfam International, *Paying the Price: Why Rich Countries Must Invest Now in a War on Poverty* (Oxford: Oxfam International, 2005), p. 72; Save the Children UK, "Private Sector Involvement in Education," submission to "The Private Sector as Service Provider and Its Role in Implementing Child Rights," Office of the High Commissioner for Human Rights, Geneva, 2002, p. 5; Save the Children UK, South and Central Asia,

"A Perspective from Nepal and Pakistan," submission to "The Private Sector as Service Provider and Its Role in Implementing Child Rights," Office of the High Commissioner for Human Rights, Geneva, 2002, p. 7; World Bank, *World Development Report 2004: Making Services Work for Poor People* (Washington: World Bank, 2003); and Oxfam International, *Paying the Price*, p. 17.

4. The reference for this section is P. Rose, "Is the Non-State Education Sector Serving the Needs of the Poor? Evidence from East and Southern Africa," paper prepared for DfID seminar in preparation for *World Development Report 2004*, 2002, pp. 6, 16, and 7 (cited with the author's permission, p.m.rose@sussex.ac.uk).

5. The reference for this section is Lauglo, "Basic Education in Areas Targeted for EFA." For further details on the research method and findings, see J. Tooley, P. Dixon, and J. Stanfield, "The Impact of Free Education in Kenya: A Case Study in Private Schools in Kibera," *Educational Management, Administration and Leadership*, 36, no. 4 (2008): 449–69.

6. References for this paragraph are Save the Children, submission to the *World Development Report 2004: Making Services Work for Poor People* (Washington: World Bank, 2003), p. 34; and Action Aid, "Response to World Development Report 2004," submission to the *World Development Report 2004: Making Services Work for Poor People* (World Bank, Washington, 2003), p. 5.

Chapter 7

1. Sources cited in this section are, in order, UNESCO, *Education for All: The Quality Imperative*, EFA Global Monitoring Report 2005 (Paris: UNESCO, 2004), p. 18; UNDP, *Human Development Report 2003* (New York: UNDP, 2003), p. 112; P. Glewwe, N. Illias, and M. Kremer, "Teaching Incentives," working paper, National Bureau of Economic Research, Cambridge, MA, 2004; UNESCO, *Education for All*, pp. 29 and 26; World Bank, *World Development Report 2004: Making Services Work for Poor People* (Washington: World Bank, 2003), pp. 24, 4, and 112; and G. B. Nambissan, "Educational Deprivation and Primary School Provision: A Study of Providers in the City of Calcutta," IDS Working Paper no. 187, Institute of Development Studies, University of Sussex, Brighton, 2003, p. 31.

2. Sources cited in this section are, in order, World Bank, *World Development Report 2004*, p. 25; and Nambissan, "Educational Deprivation and Primary School Provision," pp. 29 and 35.

3. Sources cited in this section are, in order, World Bank, *World Development Report 2004*, p. 24; Nambissan, "Educational Deprivation and Primary School Provision," pp. 20 and 21; and DfID, "The Challenge of Universal Primary Education," London, 2001, p. 23.

4. Sources cited in this section are, in order, World Bank, *World Development Report 2004*, p. 112 (emphasis added); DfID, "The Challenge of Universal Primary Education," p. 21; and Nambissan, "Educational Deprivation and Primary School Provision," p. 35.

5. UNDP, *Human Development Report 2003*; Save the Children UK, South and Central Asia, "A Perspective from Nepal and Pakistan," submission to "The Private Sector as Service Provider and Its Role in Implementing Child Rights," Office of the High Commissioner for Human Rights, Geneva, 2002, p. 5; and World Bank, *World Development Report 2004*, p. 3.

6. World Bank, *World Development Report 2004*, p. 182; and Action Aid, "Response to World Development Report 2004," submission to the *World Development Report 2004: Making Services Work for Poor People* (World Bank, Washington, 2003), p. 1.

7. Sources cited are, in order, Action Aid, "Response to World Development Report 2004," p. 2; and World Bank, *World Development Report 2004*, pp. 113, 1, 10, 11, and 6.

8. Sources cited in this section are, in order, Save the Children UK, South and Central Asia, "A Perspective from Nepal and Pakistan," pp. 8, 9, 13, and 9; Nambissan, "Educational Deprivation and Primary School Provision," p. 52; Commission for Africa, "Our Common Interest: Report of the Commission for Africa," 2005, p. 179, www.commissionforafrica.org/english/report/introduction.html; P. Rose, "Is the Non-State Education Sector Serving the Needs of the Poor? Evidence from East and Southern Africa," paper prepared for DfID seminar in preparation for *World Development Report 2004*, 2002, pp. 16, 5, 6–7, 6, Box 1, and 6–7 (cited with the author's permission, p.m.rose@sussex.ac.uk); M. Adelabu and P. Rose, "Non-State Provision of Basic Education in Nigeria," in *Nigeria: Study of Non-State Providers of Basic Services*, ed. G. Larbi, M. Adelabu, P. Rose, D. Jawara, O. Nwaorgu, and S. Vyas, commissioned by Policy Division, Department of International Development (DfID), UK, Country Studies, International Development Department, University of Birmingham, 2004, pp. 47, 47–48, 57, 64 (emphasis added), and 49; K. Watkins, *The Oxfam Education Report* (Oxford: Oxfam in Great Britain, 2000), p. 230; and UNDP, *Human Development Report 2003*, p. 115 (emphasis added).

9. See, for example, studies by G. Kingdon ("The Quality and Efficiency of Private and Public Education: A Case Study in Urban India," *Oxford Bulletin of Economics and Statistics* 58, no. 1 [1996]: 57–81); E. Jimenez, M. E. Lockheed, and N. Wattanawaha ("The Relative Efficiency of Public and Private Schools: The Case of Thailand," *World Bank Economic Review* 2, no. 2 [1988]: 139–64); E. Jimenez and others ("School Effects and Costs for Private and Public Schools in the Dominican Republic," *International Journal of Educational Research* 15, no. 5 [1991]: 393–410); and E. Jimenez, M. E. Lockheed, and V. Paqueo ("The Relative Efficiency of Private and Public Schools in Developing Countries," *World Bank Research Observer* 6, no. 2 [1991]: 205–18) that concluded that, in general, private schools outperform public schools for lower unit costs, although studies by S. Bashir ("The Cost Effectiveness of Public and Private Schools: Knowledge Gaps, New Research Methodologies and an Application in India," in *Marketizing Education and Health in Developing Countries: Miracle of Mirage?* ed. C. Colclough, pp. 124–64 [Oxford: Clarendon Press, 1997]) and G. Lassibille and J. Tan ("Are Private Schools More Efficient than Public Schools? Evidence from Tanzania," *Education Economic* 9, no. 2 [2001]: 145–72) came to contrary conclusions.

10. Watkins, *The Oxfam Education Report*, p. 230.

Chapter 8

1. Sources cited in this section are, in order, Save the Children, submission to the *World Development Report 2004: Making Services Work for Poor People* (Washington: World Bank, 2004), p. 6; Save the Children UK, "Private Sector Involvement in Education," submission to "The Private Sector as Service Provider and Its Role in Implementing Child Rights," Office of the High Commissioner for Human Rights, Geneva, 2002, p. 8 (emphasis added); P. Rose, "Is the Non-State Education Sector Serving the Needs of the Poor? Evidence from East and Southern Africa," paper prepared for DfID seminar in preparation for *World Development Report 2004*, 2002,

p. 15 (emphasis added; cited with the author's permission, p.m.rose@sussex.ac.uk); UNICEF, submission to "The Private Sector as Service Provider and Its Role in Implementing Child Rights," Office of the High Commissioner for Human Rights, Geneva, 2002, p. 6; and Save the Children UK, South and Central Asia, "A Perspective from Nepal and Pakistan," submission to "The Private Sector as Service Provider and Its Role in Implementing Child Rights," Office of the High Commissioner for Human Rights, Geneva, 2002, p. 9.

2. There is one oddity, however, that the development experts might feel reinforces their argument about the need for regulation. That is, when one visits recognized and unrecognized private schools, the recognized schools do often appear to be better than the unrecognized ones. (The evidence outlined in the next chapter reinforces this intuition.) They often appear to have better infrastructure and better-equipped classrooms. Teachers seem to speak better English. However, if becoming recognized has nothing to do with actually meeting regulations, just with the payment of bribes, then why should they be better?

It took me awhile to think this through, but it seems the answer lies in the fact that many of the ways in which recognized schools are better than unrecognized private schools are not prescribed in the detailed regulations. In Hyderabad, for instance, no regulations address the provision of learning facilities, such as televisions, tape recorders and computers, or fans. Yet with these facilities, just as with those that regulations address, like playgrounds, drinking water, and toilets, the recognized private schools seem to be better than the unrecognized schools. This suggests that the impetus for school improvement comes from other factors, not from a desire to be recognized by government. The obvious one is to meet parental demand.

But then, the development experts could counter, why don't the unrecognized schools also strive to meet parental demand in the same way, since they're also operating in the education market and will also need to keep parents happy? The reasons are not hard to find. In every study, I found that unrecognized private schools are considerably smaller and considerably newer than recognized private schools. What seems most likely to me is that the maturity of the schools, rather than regulation, is responsible for their improvement. Private schools improve as they become more mature, attracting more students, and, hence, can afford to invest in more and better facilities, and more motivated teachers. As they mature, they can also afford the informal payments to gain recognition. Why would they bother paying for recognition? Because being recognized does have its benefits: Only recognized schools can issue transfer certificates, which enable children to move from their school to the next stage. Only recognized schools can legally be examination centers.

3. Sources cited in this section are, in order, Save the Children UK, South and Central Asia, "A Perspective from Nepal and Pakistan," p. 10; UNICEF, submission to "The Private Sector as Service Provider," pp. 11–12; and World Bank, *World Development Report 2004: Making Services Work for Poor People* (Washington: World Bank, 2003), pp. 47, 49, 52 (emphasis added), 6, 55, 6–7, 115, 60, 56, 6, 8, 57, 124, 57, and 124.

Chapter 9

1. See E. A. Hanushek, "The Failure of Input-Based Schooling Policies," *Economic Journal* 113, no. 485 (2003): F64–F98; and A. B. Krueger, "Economic Considerations and Class Size," *Economic Journal* 113, no. 485 (2003): F34–F63.

2. Nandan Nilekani, *Imagining India: Ideas for the New Century* (New Delhi: Allen Lane, Penguin, 2008), pp. 92–93.

3. K. Watkins, *The Oxfam Education Report* (Oxford: Oxfam in Great Britain, 2000), p. 230.

4. UNDP, *Human Development Report 2003* (New York: UNDP, 2005), p. 115.

5. A. Mingat and C. Winter, "Education for All by 2015," *Finance and Development* 39, no. 1 (2002): 1–6; and M. Zymelman and J. Destefano, "Primary School Teachers Salaries in Sub-Saharan Africa," Division Paper no. 45, World Bank, Washington, 1989.

6. See, for example, A. Dabalen and B. Oni, "Labor Market Prospects of University Graduates in Nigeria," World Bank, Washington, 2000.

7. Gansu Statistics Bureau, *2004 Gansu Yearbook* (Beijing: China Statistics Publishing House, 2004).

Chapter 10

1. Sources cited in this section are, in order, PROBE Team, *Public Report on Basic Education in India* (Oxford: Oxford University Press, 1999), pp. 105–6; K. Watkins, "Private Education and 'Education for All'—or How Not to Construct an Evidence-Based Argument," *Economic Affairs* 24, no. 4 (2004): 11; World Bank, *World Development Report 2004: Making Services Work for Poor People* (Washington: World Bank, 2003), pp. 3, 10–11, and 33; UNDP, *Human Development Report 2003* (New York: UNDP, 2003), p. 111; World Bank, p. 4; UNDP, p. 93; K. Watkins, *The Oxfam Education Report* (Oxford: Oxfam in Great Britain, 2000), pp. 207 and 230; PROBE Team, p. 105; UNDP, p. 115; World Bank, pp. 6 and 9; Watkins, *Oxfam Education Report*, p. 232; UNDP, p. 111; World Bank, p. 33; UNDP, p. 1; World Education Forum, *The Dakar Framework for Action, Education for All: Meeting Our Collective Commitments* (Paris: UNESCO, 2000), p. 8 (emphasis added); UNESCO, *Education for All: Is the World on Track?* EFA Global Monitoring Report 2002 (Paris: UNESCO, 2002), p. 29; UNESCO, "Education for All: Meeting Our Collective Commitments, Expanded Commentary on the Dakar Framework for Action," Paris, 2000a, pp. 14 (emphasis added) and 15 (emphasis added), www.unesco.org/education/efa/wef_2000/expanded_com_eng.shtml; World Bank, p. 3; UNDP, p. 111; A. Sen, *Development as Freedom* (New York: Knopf, 1999), p. 129; World Bank, pp. 11 and 54–55; UNDP, p. 111.

2. Sources for this paragraph and the next are E. G. West, *Education and the State,* 3rd ed. (Indianapolis: Liberty Fund, 1994); A. J. Coulson, *Market Education: The Unknown History* (New Brunswick, NJ: Transaction Publishers, 1999); J. Tooley, *Reclaiming Education* (London: Continuum, 2000); J. Tooley and J. Stanfield, eds., *Government Failure: E. G. West on Education* (London: Profile Books, 2003); Education Committee, UK National Commission for UNESCO, *Education for All: United Kingdom Perspectives* (Slough: NFER, 2003), pp. 6 and 24; and B. Geldof, Foreword to *The Rough Guide to a Better World*, by M. Wroe and M. Doney (London: Rough Guides in association with DfID, 2004), pp. 5–6.

Chapter 11

1. William Dalrymple, *White Mughals: Love and Betrayal in Eighteenth-Century India* (London: Harper-Collins, 2002), pp. xliii and xliv.

2. All quotes are from Dharampal, *The Beautiful Tree: Indigenous Indian Education in the Eighteenth Century* (Coimbatore: Keerthi Publishing House, 1995), p. 355.

3. Thomas Munro, 1822, in Dharampal, p. 83.

4. T. Harris, 1822, in Dharampal, p. 88.

5. Dharampal, pp. 18–19 and 34–35.

6. Sources cited in this paragraph are, in order, Thomas Munro, 1826, in Dharampal, p. 249; Dharampal, pp. 62–63; Sivaramakrishnan, Afterword to *The Beautiful Tree: Indigenous Indian Education in the Eighteenth Century*, by Dharampal (Coimbatore: Keerthi Publishing House, 1995), p. 439; and Dharampal, p. 22.

7. Sources cited in this section are, in order, William Adam, 1841, in Dharampal, p. 268 (emphasis added); Dharampal, p. 12; and G. W. Leitner, 1883, in Dharampal, p. 349.

8. William Cooke, 1823, in Dharampal.

9. Adam, 1841, in Dharampal.

10. Dharampal seemed to have a blind spot here. He wrote that it was the "sophisticated operative fiscal arrangements of the pre-British Indian polity" that assigned tax revenue to "make such education possible" (p. 15). However, he admitted that this conclusion was "still tentative, and in statistical terms somewhat speculative" (p. 15), which was odd, given that elsewhere he had always been extremely careful to avoid any such speculation. But then his *justification* for the conclusion makes it clear why he went for it, even if not based on firm evidence: "To suppose that such a deep-rooted and extensive system which really catered to all sections of society was maintained on the basis of tuition fees, or through not only gratuitous teaching but also feeding of the pupils by the teachers, is to be grossly ignorant of the actual functioning of any system, or society" (p. 67). In other words, Dharampal was claiming that the education system must be publicly funded because he didn't believe a system of education could be anything *other* than publicly funded. In my research, of course, I'd uncovered precisely a fully functioning system of education that depended *entirely* on tuition fees and a little philanthropy. So it was not logically impossible, as Dharampal implied. It seemed, as all the evidence in his book suggested, that he'd missed a trick because of his assumption here.

11. The source cited in this paragraph is T. Fraser, 1823, in Dharampal, pp. 152–53.

12. Sources cited in this paragraph are, in order, J. Sullivan, 1822, in Dharampal, p. 100; and J. Vaughan, 1823, in Dharampal, p. 199.

13. See Dharampal, p. 66.

14. C. Hyde, 1823, in Dharampal, p. 145 (emphasis added).

15. J. Dent, 1825, in Dharampal, p. 228.

16. Dharampal, p. 355.

17. References in this section are, in order, to Philip Hartog, *Some Aspects of Indian Education Past and Present*, University of London, Institute of Education, Studies and Reports no. VII (London: Oxford University Press, Humphrey Milford, 1939), pp. vii, 11 (emphasis added), 69ff, 72, and 15.

18. A. D. Campbell, 1823, in Dharampal, p. 182.

19. References in this paragraph are to *Hansard,* June 22, 1813, quoted Dharampal, p. 75.

20. L. G. K. Murray, 1822, in Dharampal, p. 113 (emphasis added).

21. H. Vibart, 1822, in Dharampal, p. 94.

22. S. Smalley, 1823, in Dharampal, p. 144.

23. Munro, 1826, in Dharampal, p. 249.

24. Adam, 1841, in Dharampal, p. 268.

25. Ibid., p. 272.

26. Ibid., p. 273.

27. Ibid., p. 277.

28. Dharampal, p. 14.

29. References in this paragraph are to Adam, 1841, in Dharampal, p. 277.

30. House of Commons Papers, 1831–32, vol. 9, p. 468, in Dharampal, p. 383.

31. References in this and next paragraph are to Campbell, 1823, in Dharampal, pp. 179 (emphasis added), 182 (emphasis added), and 179.

32. Quoted in Dharampal, p. 260 (emphasis added).

33. J. M. D. Meiklejohn, *An Old Educational Reformer: Dr Andrew Bell* (Edinburgh: William Blackwood and Sons, 1881), pp. 1, 6, 61, and 83.

34. A. Bell, *Mutual Tuition and Moral Discipline; or Manual of Instructions for Conducting Schools through the Agency of the Scholars Themselves*, 7th ed. (London: Hatchard and Son, 1823), p. 25 or 21 (page numbers inconsistent in original; emphasis in the original).

35. References in this paragraph are to Meiklejohn, *An Old Educational Reformer*, p. 25.

36. Bell, *Mutual Tuition and Moral Discipline*, p. 23.

37. References in this and the next paragraph are to Munro, 1826, in Dharampal, pp. 251, 250, 249, and 251.

38. References in this and the next four paragraphs are to Y. Vittal Rao, *Education and Learning in Andhra under the East India Company* (Secunderabad: N. Vidyaranya Swamy, 1979), pp. 82, 82, 79, 81–82, 83–84, and 84.

39. T. B. Macaulay, "Minute of 2 February 1835 on Indian Education," in *Macaulay, Prose and Poetry*, selected by G. M. Young (Cambridge, MA: Harvard University Press, 1957), pp. 721–24 and 729.

40. References in this and the next paragraph are to Y. V. Rao, *Education and Learning in Andhra*, pp. 192 and 214–15.

41. Sources cited in this and the next two paragraphs are, in order, J. Mill, *Edinburgh Review*, October 1813, quoted in E. G. West, *Education and the State*, 3rd ed. (Indianapolis: Liberty Fund, 1994), pp. 170 and 171; 1851 Census, p. CXXXIV-V, quoted in West, *Education and the State*, p. 175; West, *Education and the State*, p. 175; E. G. West, "Nineteenth-Century Educational History: The Kiesling Critique," *Economic History Review* 36 (1983): 427; West, *Education and the State*, p. 173.

42. Dharampal, p. 355.

43. See Peng Deng, *Private Education in Modern China* (Westport, CT: Praeger, 1997); Zhiyi He, *The Socio-Economic Study on Private Education in Guangdong* (Guangzhou, China: Guangdong People's Publishing House, 2001); Thomas H. C. Lee, *Education in Traditional China: A History* (Leiden, Neth.: Brill, 2000); and Jing A. Lin, *Social Transformation and Private Education in China* (Westport, CT: Praeger, 1999).

44. J. Kenyatta, *Facing Mount Kenya* (London: Vintage Books, 1938), pp. 99, 123, 121, and 120.

45. Kikuyu Province Annual Report, 1929, p. 17.

46. World Bank, *World Development Report 2004: Making Services Work for Poor People* (Washington: World Bank, 2003), p. 15; and B. Geldof, Foreword to *The Rough Guide to a Better World*, by M. Wroe and M. Doney (London: Rough Guides in association with DfID, 2004), p. 5.

Chapter 12

1. W. Easterly, *The White Man's Burden: Why the West's Efforts to Aid the Rest Have Done So Much Ill and So Little Good* (New York: Penguin Press, 2006), pp. 1 and 384.

2. Ibid., p. 5.

3. Ibid., p. 175.

4. W. Easterly, *The Elusive Quest for Growth: Economists' Adventures and Misadventures in the Tropics* (Cambridge, MA: MIT Press, 2001), p. xii.

5. See for example, J. Leach, "DEEP Impact: An Investigation of the Use of Information and Communication Technologies for Teacher Education in the Global South," Education Paper no. 58, DfID, 2005, www.dfid.gov.uk/pubs/files/ict-teacher-educa tion-no58.asp; P. Murphy and others, *Enhancing Learning Opportunities in Africa: Distance Education and Information and Communication Technologies for Learning* (Washington: World Bank, 2002); C. Potter and A. S. F. Silva, eds., *Teachers in Action: Case Studies of Radio Learning in South African Primary Schools* (Johannesburg: Open Learning Systems Education Trust, 2002); and R. Rhodes and S. Rasmussen-Tall, "Teacher Training via Radio Is Launched in Mali," 2005, www/usaidmali.org/article. php?id=0079_EN&lan=en&skin.

6. See S. Mitra and others, "Improving English Pronunciation: An Automated Instructional Approach," *Information Technologies and International Development* 1, no. 1 (2003): 75–84.

7. Tony Halpin, *Times Educational Supplement*, February 5, 2006, www.timeson line.co.uk/tol/news/uk/article734920.ece.

8. C. K. Prahalad, *The Fortune at the Bottom of the Pyramid* (Upper Saddle River, NJ: Wharton School Publishing, 2004), p. 13.

9. Ibid., p. 37.

10. For more on Swift, see J. Tooley, "From Adam Swift to Adam Smith: How the 'Invisible Hand' Overcomes Middle Class Hypocrisy," *Journal of Philosophy of Education* 41, no. 4 (2008): 727–41.

11. References in this paragraph are to Milton Friedman and Rose Friedman, *Free to Choose* (Harmondsworth, UK: Penguin, 1980), pp. 204 and 204–5.

12. Ibid., pp. 203–4.

13. Ibid., pp. 197, 196 (emphasis added), 196–97, and 197.

Index

About the Author

Fresh out of college in the early 1980s, James Tooley went to Zimbabwe to become a public school teacher. Now an award-winning scholar featured in PBS and BBC documentaries, he has written several books, and his work has been covered in *Newsweek*, the *Atlantic*, the *Wall Street Journal*, and the *Financial Times*. Tooley's career as an academic began at the University of Oxford, his PhD is from the University of London, and he is professor of education policy at the University of Newcastle upon Tyne. He currently splits his time between Hyderabad, India, and Beijing, China, where he works with the entrepreneurs and teachers who inspired this book.

Cato Institute

Founded in 1977, the Cato Institute is a public policy research foundation dedicated to broadening the parameters of policy debate to allow consideration of more options that are consistent with the traditional American principles of limited government, individual liberty, and peace. To that end, the Institute strives to achieve greater involvement of the intelligent, concerned lay public in questions of policy and the proper role of government.

The Institute is named for *Cato's Letters*, libertarian pamphlets that were widely read in the American Colonies in the early 18th century and played a major role in laying the philosophical foundation for the American Revolution.

Despite the achievement of the nation's Founders, today virtually no aspect of life is free from government encroachment. A pervasive intolerance for individual rights is shown by government's arbitrary intrusions into private economic transactions and its disregard for civil liberties.

To counter that trend, the Cato Institute undertakes an extensive publications program that addresses the complete spectrum of policy issues. Books, monographs, and shorter studies are commissioned to examine the federal budget, Social Security, regulation, military spending, international trade, and myriad other issues. Major policy conferences are held throughout the year, from which papers are published thrice yearly in the *Cato Journal*. The Institute also publishes the quarterly magazine *Regulation*.

To maintain its independence, the Cato Institute accepts no government funding. Contributions are received from foundations, corporations, and individuals, and other revenue is generated from the sale of publications. The Institute is a nonprofit, tax-exempt, educational foundation under Section 501(c)3 of the Internal Revenue Code.

CATO INSTITUTE
1000 Massachusetts Ave., N.W.
Washington, DC 20001
www.cato.org